Visual Basic 2005
Made Simple

Visual Basic 2005
Made Simple

Stephen Morris

AMSTERDAM · BOSTON · HEIDELBERG · LONDON · NEW YORK · OXFORD
PARIS · SAN DIEGO · SAN FRANCISCO · SINGAPORE · SYDNEY · TOKYO
Made Simple is an imprint of Elsevier

Made Simple is an imprint of Elsevier
Linacre House, Jordan Hill, Oxford OX2 8DP
30 Corporate Drive, Suite 400, Burlington, MA 01803

First edition 2006

British Library Cataloguing in Publication Data
A catalogue record for this book is available from the British Library

Library of Congress Cataloguing in Publication Data
A catalogue record for this book is available from the Library of Congress

ISBN-13: 978-0-7506-6349-6

For information on all Made Simple publications
visit our website at http://books.elsevier.com

Transferred to Digital Print 2010

Printed and bound in the United Kingdom

Working together to grow
libraries in developing countries

www.elsevier.com | www.bookaid.org | www.sabre.org

ELSEVIER   BOOK AID
International   Sabre Foundation

Contents

Preface

Visual Basic has changed dramatically over the last few years, evolving from a beginners' language to a fully-fledged object-oriented programming environment. Its structures are no longer simple to understand, particularly for those new to programming, but nevertheless it makes a good starting point for anyone who wants to develop sophisticated, effective software.

Visual Basic 2005 provides a good introduction to Windows programming and can still be used to create complete Windows applications with the minimum of effort and time. Since an application's windows are 'drawn' on the screen, you can always see what the eventual application will look like, without having to guess. All of this is achieved without writing a line of code and, as a result, Visual Basic bypasses the long-winded trial-and-error approach to designing screen displays of the older programming languages.

Creating the user interface is only the start, of course, and there is still a great deal of work to be done to complete an application. Even so, the Visual Basic 2005 programming language is powerful and, once mastered, even complex tasks can be finished surprisingly quickly.

The latest version of Visual Basic is radically different to VB 6.0 and earlier versions. However, many of the principles are the same and can be applied equally well to any of the earlier versions of the product. Where there are significant variations between the versions, the differences are noted.

This new edition of the book has been revised to cover the changes made in VB 2005. There is also an additional chapter introducing Visual Basic's facilities for creating classes.

This book is aimed at those who are new to programming, or new to Visual Basic. No previous programming experience is necessary, though familiarity with the use of Windows is assumed. However, Visual Basic is a substantial programming language and, in a book of this size, it is only possible to give a brief introduction. Nevertheless, the information given here should be enough to start you on some interesting projects and to show what may be achieved with practice.

Acknowledgements

I would like to thank Mike Cash of Elsevier for his assistance and patience, and Natalia Żak for her hard work and dedication during the production of this book.

1 Overview

Installing Visual Basic

Visual Basic 2005 provides a sophisticated Windows programming environment that is capable of producing powerful programs. Since it is a 'Visual' system you can create the visible part of a self-contained Windows application in a very short time, without the need to write any program code at all. You can then add short procedures for performing specific tasks, using the powerful programming language. This book shows you how to create fully-fledged Windows applications, quickly and effectively.

Visual Basic versions

Visual Basic 2005 is an attempt updated version of Visual Basic .NET and is supplied in the following editions:

- The Express Edition is a cut-down version of Visual Basic, offering full functionality but limited application templates and design tools.

- The Standard Edition provides additional templates and further tools, such as a report viewer.

- The Professional Edition includes the full set of templates and a number of extra tools, such as a web form designer and component designer.

Installation

The easiest way to start using Visual Basic 2005 is to download the Express Edition from the Microsoft website. This edition is initially available free but a registration fee may be payable in the future.

1   Go to http://msdn.microsoft.com/vstudio/express/vb.

2   Click on Download Now.

3   Click on the Download button and follow the instructions.

At the end of the set-up process, an option will be added to the All Programs menu, leading to the main Visual Basic program.

The full Visual Basic 2005 Express Edition takes up to 1.3 Gb. If you are short of hard disk space you need only install Visual Basic Express and the .NET Framework 2.0 (requiring 500 Mb).

Running Visual Basic

The installation process will have created icons that can be used to run the application.

Visual Basic 2005 is part of the **.NET Framework**. This is a collection of languages that share a set of development tools. Visual Basic 2005 applications are developed using Visual Studio, a program used for the design of all .NET framework applications.

Starting the program

To start Visual Basic:

1   Click on the Start button to display the Start menu.

2   Move the pointer to All Programs.

3   Click on the Microsoft Visual Basic 2005 Express Edition option.

Take note

The operation of Visual Studio the same in all versions of Windows. In this book, the illustrations are taken from the Express Edition in Windows XP but the same principles apply in other versions of Windows.

Registration

The first time you load Visual Basic 2005, you should register the product. Although you do not have to register immediately, you must do so eventually or you will no longer be able to run Visual Basic.

To register Visual Basic:

1   From the Help menu, select Register Product.

2   Enter your Microsoft Passport details (e-mail address and password). If you do not have a passport, follow the instructions to set one up.

3   Fill in the registration details.

4   At the end of the registration process, you will be given a Registration Key. Copy this key to the Registration dialog.

After successfully completing registration, you will receive an e-mail confirming that the product has been registered.

Click to register VB

Enter key on completion of registration

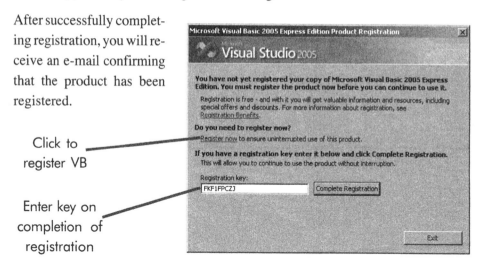

Take note

You can run the program for a limited time on any particular machine without activating it. After that, you must register to continue using Visual Basic. Full details of the registration process and benefits can be found at http://msdn.microsoft.com/vstudio/express/register.

Starting a new project

As you enter the application, the Visual Basic window is displayed, with the Start Page tab open and, within this, the Recent Projects pane. If this is the first time you have run the program, the Recent Projects pane will be empty. To create your first application:

1   Click on the New Project button. The New Project dialog is displayed.

New project
button

2   Check that the Windows Application icon is highlighted.

Start new
project

Enter Project
name

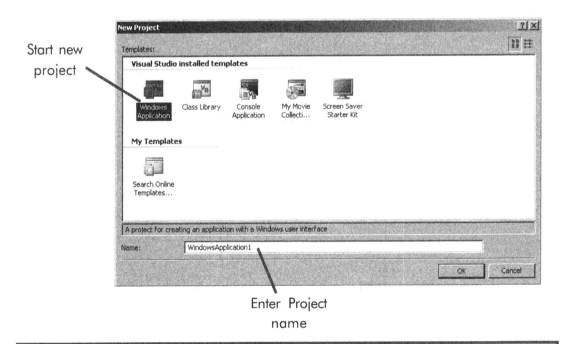

Take note

You can create several types of project, such as class libraries and console applications. For more information on these, see the on-line help.

3   Enter a Name for the application.

4   Click on OK to create the new project. The location for the project will be selected when you first save the files.

You now have a blank application, ready to customise.

Saving the project

Before going any further, you should save the project and select a location for the project files:

1   In the Visual Studio window, select File|Save All.

2   If you do not want to save your project in the default location, click on the Browse button to choose a new location.

3   Check the 'Create directory' box if you want to create a directory for the files. The folder name is the same as the solution name.

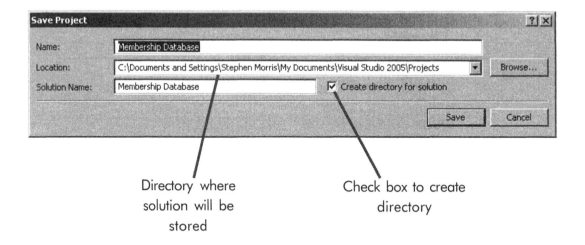

Directory where
solution will be
stored

Check box to create
directory

4   Click on Save.

The solution directory is created, along with a number of subdirectories. A number of files will be created here and updated as you develop your project. In general, you should not make any changes to these files from outside Visual Basic.

Visual Studio

After creating an application, a new tab (Form1.vb [Design]) is added to the Visual Studio window. This is where you will design the **interface** for your application; the interface comprises the windows that the end user will see.

The main Visual Studio window contains a number of other windows. Initially, four of these are open; others will pop up as you develop your application.

Main window

Solution Explorer window

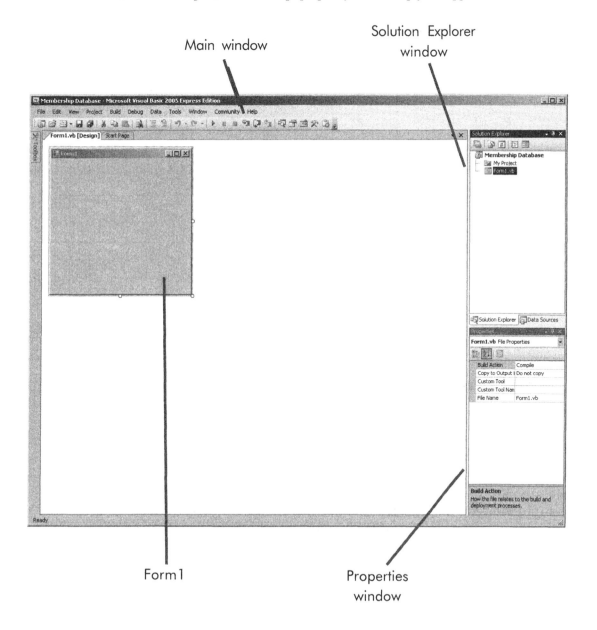

Form1

Properties window

Main window

The **main window** contains all the elements you would expect to find in a Windows application:

- The **title bar** contains the name of your new project and tells you that you are in Visual Basic 2005. On the right are the usual buttons for minimising, maximising and closing the window.

- The Visual Studio **menu bar** includes 11 drop-down menus. Many of the options in these menus are described later in the book.

- The **toolbar** contains a row of icons that provide shortcuts to the most frequently used Visual Basic operations.

Title bar

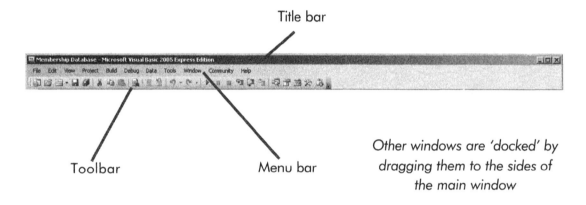

Toolbar   Menu bar

Other windows are 'docked' by dragging them to the sides of the main window

Below the toolbars are two **tabs**:

Navigation

- The first tab, Form1.vb [Design], is where you will design the first window for your application.

- The second tab, Start Page, was the tab that appeared when you entered Visual Studio. Click on this tab and you will see the same display as before. Here you can start a new project or change to an existing project.

Other tabs will be added as the application progresses. If there are too many tabs to fit the display, the buttons on the right let you navigate between them.

Design windows

The main Visual Studio window can contain a number of other **design windows**. Initially, the design windows are 'docked' at the sides of the Visual Studio display or are represented by buttons. There are a number of options for how these windows can be displayed and these can be confusing at first. The appearance of the windows can be changed to suit your method of working:

- The windows can be kept open at all times (as is the case initially with the Solution Explorer and Properties windows on the right).

- The windows can be made to 'float' to any position on the screen.

- The windows can be **hidden** so that they appear as buttons down the side of the Visual Studio display (as for the Toolbox button below it).

- The windows can be closed. (There are a number of closed windows, which will be displayed as they are needed.)

Open windows

When a window is open, you can change its appearance:

- The width of the window can be changed by dragging the edge opposite the docked edge.

- The window can be made to 'float' by dragging the title bar into the main window.

Floating Properties window

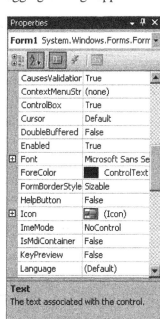

Docked Properties window

9

- The window can be hidden by clicking the ▣ (Auto Hide) button on its toolbar; the window will then appear as an icon at the edge of the Visual Studio display.

- The window can be closed by clicking on its ☒ (Close) button.

Floating windows

A floating window can be changed to suit your requirements:

- The window can be moved by dragging its title bar or resized by dragging any of its edges.

- The window can be docked by dragging it to any edge of the Visual Studio display.

- The window can be docked with another window by dragging it onto the top part of the second window. (Initially, the Solution Explorer and Properties windows are docked together in this way.)

- The window can be closed.

You can also dock or undock a window by double-clicking on the title bar.

Hidden windows

Several options exist for the hidden windows:

- If you move the mouse pointer over the window's button, the window is temporarily displayed (as a docked window). When you move the pointer away, the window is hidden again; the button for this window is enlarged to show the window name, while the other buttons are reduced in size.

- You can keep the window permanently open (and docked) by clicking on its ▣ (Auto Hide) button. The button image changes depending on whether the window is temporarily or permanently open.

Click to open window permanently

Move pointer over button to show hidden window

Closed windows

A closed window can be opened by selecting the relevant option from the View menu (or pressing the corresponding shortcut key). For example, to re-open the Properties window, select View|Properties Window (or press function key [F4]).

Window tabs

To add a further layer of complication, design windows can be combined into a single window with multiple tabs. For instance, the Solution Explorer window that you see initially also contains the Data Sources window. If you click on the Data Sources tab, this window is brought in front of the Solution Explorer window.

Data Sources window

Tip

If the Start Page tab has been closed you can redisplay it at any time using View|Other Windows|Start Page.

Click on the Solution Explorer tab to get the Solution Explorer window back again.

It is up to you how the windows are combined:

● Drag a tab off a window to create a separate open window.

● Drag an open window onto the tab area of an existing window (with tabs) to add the window as a new tab.

● Drag an open window onto the title bar of an existing window with no tabs to create a multi-tabbed window.

● Drag a tab to a new position within the row of tabs to change the order of the tabs.

● Drag a tab from one set of tabs to another.

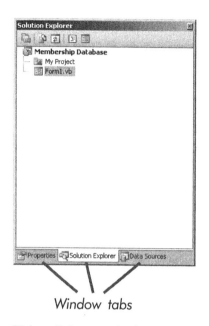

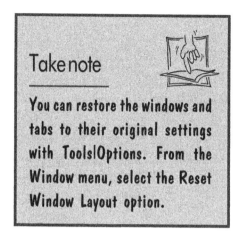

Take note

You can restore the windows and tabs to their original settings with Tools|Options. From the Window menu, select the Reset Window Layout option.

Window tabs

Using all these methods, you can set the appearance of Visual Studio to suit the way in which you want to work at any time.

Form Design tab

A Visual Basic application usually consists of one or more windows. At the design stage, these windows are called **forms**. To start you off, Visual Studio supplies a single form, called Form1. This form will be renamed and resized when you begin to develop the application; other forms will be added as required. The forms are held in separate tabs on the main Visual Studio window.

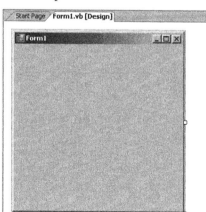

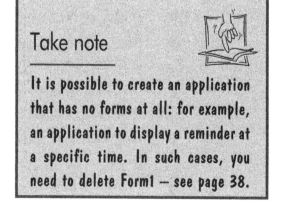

Take note

It is possible to create an application that has no forms at all: for example, an application to display a reminder at a specific time. In such cases, you need to delete Form1 — see page 38.

Toolbox window

Any window contains a number of different objects: buttons, text boxes, labels and so on. These are called **controls**. When you are creating a window within Visual Studio, these controls can be added by dragging them from the Toolbox window. The Pointer object at the top of the toolbox is used for selecting existing controls so that they can be moved, resized or changed in some other way.

The toolbox controls are described in detail in Chapter 3.

Start by making the toolbox into a docked window by placing the cursor over the Toolbox button and then clicking on the ▣ (Auto Hide) button.

The controls are divided into a number of categories (Common Controls, Containers etc.) Click on the ⊞ button next to a category to display its contents; click on ⊟ to hide them again.

Title bar: when docked, drag to move toolbox to new position

Common controls (collection of controls)

Pointer: select existing controls

Standard controls

Toolbox

Other controls

Show contents

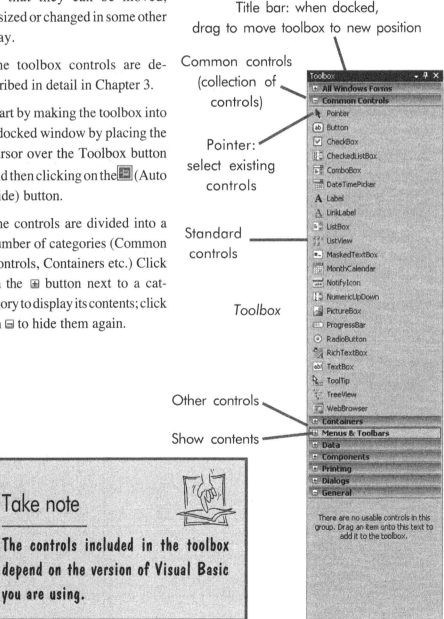

Take note

The controls included in the toolbox depend on the version of Visual Basic you are using.

Solution Explorer window

For each window in your final application there is a corresponding Visual Basic form, and each form has its own file on disk. Usually, there is also at least one file containing the program code for the application and, if your forms use any third party tools, these will be held in additional files. Finally, there are a number of files used by the system. All these files go together to make up the **project** from which a distributable program is compiled.

For large applications, you may have several projects, forming a **solution.**

The Solution Explorer window lists the projects that make up the solution and the files in each project. The files are listed in a tree structure, similar to that used for Windows Explorer.

You can add existing files to a project or remove files. A file can be part of more than one project; for example, you may use the same window in two independent applications. Files can be removed from a project if they are no longer required.

At this stage, the Solution Explorer contains just one project (My Project) and the file for Form1.

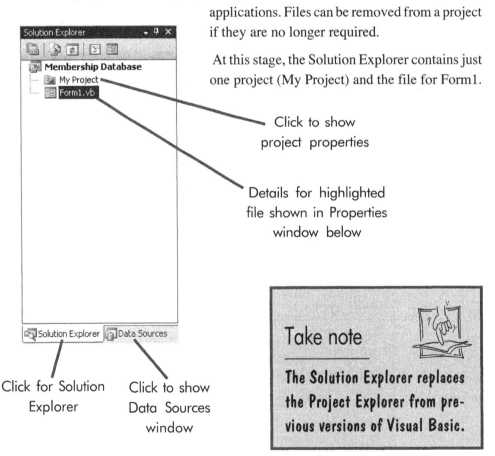

Click to show
project properties

Details for highlighted
file shown in Properties
window below

Click for Solution
Explorer

Click to show
Data Sources
window

> **Take note**
>
> The Solution Explorer replaces the Project Explorer from previous versions of Visual Basic.

Data Sources window

The Data Sources window, which is currently available as a tab on the Solution Explorer window, lists the sources of data available to an application: for example, external database files and web sources.

Close the Data Sources window. You can redisplay the window with Data|Show Data Sources.

Properties window

Each form, and each control on a form, has a set of **properties**. These determine the appearance of the form or control and the way in which it behaves. A form has properties that specify how big it is and where it is on the screen, whether it is visible when the application starts, whether it has Minimise and Maximise buttons, and so

Form or control whose properties are shown

Property

Setting

Properties by category

Properties in alphabetical order

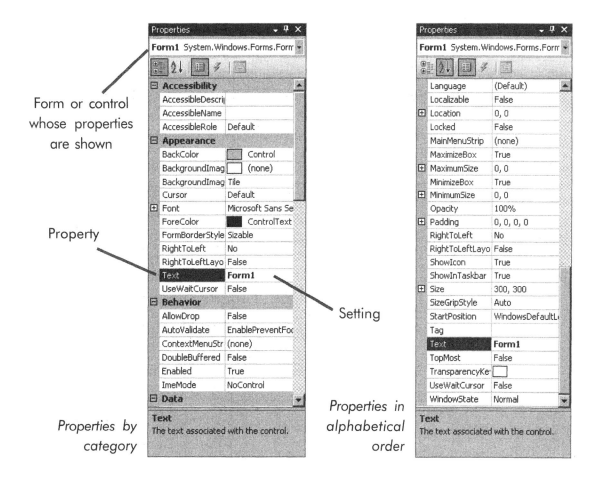

on. Most controls have a large number of properties, some of which are similar to those of forms. For instance, a button has the same size and position properties as

a form but also includes properties to determine which keys can be used to activate it. Each type of control has a different set of properties. For each control, you can change the settings of individual properties (so all buttons have the same properties but their settings are different).

The Properties window displays the properties for the selected form or control, and allows you to change their settings. The properites are listed on the left, with

Take note

Some properties can also be changed more simply; for instance, the position or size of a form or control can be altered by dragging the object or its borders.

the corresponding settings on the right. Some of the more important properties are described in Chapters 2 and 3.

Initially, the properties are divided into categories: for instance, those that determine the appearance of the object and those that specify its behaviour. However, this format can be confusing, so you can list all the properties in alphabetical order by clicking on the button. To return to the listing by category, click on .

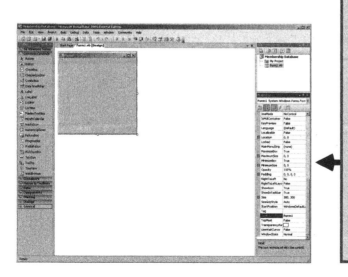

Tip

To make the screen as uncluttered as possible, maximise the main window, dock the toolbox and reduce its width, close the Data Sources window and dock the Solution Explorer and Properties windows. Reduce the height of the Solution Explorer window.

Getting help

Visual Basic contains a wide range of controls and other elements. Deciding which ones to use can be a problem. However, Visual Studio holds all the information you will need in the form of on-line help. The information available includes help specific to Visual Basic and the more general MSDN Library. Because the help is very extensive you may have chosen not to install the MSDN files; these are still available, provided you are connected to the Internet.

The easiest way to get help is via the Help menu:

1   From the Help menu, select Index.

2   In the 'Look for' box, type the word or phase for which you need help.

3   Click on the appropriate topic: for instance, the Form Designer window or an item on the Toolbox or Properties windows.

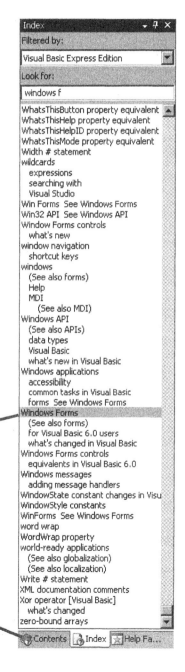

Click on an item to show corresponding help

Click on Contents tab for structured list of help topics

4 Click on a topic in the Index window. The relevant help page is shown as a tab in the main window.

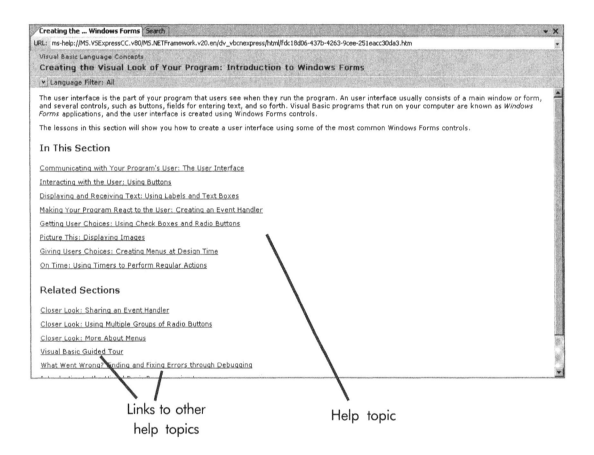

Links to other help topics   Help topic

5 You can move to another help topic by clicking on one of the blue, underlined phrases. You can move backwards and forwards between the topics you have viewed by clicking on the buttons on the left of the Web toolbar.

6 When you have finished with the help screen, remove it by clicking on the Close button; alternatively, click back on the Visual Studio window to keep the help page open.

You can also get on-line help in other ways:

● Select Help|Contents. This opens the Help Contents window, where a number of 'books' are displayed. Double-clicking on the books and the topics they contain eventually takes you to a help screen. The 'Sync with Table of Contents' button on the Web toolbar allows you to find the current help topic in the Contents list.

Synchronise with Contents

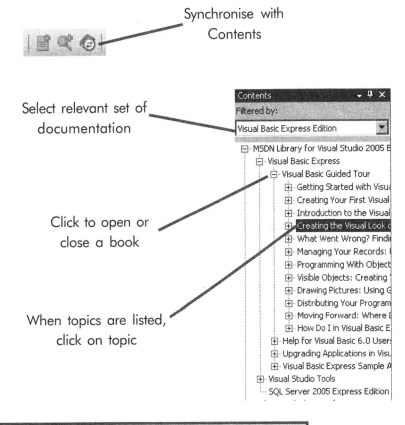

Select relevant set of documentation

Click to open or close a book

When topics are listed, click on topic

Tip

Change the entry in the Filtered By box to Visual Basic. This restricts the help to topics specific to Visual Basic, making it much faster to find the topic you want.

- Select Help|Search to search the help for a particular word or phrase. Matching topics are listed in the Search tab. Double-click on a topic to display the corresponding help. You can reduce the number of topics found by specifying a particular part of the extensive help (e.g. Visual Basic).

- The best access point for help is the MSDN library. To display this help, enter http://msdn.microsoft.com/library at the top of any help tab. Then select from books and topics in the left-hand pane.

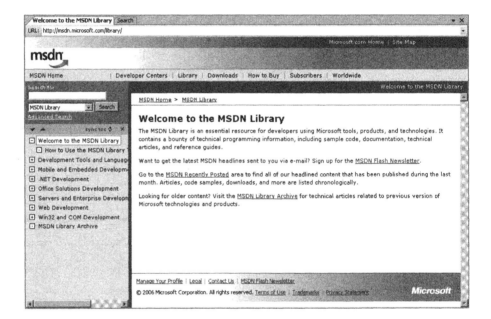

- Save the MSDN contents page for future use by clicking on the 'Add to Help Favorites' button. To redisplay the help page, select it from the Help Favorites tab.

- Click on an object and then press function key **[F1]** (context-sensitive help) to go straight to the topic relating to your current activity. For instance, if you click on a window and press **[F1]** you will get information on that window.

You can also get context-sensitive help on error messages and individual keywords when writing code.

Leaving Visual Basic

You can get out of Visual Studio at any time, either temporarily (while you work on some other application) or permanently.

Suspending Visual Studio

To suspend Visual Studio temporarily, click on the Minimise button on the main window and then start another application.

To get back into Visual Studio, use one of these methods:

● If Visual Studio was minimised, click on the project's taskbar button.

● If any part of the Visual Studio window is visible, click on it.

● Press **[Alt-Esc]** or **[Alt-Tab]** repeatedly to cycle through the open applications until Visual Studio is active.

The program will be exactly as you left it.

Exiting Visual Studio

To close down Visual Studio altogether, select File|Exit. Alternatively, click on the Close button on the main window. If you have made any changes to the current project you are asked if you want to save them:

● Click on Save (or press **[Enter]**) to save the changes.

● Click on Discard to abandon the changes – no further confirmation is requested.

● Click on Cancel (or press **[Esc]**) to continue working in Visual Studio.

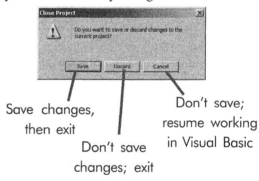

Save changes, then exit

Don't save changes; exit

Don't save; resume working in Visual Basic

If you attempt to close down the computer without ending Visual Studio, Windows will close Visual Studio for you and the same options will be given for any unsaved projects.

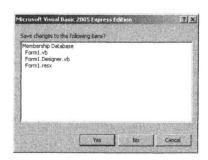

Restarting Visual Studio

You can add Visual Basic to the Start menu by right-clicking on the entry in the All Programs list and selecting 'Pin to Start menu'. You can then re-run Visual Basic by simply clicking on the Start button and then on the Visual Basic icon.

Click to restart

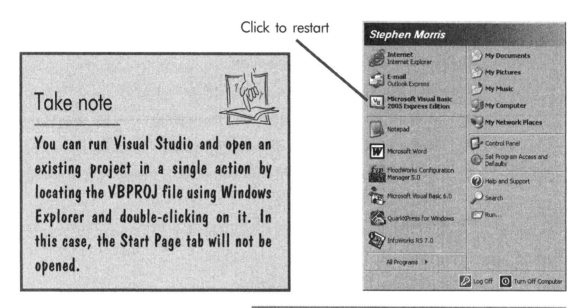

Take note

You can run Visual Studio and open an existing project in a single action by locating the VBPROJ file using Windows Explorer and double-clicking on it. In this case, the Start Page tab will not be opened.

The projects you have worked on recently are listed in the Visual Studio Start Page. Click on a project name to open it.

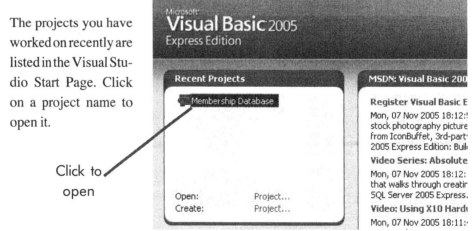

Click to open

To open a project that is not included in the Start page:

1   On the Start Page, click on the Open File button.

2   Locate and open the project directory.

3   Click on the file with an SLN extension and then on Open.

Upgrading old projects

There are big differences in the format of application files between previous versions of Visual Basic (e.g. VB 6.0) and Visual Basic .NET. There are also differences between VB .NET and VB 2005. However, Visual Basic lets you upgrade an existing application without too much difficulty:

1 Create the directory where you want to store the upgraded project. (The upgrade process does not do this automatically for you.)

2 On the Visual Studio Start Page, click on athe Open File button and select the project to be upgraded.

3 The Visual Studio Conversion Wizard starts. Click on Next to start the wizard.

4 Decide whether or not to create a backup of the existing project. Click on Next to continue.

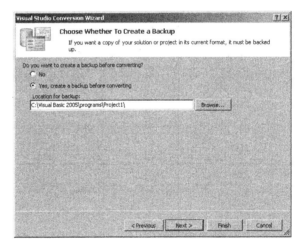

5 A summary is displayed. Click on Finish to start the conversion process. The upgrade may take quite a while for large projects.

6 On completion, the new version of the project is displayed in the Solution Explorer window and the application can be edited as required. Included in the Solution Explorer is a file called _UpgradeReport.htm, which gives details of the upgrade process and any errors that were encountered.

7 Click on the Save All button to save the upgraded application, accepting the default name suggested for the solution filename.

Exercises

1 Start Visual Basic and create a project called Member Database, saving it in the hard disk's root directory.

2 Reset the windows and tabs and their original settings. Identify the windows that are displayed.

3 Make the Toolbox into a pernament docked window and resize it to make it take less space. Make the Data Source window into a floating window, then close it. Maximise the main window. Display the properties in alphabetical order.

4 Search for help relating to the Properties window. Afterwards, close the help page and any open windows.

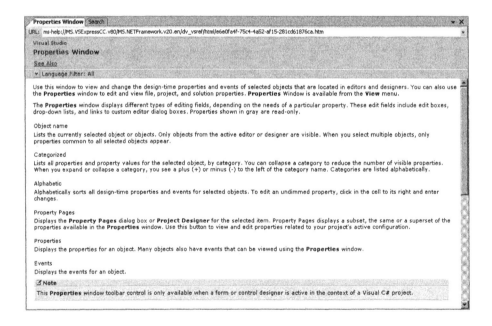

5 Minimise the main Visual Studio application and then re-activate it.

6 Exit Visual Studio, saving any changes.

For help with these exercises, see page 292.

2 Forms

The first form

Any Windows application is made up of one or more distinct **windows**. A window can be used to display information, to allow the user to enter data or to provide options for the user to select. At the development stage, the windows that make up a finished Visual Basic application are called **forms**. The forms you create become the windows through which the user accesses your application.

It is up to you, when designing a form, to decide how the window will behave: whether it is on-screen initially; whether the user can minimise or resize it; what objects it displays; and so on. However, you should remember that once a window has been displayed it is the user who decides the order in which things happen and when the window will be closed down. The more objects (buttons, scroll bars, text boxes etc.) you put on a form, the less control you have over the user's actions.

A form starts off as an empty window, which may have a title bar and control buttons (Control-menu box, Minimise button, Maximise button, Close button). Within this, you may add other objects: buttons, lists, check boxes etc.

Form files

The details of each form are stored in two **form files**, with extensions of **vb** and **resx**. These hold information such as the initial size of the form and its position, the objects on the form and so on.

Take note

Forms are also used for most dialog boxes (e.g. those to select a file or enter a password) though some simple message boxes can be created as and when required within the code (see page 143).

Tip

Because a form is totally self-contained (the form file contains both a description of the form and all the code attached to it), the same form can be re-used in other applications. This means that all your applications can have the same 'look and feel', as well as reducing the amount of time you spend creating applications.

There will usually be some Visual Basic code attached to the form, determining how the application will respond when the user takes action on the window's controls. For instance, when the user closes the window, the code attached to the form should take any necessary action on data that has been entered and then remove the window. The code for a particular form is stored in the corresponding **vb** file.

The forms in an application are listed in the Solution Explorer window.(To display the Solution Explorer, if it has been closed, select View|Solution Explorer.)

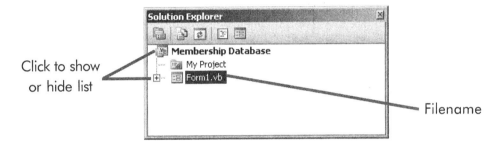

Click to show
or hide list

Filename

Form1

Visual Basic supplies a default form to start the project: Form1. You can use this as your application's front-end window. You can increase or decrease the size of the window by dragging the handles on the form's edges and corners.

Other changes to the window and the way in which it behaves are made by altering the form's properties.

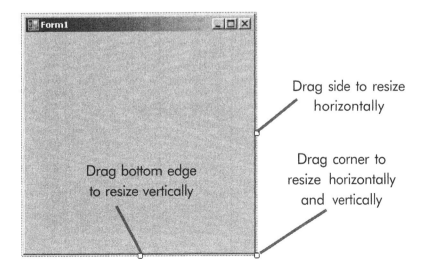

Drag side to resize
horizontally

Drag corner to
resize horizontally
and vertically

Drag bottom edge
to resize vertically

Form properties

The appearance and behaviour of a window are determined by the corresponding form's **properties**. These specify such details as the size and position of the window and whether it can be minimised or closed. For each property, there is a single **setting**.

When you click on Form1 in the main window, the properties are listed in the Properties window, in the left-hand column. The corresponding settings are shown on the right. Any property can be changed by clicking on the appropriate item. In some cases, there are a fixed number of options and you must choose from a drop-down list; for others, a value for the setting can be typed in directly.

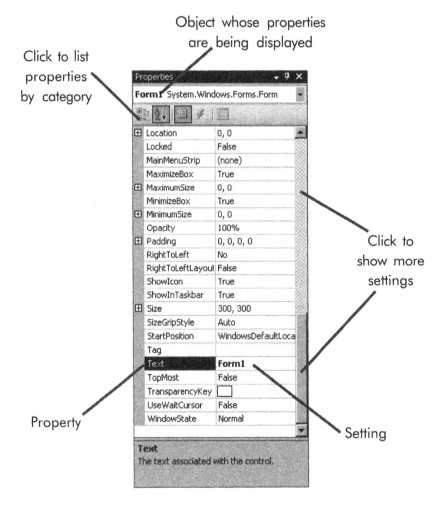

Object whose properties are being displayed

Click to list properties by category

Click to show more settings

Property

Setting

Name and Text

The **Name** of the form is the name that appears in the Solution Explorer window; the **Text** is the piece of text that appears in the title bar (for the front-end window, this is usually the application title). Either of these properties can be changed by clicking on the existing setting and typing over it.

The Name property is shown in brackets so that it appears at the top of the alphabetic property list. Its setting should be changed to something that will tell you what the form does.

Adopt a suitable convention for naming forms and controls. For example, identify forms by setting the first three characters to be 'frm', such as 'frmFront' for the front-end window. The Name will be used when referring to the form in the code.

Take note

In earlier version of Visual Basic the Text property was called the Caption property.

Form Name

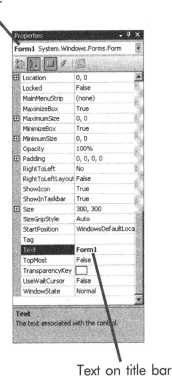

Text on title bar

Tip

The values you have changed are shown in bold type; the settings in normal type represent default values. If you change a value back to the default, it returns to normal type.

Take note

Although the properties are set as you develop the form, you can also write code to change them while the application is running — see page 89.

The border style

The **FormBorderStyle** property specifies the type of border and the elements that may appear in the title area. The most useful options are:

None
There is no border; the window has no title bar or control buttons – useful for message boxes.

FixedSingle
The window may have a title bar, Control-menu box, Close button, Minimise button and Maximise button. The user cannot change the window size by dragging the border. This style is used for windows with a fixed number of controls (e.g. data-entry forms).

Fixed3D
As for FixedStyle but with a three-dimensional border.

Sizable
The window may have any of the Fixed Single controls and may also be resized by the user. This is the default for all new forms and is used anywhere that the user may need to resize the form (e.g. text windows, spreadsheets, pictures).

FixedDialog
The window is a dialog box. It may have a title bar and Control-menu button but cannot have the other control buttons. It cannot be resized by the user.

Two other options, **FixedToolWindow** and **SizableToolWindow**, are used in the creation of toolbars. For more information on these options, see the on-line help.

To select a border option, click on FormBorderStyle. A down-arrow button appears on the right of the current setting. Click on this, and a drop-down list is displayed. Click on one of the options in the list to change the setting.

Previous versions of VB had a BorderStyle property rather than FormBorderStyle.

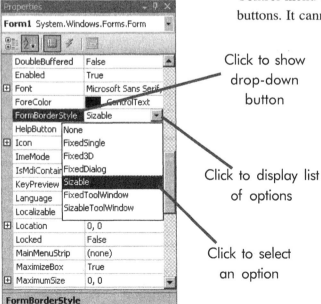

Click to show drop-down button

Click to display list of options

Click to select an option

Title bar and buttons

If FormBorderStyle is None, the window will have no title bar and therefore no buttons. For any other setting a title bar is displayed and may contain the usual Windows buttons. The inclusion of a Control-menu box, Minimise button and Maximise button are determined by the settings of the **ControlBox**, **MinButton** and **MaxButton** properties respectively.

Each of these properties has two possible settings: True or False. The True setting indicates that the button is included (and therefore that the user may click on it); False means that the button will not be available.

The Close button is included only when there is a Control-menu box.

The **ShowInTaskbar** property determines whether an icon for the form is added to the Windows taskbar. If the property is set to False and the form is minimised, it will appear as a small window in the bottom left of the screen.

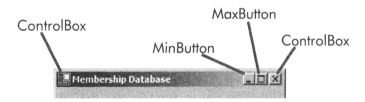

Size and Position

The size of a form can be altered by dragging its borders and is held in the **Size** property.

This property is actually a combination of two independent properties:

Width   Width of form (including borders)

Height   Height of form (including borders and title bar)

For a more precise form size, the Width and Height can be entered directly in the Properties window. Entering the settings directly also ensures consistency between windows.

You can set the property directly in two ways:

● Click on the Size setting and enter values for width and height, separated by a comma.

● Click on the ⊞ button to the left of the Size property and then enter the Width and Height individually.

All sizes are measured in pixels. Therefore the physical size of the window will depend on the resolution of the end user's screen.

For high-resolution screens, windows will be smaller and take up less space on the screen; text appears much smaller and more can be fitted on the screen.

The initial position of the form in the screen is determined by the **StartPosition** property, which can take the following values:

WindowsDefaultLocation	The position is set by Windows when the program starts. (This is the default setting for all new forms.)
WindowsDefaultBounds	The position and size are set by Windows when the program starts.
CenterScreen	The window is centred on the screen.
CenterParent	The window is contained in another window and is centred within that window.
Manual	The position is determined by the Location property.

Tip

When developing on a high-resolution screen, remember that end users may have screens of lower resolution. Either make sure that windows will have an initial position towards the left and top of the screen, or get the user's screen dimensions and use them to calculate the position and size at run time – see Chapter 4.

Set the value by clicking on StartPosition and then selecting from the drop-down list. If you choose **Manual**, you must also set the **Location** property, which is a combination of two other properties:

X   Distance from left-hand side of screen or parent window

Y   Distance from top of screen or parent window

Both properties are specified in pixels. As for the Size property, you can either enter the Location values separated by a comma or specify the X and Y values individually.

Take note

Visual Basic 6.0 allowed you to use a variety of scales; in Visual Basic 2005 all sizes must be given in pixels.

Visible and Enabled

A window should be displayed only when it is needed; this is controlled by the form's **Visible** property. When Visible is True, the window appears on the screen in its predefined position; when Visible is False, the window is hidden. Usually, the first form is visible; making the first form invisible when the program starts up requires some additional programming (see 'Making a Startup Windows Form Invisible' in the MSDN help for details). Other forms are usually displayed as needed and then hidden or closed when no longer required. As with most properties, the settings can be changed when the program is running.

Only one window can be **active** at a time; the colour of the title bar is used by Windows to show which window is active. Clicking on a window makes it active (and deactivates all other windows).

Even though a form is visible, you may not want the user to be able to access it. For instance, when a dialog box is displayed, you may not want the user to click on the window behind it until the dialog is closed. When the **Enabled** property for a form is True, users can click on the corresponding window to make it active; when the property is False, clicking on the window has no effect.

Saving the form

Like all other computer applications, you should save your work regularly. It can take a long time to set up a form just as you want it and it takes only a few seconds to save it.

As described above, the details of the form will be saved in a pair of form files. These files hold everything that is needed to construct the form: its properties, its controls and their properties, and the code attached to the form.

The form files have been created in the project directory, with the default name Form1. Before beginning the task of customising the form, you should give it a more appropriate name. To save the current form with a new name, select File|Save *formname.vb* As from the Visual Studio menu bar. The project directory is shown and you can give the file a suitable name (e.g. frmFront.vb for a form named frmFront). If you type a new name, Visual Basic will add a VB extension. Remember that you are choosing a name for the form, not for the project as a whole. Visual Studio will also create the corresponding RESX file.

After saving the file, the filename you specified appears in the Solution Explorer window.

You should change the Name property for the form to match the filename; you should also change the Text property so that suitable text is displayed in the title bar.

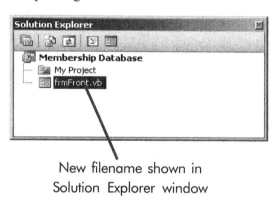

New filename shown in
Solution Explorer window

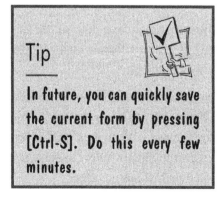

Tip

In future, you can quickly save the current form by pressing [Ctrl-S]. Do this every few minutes.

Take note

The original Form1 files will also still exist in the project directory and can be deleted.

Adding new forms

Most applications need a number of windows, and the forms for these can be created in much the same way as the first form. To add a new form, select Project|Add Windows Form from the Visual Studio menu, click on the Windows Form icon (if not already selected), type a filename for the form and then click on Add.

New Windows form

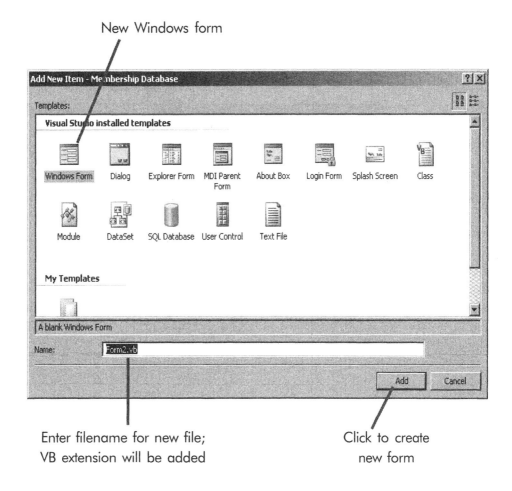

Enter filename for new file;
VB extension will be added

Click to create
new form

A blank form is displayed in a new tab, with the same default settings as the original Form1. An entry for this form will have been added to the Solution Explorer window.

The property settings for either form can be changed by clicking on the appropriate tab in the Visual Studio window and then changing the values in the Properties window.

The Name for the new form is set to match the filename, so does not need to be changed. The Text property should be changed to something that describes the purpose of the form.

Text property
for form

Filename; Name property is the
same (without extension)

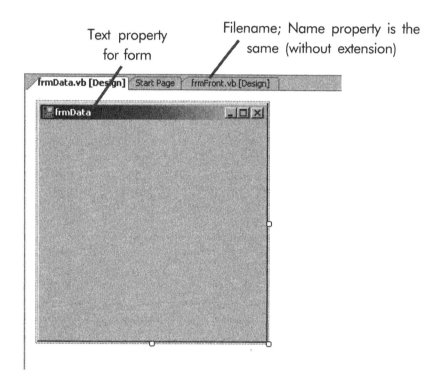

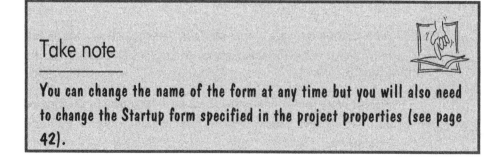

Take note

You can change the name of the form at any time but you will also need to change the Startup form specified in the project properties (see page 42).

The following table lists suitable property settings for three different types of form that might be used in an application:

Property	Data Entry Window	Text Entry Window	Message Box
(Name)	frmData	frmText	frmMess1
Text	Data Entry	Text Entry	Error
Location:			
X	100	200	300
Y	200	100	300
Size:			
Width	480	512	400
Height	480	300	120
BorderStyle	FixedSingle	Sizable	FixedDialog
ControlBox	True	True	False
MinButton	True	True	False
MaxButton	False	True	False

Having set up the new forms, each one should be saved with File|Save (or press **[Ctrl-S]** or click on the Save icon on the toolbar). This option saves the **current** form, so make sure you have clicked on the tab for the form you want to save.

Keep all forms for the project in the same directory.

Tip

Most message boxes are created when needed within the code, as illustrated on page 143.

Adding existing forms

Existing form files can be added to the project at any time. Select Project|Add Existing Item and then choose the file with VB extension from the file list. In this way, you can restore forms that were previously removed. You can also add in forms that were created for other projects.

Removing forms

If a form is no longer needed, it can be removed from the project:

● The form can be permanently deleted. On the Solution Explorer window, right-click on its form name and then select Delete from the pop-up menu. You are asked to confirm the action, following which the form is removed from the project and the two form files are deleted from the project directory.

● Depending on the type of project, the form may be temporarily excluded. On the Solution Explorer window, right-click on the form name and then select Exclude From Project (or use Project|Exclude from Project). Although the form is removed from the project, the form file itself is unaffected and can be restored later if required.

Form being removed
(files also deleted)

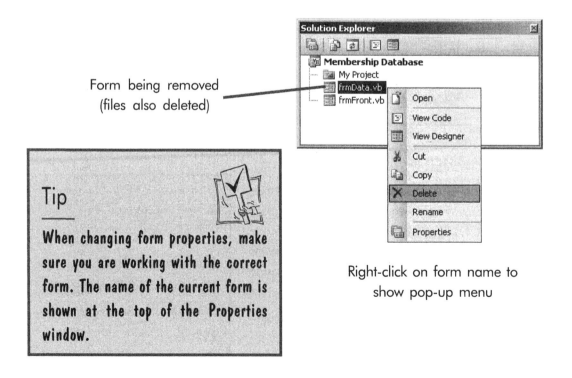

Right-click on form name to
show pop-up menu

Tip

When changing form properties, make sure you are working with the correct form. The name of the current form is shown at the top of the Properties window.

Restoring a form

To restore a form that has been previously excluded:

1   Select Project|Show All Files. The list in the Solution Explorer is expanded. Among the new items (which were previously hidden from view) is the excluded form file, next to a white icon.

2   Right-click on the file and select Include In Project (or use Project|Include In Project). The form's icon is restored in the Solution Explorer list.

3   Select Project|Show All Files again, this time to hide the other (system) files.

4   There is currently no tab on the Visual Studio display for the form, so double-click on the VB file in the Solution Explorer to display the form again.

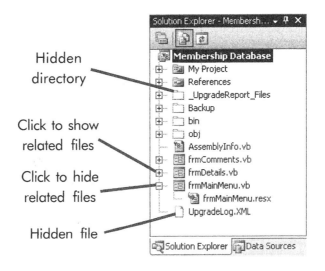

Hidden directory

Click to show related files

Click to hide related files

Hidden file

Tip

You can copy standard form files to another directory for use with a different project. These can then be added to the new project.

You can also copy an entire project (including all its files) to a new directory and then change the project name and use this as the basis for a new project.

Saving and running

Usually, an application is made up of several windows, each of which is created from a form in a VB file. The application as a whole has a **project file**, which defines the forms and other files that go together to make up the finished project.

The project is defined by a number of files in the project directory; the main file has the name given to the project initially and the extension VBPROJ.

The project has two properties: the filename and its location. You can change the name of the project at any time by clicking on the project name at the top of the Solution Explorer and then changing the Project File setting in the Properties window. The immediate effect is that the name changes in the Solution Explorer and the two physical files are renamed.

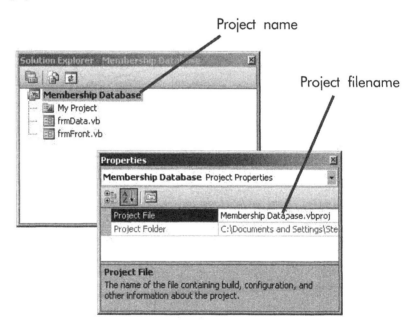

The project comprises part of a solution (which may contain other projects as well). The solution is defined in two further files, with SLN and SLO extensions. Initially, the name of the solution is the same as the project name.

The solution also has a number of properties, which you can display by clicking on the solution name at the top of the Solution Explorer. You can change the Name of the solution in the Properties window; the names of the solution files are updated immediately but there is no change to the project filename or project folder name.

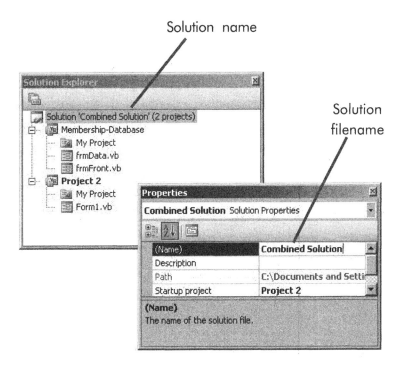

Solution name

Solution filename

You can save any changes to the project or solution by clicking on the appropriate item in the Solution Explorer and then selecting the relevant Save option from the File menu. Any changed forms are saved at the same time.

More simply, you can save all your changes (to forms, the project and the solution) at any time by selecting Form|Save All or by clicking on the Save All button on the toolbar.

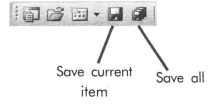

Save current item

Save all

If you have set up a SoureSafe database, you will also be asked if you want to save the project in SourceSafe. This is a file management system, which stores previous versions of your files so that you can recover them at any time. SourceSafe is particularly useful if several people are working on a project at the same time. For information on SourceSafe and setting up a SourceSafe database, see the on-line help.

The Start-up form

Visual Studio needs to know which form you want to display first when the program is run. By default, it assumes this will be Form1. However, if you have renamed this form or want to use a different form, you must tell Visual Studio the name of the new start-up form:

1   Right-click on the project name in the Solution Explorer and select Properties.

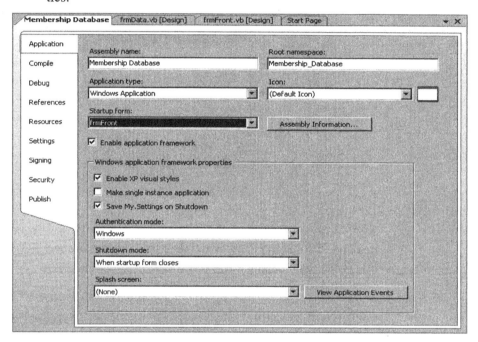

2   Click on the 'Startup form' object drop-down box and select the relevant form.

3   Click on OK.

Take note

You can also select a code file to be the startup object if you do not want to display a form initially. For more information, see the on-line help.

Running the application

To test the program, select Start Debugging from the Debug menu (or press **[F5]**). An Output window appears at the bottom of the Visual Studio window and a few messages will flash by (if the window has been selected for display).

The first window should pop up very quickly. It may not appear very impressive but all the buttons on the window should behave as you would expect. The Minimise and Maximise buttons (if included) reduce the application to an icon or blow it up to full-screen size, respectively. The window can be moved or resized (depending on the setting for BorderStyle). Other windows are not visible yet – you need to add some program code before they can be seen.

The Visual Studio window is still open, behind Form1, but you cannot make any changes to your application. The title bar shows that it is '(Running)' and some of the windows are hidden.

Visual Studio visible in background

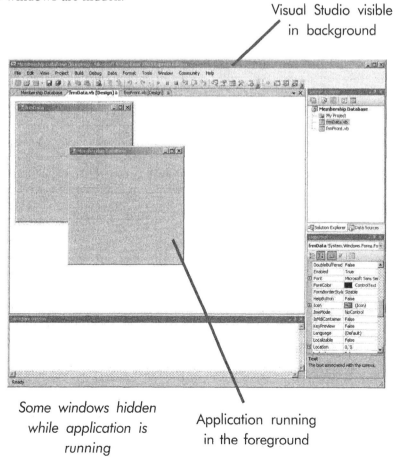

Some windows hidden while application is running

Application running in the foreground

You can close the application by clicking on the Close button in the top right-hand corner of the window. You will be returned to the Visual Studio window, where you can continue building your application.

The Output window shows details of how the program was compiled. If the window is not visible, select View|Other Windows|Output. By clicking on the drop-down box at the top of the window you can choose between the Build and Debug messages. You can close this window at any time.

Click to select either Debug or
Build messages

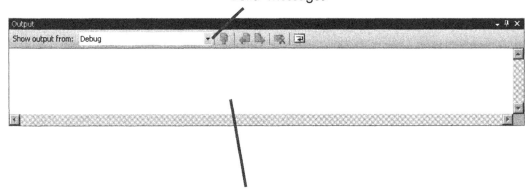

Messages will show actions
carried out while the application
was running

Tip

If you cannot close down your application for any reason, you can always do so by switching to Visual Studio and selecting Debug|Stop Debugging. This will exit your application, closing any open windows and giving you full access to Visual Studio once again. No harm will come to your application when you do this.

Debug options

There are two ways of starting your application:

- Selecting Debug|Start runs the program with debugging turned on, so that you can interrupt the program at any time and find out how it is operating.

- Selecting Debug|Start Without Debugging runs the program independently of Visual Studio. You cannot interrupt the program but you are able to carry on working in Visual Studio. In this case, the Output window shows only the Build stage of the compilation.

Build window

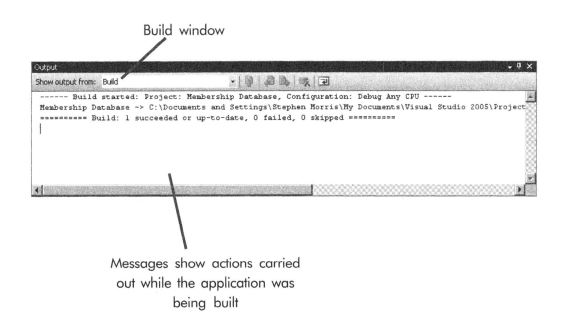

Messages show actions carried out while the application was being built

EXE files

When you build and run an application, an EXE version of the application is also built. This file can be found in the 'bin' subdirectory of your project directory.

You can run the EXE file at any time, even when Visual Studio is not running. However, you should take care to ensure that the program is not going to 'hang'; you will not be able to break into it via Visual Studio and the only option will be **[Ctrl-Alt-Del]**.

Exercises

The exercises in this book build up an application for storing membership details for an organisation. This application can be modified to suit many other purposes, such as a contacts database or a program to store records of correspondence.

1. Open the Membership Database project.

2. Modify the front-end form, so that it has a Minimise button but no Maximise button. The form should be of fixed size, with a suitable title. Name it 'frmMainMenu' and save it in a file called frmMainMenu.vb.

3. Create a form for entering data, again with no Maximise button and of fixed size. Name it 'frmDetails' and save it with a suitable filename.

4. Create a form for entering text. This form should be sizable. Name it 'frmComments' and save it with a suitable filename.

5. Change the Name of the project to 'Members' and its filename to Members.vbproj.

6. Save the changes.

7. Set the front-end form as the start-up form. Save the changes.

8. Run the application to check that the front-end window is displayed correctly. Save the changes. Close the Output window.

For help with these exercises, see page 293.

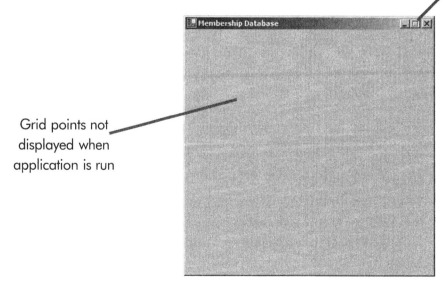

Maximise button not available

Grid points not displayed when application is run

3 Controls

Object-oriented programming

In a very short time, you have built a fully functioning Windows application – something that would take you many weeks to accomplish if you had to do it from scratch. This has all been achieved with the object-oriented programming structures that underly Visual Basic. This section gives a very brief introduction to object-oriented programming (OOP).

Objects and their use

In traditional programming systems, a program consists of a linear series of instructions, through which control flows in an ordered and predictable manner; data is stored separately from the program. Object-oriented programs, on the other hand, have a much looser structure, in which programs and data are bound together in independent units and control lies firmly in the hands of the user.

The windows in your application and their components – buttons, labels, scroll bars, menus etc. – are all **objects**. An object is self-contained; it comprises both the procedures to perform its required tasks and the data that these procedures need. In a process called **encapsulation**, the procedures and data are insulated from the rest of the program. There should be no danger of control jumping unexpectedly from one object's procedures into the middle of those of another object; nor should it be possible for one object to inadvertently change the data belonging to another object.

Information – data and instructions – is passed between objects in the form of **messages**. For instance, when a button is clicked, Windows sends a particular message to the button object. The button-click procedure is executed and another message is sent back to say that the action has been processed.

All objects of the same type come from the same **class**. The class defines the procedures and data for the object. Visual Basic uses a set of related classes called the **.NET Framework Class Library** and all objects in your programs will be derived from one of these classes. This library is made up of a number of **namespaces**. Each namespace contains a collection of classes.

For instance, all buttons come from a class called Button in the System.Windows. Forms namespace. The class is a template for objects of that type; individual objects are created as **instances** of that class.

The appearance of an object – and to a certain extent its behaviour – is determined by its **properties**: specific data values encapsulated within the object. For example, two windows from the same class may have different text in the title bar; whether or not they can be minimised is determined by the value of another property.

When a class has been defined, a new class can be derived from it. Initially, the new class will have all the procedures and data from the original class (the **base** class); this is called **inheritance**. Some of the data structures and procedures are changed in the new class, giving its objects different behaviour and appearance to those of the original class.

For example, Button is derived from a general class of controls called ButtonBase; Button has all the features of ButtonBase but modifies and extends them to produce a variety of buttons. ButtonBase is, in turn, derived from System.Windows.Forms.Control.

Similarly, RadioButton and CheckBox are derived from ButtonBase and result in buttons that have a slightly different appearance and behaviour.

TextBox and RichTextBox are both derived from System.Windows.Forms.TextBoxBase, which is also derived from System.Windows.Forms.Control. TextBoxBase modifies the class in slightly different ways to produce text boxes and rich text boxes respectively. Therefore, Button, TextBox and CheckBox share many characteristics but have their own unique features; this is known as **polymorphism**.

Most classes in the library are derived from a single class, Control, and together they form a **class hierarchy**.

Take note

You can find out more about any of these classes by searching for the class name in the on-line help. To see the full class hierarchy, search for 'System.Windows.Forms namespace'. Full details of the hierarchy can be found in the MSDN help at .NET Developer/.NET Framework SDK/.NET Framework/Reference/Class Library/System.Windows.Forms.

Adding controls

All windows have one or more **controls**. These are objects that display information or allow the user to perform an action: for instance, buttons, text boxes, option buttons and scroll bars.

Any combination of controls can be placed on a form but you should remember that when the application is run the user will be free to use the controls in any order (subject to any restrictions you impose at development time).

For example, the message box that is displayed if you try to delete a form contains, in effect, four controls: two buttons (marked OK and Cancel), a label (containing the text of the message) and an image control (containing the icon). The program forces you to click on one of the buttons but it's up to you which you choose. The action taken by the program depends on which button is clicked. (In fact, message boxes are created in a special way.)

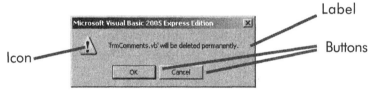

Icon   Label   Buttons

The toolbox

Visual Studio supplies a number of standard controls for use on forms. These are represented by icons in the Toolbox. Controls can be added to a form in three ways:

- Double-click on the control in the Toolbox to create an object of default size in the top left-hand corner of the form.

- Click on the control and then click on the form to create an object of default size at that point on the form.

- Click on the control in the Toolbox, then drag the pointer over the area of the form to be covered by the control.

Whichever method you use, you can change the size and position later (see *Control properties* below). The standard controls are described from page 65 onwards.

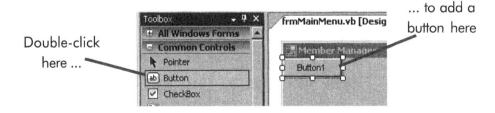

Double-click here ...   ... to add a button here

50

Control properties

The appearance and behaviour of a control is determined by its **properties**, in the same way as for a form. The properties include not only cosmetic items – the size, colour and position of the control, for example – but also those characteristics that affect the way a control is used: whether it is enabled, the user actions that are allowed etc.

The properties are different for each type of control and in each case the system provides a default. Most defaults are quite satisfactory so there are usually only a very few properties that need to be changed.

As for forms, you will set the properties when developing the project but they may also be changed while the application is running.

Some properties apply to most or all of the controls – for instance, every control has a Name – and most can be changed. The most important properties are described below for the standard controls.

A number of other, more advanced properties are included in most controls and may be useful when an application reaches a later stage of development. You are unlikely to use these properties often but it is worth knowing they are there.

Changing properties

To change the properties for a control, first click on the control so that it is selected. Small square 'handles' will appear at each corner and in the middle of each side. The Properties window will show the properties for the selected control. This will include the name of the control at the top (initially a default name, consisting of the control type and a number); you will see the properties that are listed change each time you select a different type of control.

Remember that all controls of the same type will have the *same properties* but each control of that type will be given *different settings*. Therefore, when you click on different controls of the same type you will see the same list of properties but with different settings in each case. For example, all buttons have Name, Width and Text properties; the settings for one button may be btnOK, 128 and OK respectively, and for another, btnHelp, 96 and Help.

To change the control properties, click on a control and then on a property in the Properties window. Then either type a new setting in the right-hand column or (where appropriate) select the setting from a drop-down list.

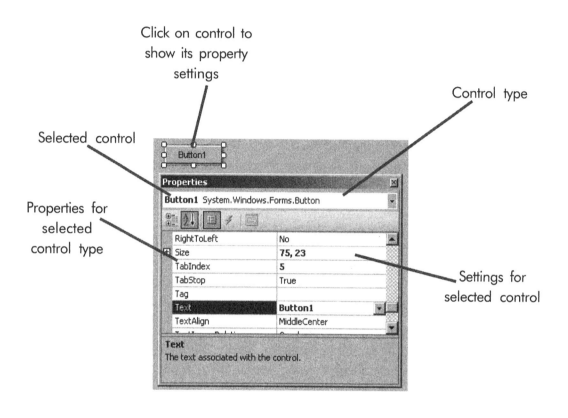

Click on control to
show its property
settings

Control type

Selected control

Properties for
selected
control type

Settings for
selected control

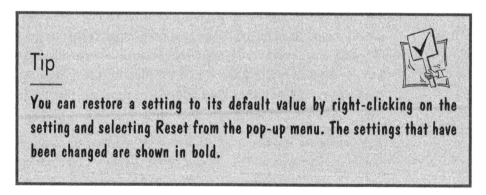

Tip

You can restore a setting to its default value by right-clicking on the setting and selecting Reset from the pop-up menu. The settings that have been changed are shown in bold.

Deleting controls

To remove a control from the form, click on it (so that square 'sizing handles' are shown on the corners and sides) and then press the **[Del]** key.

Multiple properties

You can select a group of controls in one of the following ways:

- Hold down the **[Shift]** key and then click on two or more controls. Each time you click on an additional control, the other selected controls are identified with white sizing handles.

- Move the pointer to a blank area of the form and then drag it over the controls. Any control that is at least partly covered by the marked rectangle is given sizing handles.

- A control can be removed from the group by holding down **[Shift]** and clicking on it again.

This method is normally used for dragging controls to another part of the form but it can also be used for changing the settings for all the marked controls at the same time. If you change a setting in the Properties window, the setting is applied to all selected controls; for instance, you can change the width of a group of controls.

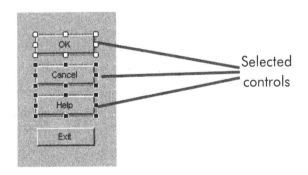

Selected controls

Tip

You can find out what any property is used for by looking for the relevant entry in the System.Windows.Forms section in the MSDN library. Every control has an entry in the on-line help, giving an overview and a link to a list of all the control's members (including the properties).

Common properties

A large number of properties are common to all or most controls; these provide the basic functionality of the controls. Each type of control has its own additional properties, which regulate those features that are peculiar to the control. For instance, most controls can have their size and position changed but only a text box has a PasswordChar property, which allows the box to be used for entering a password. The most useful common properties are described here.

Name

Every control has a **Name**, which is used when referring to the control in a procedure (for instance, when changing the control's properties at run time). Visual Studio gives each new control a default name, consisting of the control type and a number: Button1, Button2, ..., Text1, Text2 etc.

You should change these names to something more meaningful. Although you could keep the defaults, you should change the Name for all controls, even those you think you are unlikely to use in your program.

The rules for names are as follows:

● Names may consist of letters, numbers and underscore (_) characters; no other characters or spaces are allowed.

● Names must start with a letter. You can use numbers or underscores anywhere in the Name apart from the first character.

● Upper and lower case letters are treated as being the same but a mixture can be used to make the name easier to identify (btnSaveAs is more recognisable than btnsaveas but both refer to the same control).

● Names can be any length but for ease of use you should keep them much shorter than this.

To make it easier to identify controls from their names, you should adopt a suitable naming convention. A common convention is that the first three characters are lower-case letters and indicate the type of control; all buttons begin 'btn', all text boxes 'txt' and so on. A suggested naming convention is given in the on-line help. If you adopt the standard naming convention, keep to it for all controls.

You should change the Name for all new controls, even those you think you are unlikely to use in a procedure. For instance, labels may originally be fixed but later on you may want to vary them when the program is running.

If you enter a name that is invalid, Visual Studio displays an error message.

Click to show
description of
error

Clicking on the Details button displays a brief description of why the button is invalid – though some descriptions are more helpful than others!

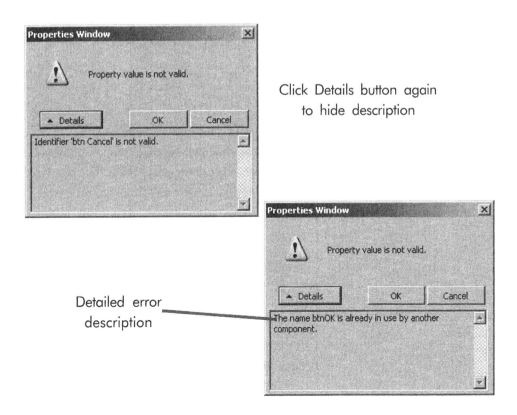

Click Details button again
to hide description

Detailed error
description

Text

Many controls have a fixed item of text that appears on the surface of the control: for example, buttons, check boxes and labels. The fixed text is held in the **Text** property. The restrictions on the Name do not apply to the Text; this is a purely cosmetic piece of text and you can enter whatever you like.

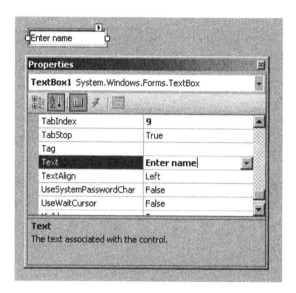

You can include an & in front of any character in the Name to denote that character as an **access key**. When there is an access key, the user can 'click' the control by pressing **[Alt]** and the access character together. For example, if the access key is S, the control can be clicked by pressing **[Alt]+[S]**. The access key character is underlined in the control's caption. If you need to include an & in the Text itself, type '&&'; only one & will be displayed.

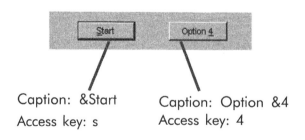

Caption: &Start
Access key: s

Caption: Option &4
Access key: 4

It is usual to select the first letter of the Text as the access key, unless that letter has already been used by another control on the same form (in which case you can select any suitable character in the Text).

If two controls have the same access key, pressing that combination will select each one of them in turn. However, this is confusing for users and should be avoided!

Other controls allow users to type an entry. These also have a **Text** property, which holds the user's input. In some cases, you can set a default value for the Text property, which is shown when the form is first displayed and which the user can then overwrite. For other controls, the Text property cannot be set during development but you can change it (and the user can add text) while the application is running.

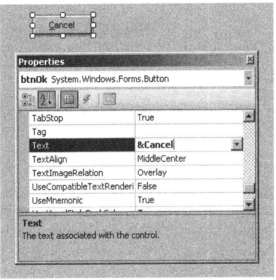

You can add read-only controls to the form (where the user cannot change the text) by changing the controls' Enabled property to False (see page 64).

Take note

In earlier versions of Visual Basic, the Text property was referred to as the Caption property.

Size and Location

The size and position of a control are determined by the same set of four properties as for a form: **Width** and **Height** for the size, **Left** and **Top** for position. As for forms, you can enter these properties individually or use the combined properties, Size and Location. Left and Top give the position of the top-left corner of the control relative to the top-left corner of the inside of the form.

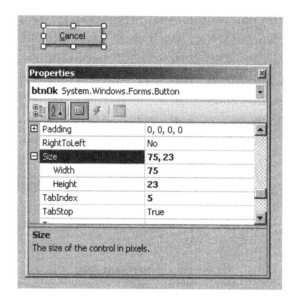

These properties can be changed either by dragging the sizing handles on the corners and sides of the control or by entering new settings directly. Usually, dragging the sizing handles is satisfactory, as it enables you to set the size and position by eye. For precise settings, however, the values can be adjusted in the Properties window.

The size and location of controls are measured in pixels, as for forms.

When developing a form there is a background grid of points for aligning controls. If you change the control size or position by dragging, the control corners 'snap' to the nearest grid points. The grid can be changed (or switched off) by choosing Tools|Options and clicking on the Windows Form Designer folder on the left; the Width and Height of the grid square can be changed and the grid snap can be turned off.

Spacing of grid points (pixels)

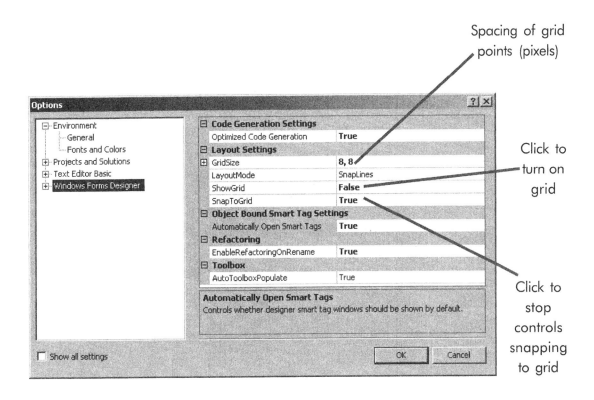

Click to turn on grid

Click to stop controls snapping to grid

Fonts

If a control displays text, you can change the appearance with the **Font** property.

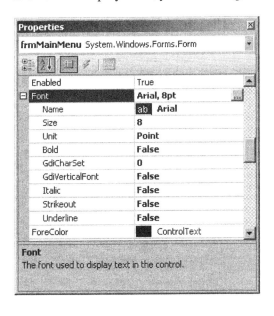

In the same way as for Size and Location, Font is actually a combination of subsidiary properties. When you click on the ⊞ box to the left of the property, the list is expanded to show the items that make up the property.

When you click on the property, a small button with three dots appears on the right.

Clicking on this displays the Font window, from which you can select the font, the style (bold, italic etc.) and the point size. You can also apply strikeout (a line through the middle of the text) and underline.

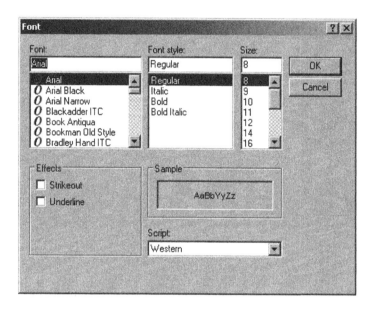

After making the necessary changes in the Font window click on OK to update the corresponding settings.

Tip

If you click on the Font list and move up and down using the arrow keys, the Sample box shows you what the text will look like.

Tip

Use only the standard Windows fonts, so that your application will always look the same, regardless of the machine running it. If you use third-party fonts, you must be prepared to supply these with your application.

Colour

The control's background colour is set by the **BackColor** property. For controls that display text or graphics, the colour of these is determined by **ForeColor**. The values for colours can be entered in one of two ways:

●   Selecting from a palette

●   Entering an RGB colour number

The easiest way to choose a colour is by clicking on the drop-down list in the setting box. You can select a colour from one of three tabs:

●   The Custom tab contains a grid of coloured boxes.

●   The Web tab includes a list of colours that are safe to use on forms that will be displayed on the Internet. (Other colours will not necessarily display effectively on every Web browser.)

●   The System tab lists the colours that are selected on the Windows Display Properties dialog. The colours on your application will change according to the choices made by the user when setting up Windows.

When you click on a colour, either the colour name or a series of numbers is entered in the setting box. The main disadvantage of these methods is that the range of colours is limited.

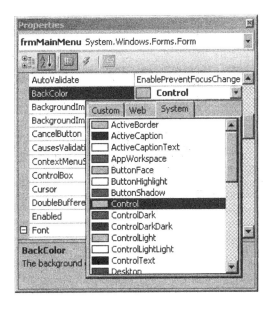

Each colour on the screen is made up of three components – red, green and blue – in differing intensities. The colour is represented by a number in the form rr, gg, bb where rr is the red component, gg green and bb blue. Each component can have a value between 0 (no colour) and 255 (full intensity). The midpoint is 128. This is the RGB code.

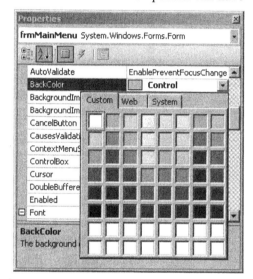

You can increase the number of available colours by entering an RGB code directly:

1   In the colour dialog, click on the Custom tab.

2   Right-click on one of the blank squares at the bottom of the palette.

3   Define the colour either by clicking on the large multi-coloured box or by entering specific values for the Red, Green and Blue components of the colour.

RGB values
shown for setting

Define new
colour

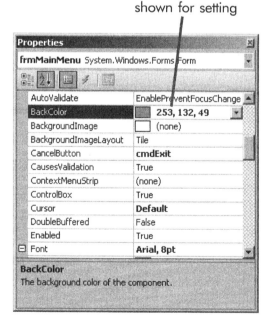

Tab stops and focus

When the user clicks on a window, the window is said to have the **focus**; that is, it is the active window. The title bar of the window with the focus has a different colour to the others. (In the default Windows colours, the window with the focus has a blue title bar, the rest are grey.) Only one window can have the focus at any one time.

Similarly, one (and only one) control on the window has the focus. This is usually indicated by a thicker border around the control, by highlighting or by the appearance of a cursor in text boxes.

When the user presses the **[Tab]** key, the focus moves from one control to the next. The order in which the focus moves is determined by two properties: **TabStop** and **TabIndex**. The TabStop setting specifies whether or not the control can have the focus (a setting of True if it can), while TabIndex gives the order in which the controls have the focus. Each control on the form has a unique tab index number. Initially, the tab index numbers match the order in which the controls were added to the form.

To change the tab order, change the TabIndex setting for a control. All the index numbers will be updated to take account of the new order. For example, if there are four controls on the form, the index numbers will be 0, 1, 2 and 3. To move the last control into second place, change its index number from 3 to 1. The system will then renumber the two controls in the middle from 1 and 2 to 2 and 3 respectively. By changing the tab index for several objects, you can put the controls into any order you like.

Take note

All controls have a TabIndex number but those for which TabStop is False are ignored. No two controls on a form can have the same TabIndex.

Tip

Don't worry about the tab settings until the form is complete — then you can set the tab index for all the controls at once, when you have a better idea of the order you want.

Visible and Enabled

The **Visible** property determines whether the control can be seen and **Enabled** decides whether it can be used. As a general rule, it is less confusing for the user if controls are always visible but not necessarily enabled. When a control is not enabled (its Enabled setting is False), any text displayed on it is grey and clicking on the control has no effect. Naturally, if a control is not visible (its Visible setting is False), the user cannot click on it and its Enabled property is irrelevant.

For example, you may have a Save button on your form that is enabled only when new data has been entered in text boxes. (The alternative would be to make the Save button visible when a change is made to the data but a button suddenly popping up on the window is disconcerting for the user.)

The Enabled property can also be used for making a text box read-only. If you set Enabled to False the user can see the text but cannot change it.

The Visible property may be used where the value of one control affects the applicability of others. For instance, on an accounts form a pair of radio buttons may allow you to choose between a payment and a receipt. Other controls on the form – such as a text box for the cheque number – will be made visible depending on the radio button that is clicked. When the user clicks the payment button, the cheque number is made visible; when the receipt button is clicked, the Visible property for the cheque number box is set to False while a text box containing the delivery date could be made visible

In another case, a button may be clicked to display additional information in the window; when the button is clicked, the Visible property on a text box could be set to True.

Tip

Two controls may occupy the same space on the form, providing they are never both visible at the same time. For instance, the same area may be used for a cheque number for payments and the delivery date for receipts.

Standard controls

The Visual Studio toolbox contains a large number of standard controls. Click on the arrows above and below the list of items to move the list up or down. Click on the horizontal tabs to view other lists of components. The diagrams below show the full set of controls available for Windows forms.

The toolbox may show other controls, depending on the Visual Studio version that is being run and any controls that have been added. Visual Studio allows you to add other controls using Project|Add User Control but the standard toolbox should contain enough controls for most applications.

To find out more about any control, locate the relevant topic in MSDN help. This displays a list of all the control's properties etc. For a more general description, click on the Overview link at the top of the help page.

Take note

The pointer icon at the top of the Windows forms list is not a control. Click on this icon when you want to select an existing control in order to make changes to the control's properties.

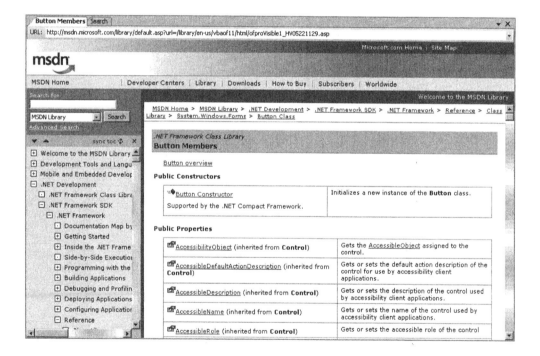

Buttons

Buttons are used for performing actions. A procedure is attached to each button and is executed when the user clicks on the button. You cannot decide the order in which buttons are clicked but you do have full control over the action taken once the user has clicked a button.

The text that appears on the surface of the button is held in the **Text** property.

Each form has two settings that affect the behaviour of its buttons:

● The **AcceptButton** property identifies the button that is activated when the user presses the **[Enter]** key; usually, this is the OK button. Select the appropriate button from the drop-down list of all buttons included on the form so far.

● In a similar way, you can select a button in the **CancelButton** property; this is the button that is activated when the user presses the **[Esc]** key (usually the button for which the Text is 'Cancel').

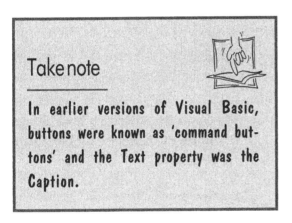

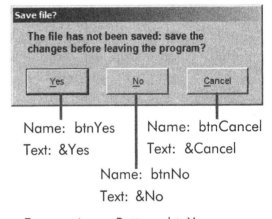

Name: btnYes   Name: btnCancel
Text: &Yes   Text: &Cancel

Name: btnNo
Text: &No

Form: AcceptButton: btnYes
          CancelButton: btnCancel

Labels

The **label** control adds text to the form: titles, instructions, text for data-entry boxes and so on. The user cannot do anything with these controls but you may wish to change the text itself at run time; for example, after a file has been selected a label may be used to display the filename.

The text of the label is held in the **Text** property. The position of the text within the label area is set by the **TextAlign** property.

You can place the text on the left, centre or right of the label area, and at the top, middle or bottom. The alignment is chosen by clicking on the setting and then on the appropriate grey rectangle on the drop-down box.

If the text will not fit in the label area, setting **AutoSize** to True allows the label to expand its area if necessary.

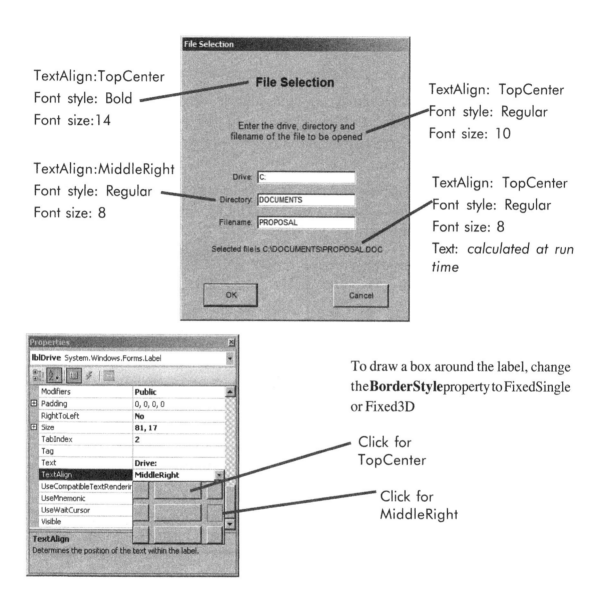

TextAlign:TopCenter
Font style: Bold
Font size:14

TextAlign: TopCenter
Font style: Regular
Font size: 10

TextAlign:MiddleRight
Font style: Regular
Font size: 8

TextAlign: TopCenter
Font style: Regular
Font size: 8
Text: *calculated at run time*

To draw a box around the label, change the **BorderStyle** property to FixedSingle or Fixed3D

Click for
TopCenter

Click for
MiddleRight

Text boxes

The **text box** provides the simplest method for the user to enter data. When the control has the focus, a vertical cursor is displayed and the user can make an entry.

The **Text** property contains the user's entry when it is complete; by setting this property during development you can supply a default value, which the user can either leave as it is or change.

68

By default, the **BorderStyle** property is Fixed3D, resulting in a box drawn around the edge of the text area. Change this to FixedSingle for a simple box or None to remove the box.

The lack of a any sort of fixed text means that text boxes cannot be given an access key directly. However, you can get round the problem by placing a label control next to the text box; since a label control cannot be clicked, the access key on the label acts as an access key for the text box.

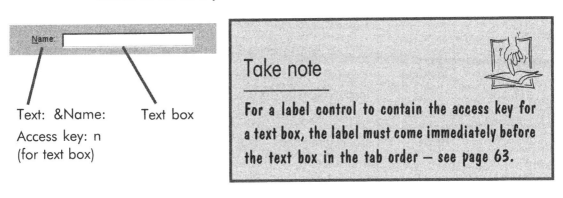

Text: &Name:

Access key: n
(for text box)

Text box

Take note

For a label control to contain the access key for a text box, the label must come immediately before the text box in the tab order – see page 63.

MultiLine determines whether text can spread over more than one line. A value of True means that text will wrap from one line to the next when the edge of the box is reached; a new line will be started when the user presses **[Enter]**. A value of False means that the text always stays on a single line (with long items of text scrolling out of view at either end of the box).

The **TextAlign** setting places text on the left or right of the box, or centres it.

The **Locked** property, if set to True, stops the user from changing the text.

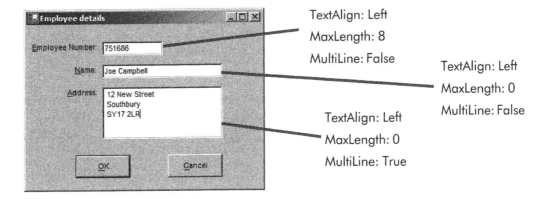

TextAlign: Left
MaxLength: 8
MultiLine: False

TextAlign: Left
MaxLength: 0
MultiLine: False

TextAlign: Left
MaxLength: 0
MultiLine: True

MaxLength sets a limit to the number of characters that can be entered in the box. For instance, a setting of 8 could be used when entering a password. If MaxLength is 0 (the default), the amount of text is limited only by the computer's memory.

For large amounts of text, where MultiLine is True, you may want to add scroll bars. The **ScrollBars** property can take the following settings:

None	No scroll bars. Use this when the amount of text is limited.
Horizontal	Horizontal scroll bar. The user can keep typing to the right, beyond the end of the box. Use where there are no paragraphs (e.g. program code).
Vertical	Vertical scroll bar. This is the most useful option, giving a clear indication of how much text has been typed and where the cursor is, relative to the text as a whole.
Both	Both scroll bars. Use this for text that can spread in both directions.

If there is no horizontal scroll bar, the text for a multi-line box automatically wraps to the next line when the right-hand edge of the box is reached. However, when there is no vertical scroll bar, the text will still scroll upwards when the box is full, unless you set MaxLength. Therefore, you should usually have a vertical scroll bar for multi-line text.

The **PasswordChar** property is useful when asking the user to enter a password. The setting can be any single character (though it is usually *); this character will be displayed regardless of what the user types but the actual entry will be held in the Text property.

Radio buttons and check boxes

Radio buttons and check boxes provide two different methods of giving the user choices.

Radio buttons usually appear in groups of two or more, and all the buttons on a form are interrelated (unless they split into groups – see page 72). The control consists of a circle with a piece of text next to it. The text is held in the **Text** property.

The **TextAlign** property has the same options as labels, allowing the text position to be set both horizontally and vertically. The **Checked** property has a setting of either True or False, depending on whether or not the button has been selected. Only one button can be selected at a time, so when the user clicks on a radio button the Value for that button is set to True and for all other buttons to False.

Check boxes work in a similar way to radio buttons, the main difference being that they operate independently of each other. As a result, the user may select several boxes at the same time by clicking on them – or turn all boxes off.

The check box has three possible states, defined by the **CheckState** property:

Unchecked	The box is empty.
checked	The box contains a black tick.
Indeterminate	The box contains a grey tick.

You can choose any of these values to be the setting that is displayed when the program is run. The options available to the user depend on the setting of the **ThreeState** property. When ThreeState is True, clicking on the check box takes the user through each of the three states in turn; when False, the box can only be Checked or Unchecked.

Check boxes:

Checked: True
CheckState: Checked
ThreeState: False
Enabled: True

Checked: False
CheckState: Unchecked
ThreeState: False
Enabled: True

Checked: True
CheckState: Indeterminate
ThreeState: True
Enabled: False

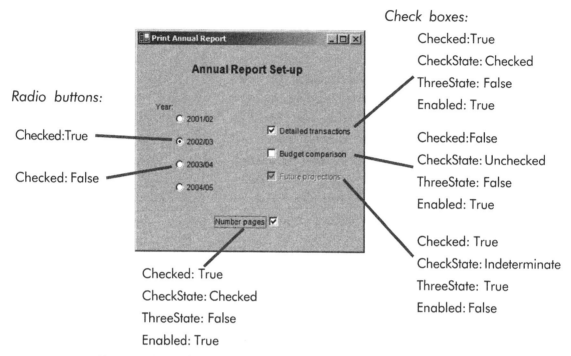

Radio buttons:

Checked: True

Checked: False

Checked: True
CheckState: Checked
ThreeState: False
Enabled: True

There is also a **Checked** property; this is True when CheckState is Checked or Indeterminate, otherwise it is False. Changing the value of Checked will affect the setting of CheckState, and vice versa.

At the development stage, you can set CheckState to Indeterminate even when ThreeState is False. This is useful if an option is to be shown as selected by default and you do not want the user to change it. In such cases you will usually also set Enabled to False.

Group boxes

Group boxes allow you to group controls together. From a functional point of view, group boxes are needed if you want more than one set of radio buttons on a screen. Radio buttons inside a group box act independently of any other buttons. For this to work, you must add the group box to the form first and then insert the radio buttons within the borders of the group box.

Take note

Group Boxes were called 'frames' in earlier versions of Visual Basic.

Select exactly one button from this group

Select box independently of others on form

Select any number of boxes from this group

Greyed boxes cannot be selected (Enabled = False)

Select exactly one button from this group

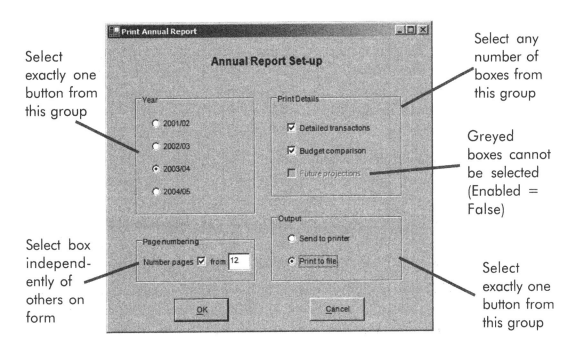

Print Annual Report

Annual Report Set-up

Year
- ○ 2001/02
- ○ 2002/03
- ◉ 2003/04
- ○ 2004/05

Print Details
- ☑ Detailed transactions
- ☑ Budget comparison
- ☐ Future projections

Page numbering
Number pages ☑ from 12

Output
- ○ Send to printer
- ◉ Print to file

[OK]   [Cancel]

Group boxes can also be used to improve the appearance of the window. Apart from radio buttons, any other group of controls can be placed within a group box, though this has no effect on the way they function.

The group box **Text** is the piece of text overlaid on the top left-hand corner of the group box.

Take note

The buttons must be drawn within the group box borders; you must not create the buttons by double-clicking on the toolbox and then dragging the buttons inside the box.

Tip

If you add a group box later, you can put it behind existing controls with Format|Order|Send To Back.

The Format|Order|Bring To Front option displays the current control on top of any others that share the same space.

Scroll bars and progress bars

Scroll bars (HScrollBar and VScrollBar) frequently appear on text boxes but you can also add them in other places. They can be added on their own (for instance, to indicate the progress of some activity or as an alternative data entry method), though standalone scroll bars tend to look rather peculiar. More usually, they can be attached to the edge of windows (for instance, one displaying part of a bitmap). In such cases, the properties are usually set while the program is running.

The **Minimum** and **Maximum** properties give the limits of the values that can be represented by the scroll bar; the **Value** represents the current position of the button on the scroll bar, as a proportion of the distance from one end of the scroll bar to the other. For instance, suppose that Minimum is 100 and Maximum is 200. When the button is at the top (or left) of the scroll bar, the Value is 100; when at the other end, the Value is 200; and in the middle of the bar, the Value is 150.

SmallChange specifies the amount by which Value will change when an arrow at the end of the scroll bar is clicked; **LargeChange** gives the change in Value when the bar itself is clicked (between an arrow and the scroll button).

In the illustration below, two procedures are used: the first sets the Text value of the text box to the scroll bar Value when the scroll bar is adjusted; the second revises the scroll bar Value (and hence the position of the button on the scroll bar) when the Text in the text box is changed. Information on procedures is given in Chapter 4.

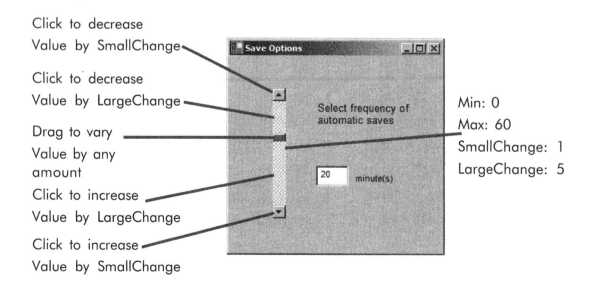

Click to decrease
Value by SmallChange

Click to decrease
Value by LargeChange

Drag to vary
Value by any
amount

Click to increase
Value by LargeChange

Click to increase
Value by SmallChange

Min: 0
Max: 60
SmallChange: 1
LargeChange: 5

The **TrackBar** is the modern equivalent of the standalone scroll bar and is the standard control for tasks where a value must be selected from a range. The bar has a set of marks on a horizontal scale, with a button indicating a proportion of the maximum value (for instance, the volume level in a music program or the proportion of a task that has been completed).

The control has **Minimum**, **Maximum**, **SmallChange**, **LargeChange** and **Value** properties that are identical to those of the scroll bars.

The **Orientation** property determines whether the track bar is **Horizontal** or **Vertical**. The **TickFrequency** lets you set the number of ticks on the scale.

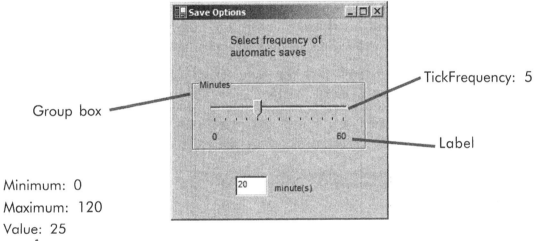

The **ProgressBar** is another similar control but is used for informing the user rather than giving the user the ability to make changes. The control has **Minimum**, **Maximum** and **Value** properties that specify the range and determine the current value within the range. The proportion represented by Value is indicated by coloured blocks that advance from left to right.

The **NumericUpDown** control provides a way for the user to select a value in a range, where there is no necessity to change the value from within the program (though, of course, you can do so if you need to). The control consists of a box displaying a numeric value, with up and down arrows to the right. Clicking on the arrows increases or decreases the value.

The control has **Minimum**, **Maximum** and **Value** properties, with Value usually determined by the user. The setting that you give to Value at the design stage is the number that is displayed initially.

The **DecimalPlaces** property allows you to specify decimal values, with the Increment setting giving the amount by which the Value changes with each click of the arrows. For large numeric values you can specify that **ThousandsSeparator** is True, so that the thousands are separated from the last three digits by a comma (or whatever character the user has selected on their Windows Regional Options).

The size of the text (and hence the height of the box) is determined by the **Font** property; you can set the **Width** to any value.

If **ReadOnly** is False, the user can type a value in the text box (which has a white background); if True, the user cannot enter a value directly and the box is grey.

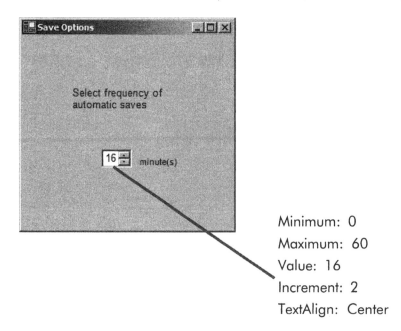

Minimum: 0
Maximum: 60
Value: 16
Increment: 2
TextAlign: Center

Other controls

In addition to the simple controls described above, there are a number of other standard controls on the toolbox:

- The **picture box** control allows you to add bitmaps; picture boxes also provide simple drawing facilities (see page 274).

- The **timer** lets you generate events at predefined times. (Add the control to the form and then set the Interval between timer events, giving a value in milliseconds.) (See page 281.)

- **List boxes, checked list boxes** and **combo boxes** allow you to choose from lists. Variations are provided by **list views** and **tree views** (see page 99).

- A number of controls provide standard Windows dialogs, such as those for opening files, saving files, changing font or colour, or accessing the printer (see page 244).

In addition to these, there are many other controls for performing more specialised tasks. Some of these are supplied on the Toolbox tabs; many others are available from third-party suppliers. Additional controls are added with the Project|Add New Item option.

Re-running the application

Try out some of these controls (examples are given over the page). You can see what your application will look like by pressing **[F5]** to run it. Clicking on a button won't do anything but you will see the button change as it is clicked. You can click on a radio button, and check boxes can be switched on or off.

Always save the project before running it. Occasionally, the system may 'hang' but providing you have saved your work, this should not be a problem. Remember that you can get out of an application by switching to Visual Studio and selecting Debug|Stop Debugging.

By this stage you should be able to create a fairly impressive 'front end' to your application – all without writing a line of code. Now, to make the windows and controls respond to the user's actions, you need to start adding program code.

Exercises

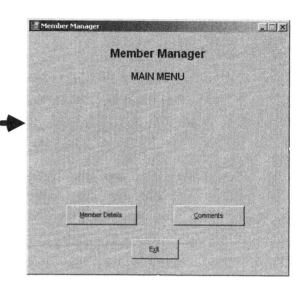

1   Add labels and buttons to the front-end form, as shown here. The Exit button should be set up so that it is activated by pressing the **[Esc]** key.

2   Create a password form. When text is typed into the text box it should show as asterisks.

3   Add controls to the Details form.

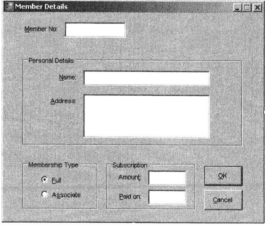

4   Add a text box and buttons to the Comments form.

5   Save all files and test the application. (At this stage only the front-end window will be displayed and the buttons will be ineffective.)

For solutions to these exercises, see page 295.

4 Coding events

The event-led environment

In traditional programming languages, the programmer is in complete control while the program is running. The program consists of a linear sequence of coded instructions, with branches to particular points in the program. At each stage of the program, the user is offered a limited number of options and the program branches to the relevant section of code, according to the choice that has been made. If the code has been written correctly, there should be no surprises.

Windows programming languages, such as Visual Basic, start from a very different viewpoint. At any one time there will be many **objects** on the screen: windows, buttons, menus, text boxes and so on. The user is free to click, drag or type on any object and, in most circumstances, is not constrained to follow a linear path through a fixed sequence of actions.

This **event-led** environment requires the programmer to take a completely new approach. Rather than trying to confine the user to a limited number of actions, the programmer must create an application that reacts correctly to whatever the user does. This is not as daunting as it sounds; there are, of course, ways of limiting the user's scope (for example, making forms and controls invisible or greying out check boxes) but the simplest action is to do nothing.

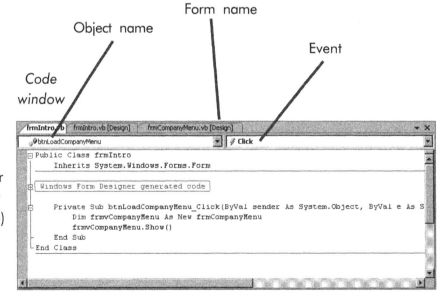

Form name

Object name

Event

Code
window

Procedure for
object/event
(see page 85)

For each object on the screen there are a number of possible **events**. Some of these are generated by the user: for instance, clicking or double-clicking the mouse-button, dragging an object across the screen or pressing a key. Others arise as a result of some other event occurring in the system: for example, a window opening or closing, a control getting or losing the focus, or the system time reaching some predefined value. You can also force an event to occur by including suitable instructions in your program.

The code to respond to these events is contained in Visual Basic **procedures**. For any object, there is a procedure for each possible event; initially, every procedure is empty, so nothing happens when the event occurs. Theoretically, you could create a procedure for every event but in practice you will only fill in the procedures for those events that are of interest.

For example, a button's events include being clicked, getting and losing the focus, and the mouse button being pressed and released. However, you may only want to provide code for the Click event; any other events would be ignored.

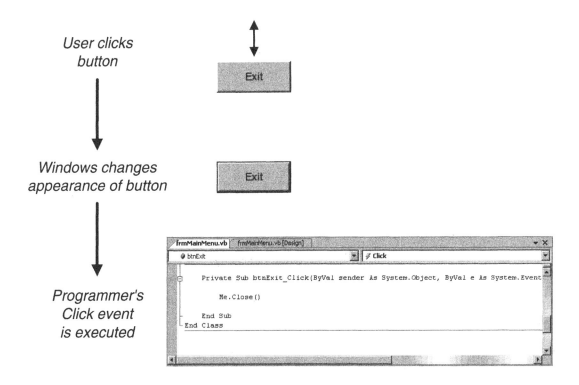

User clicks button

Windows changes appearance of button

Programmer's Click event is executed

Each event results in some action being taken by Windows itself. For instance, clicking on a button causes it to change its appearance while the mouse button is held down; clicking on a window's Minimise button reduces the window to an icon. These actions are encapsulated in the objects' definitions; they are part of the code that you get when you choose those objects.

In these cases, you cannot alter the object's behaviour but you can add to it; for example, you may activate a new form when the command button is clicked or display a message when a form is minimised.

Therefore, the next task, after creating the user interface, is to decide the events that are to be handled and create the appropriate procedures.

Common events

A number of events are common to most of the standard Visual Basic controls. (This is because of the way objects are related, allowing behaviour in one class to be inherited by those classes that are derived from it.)

A brief description is given here but for a full list of events view the relevant topic in the MSDN library. This contains a help page listing all an object's members: the properties, events and methods (described on page 95). The first item in the list is the Constructor, a special method that is used to create an instance of the object. Next come all the object's properties, followed by the methods and then the events.

For a full description of any event, click on the event name.

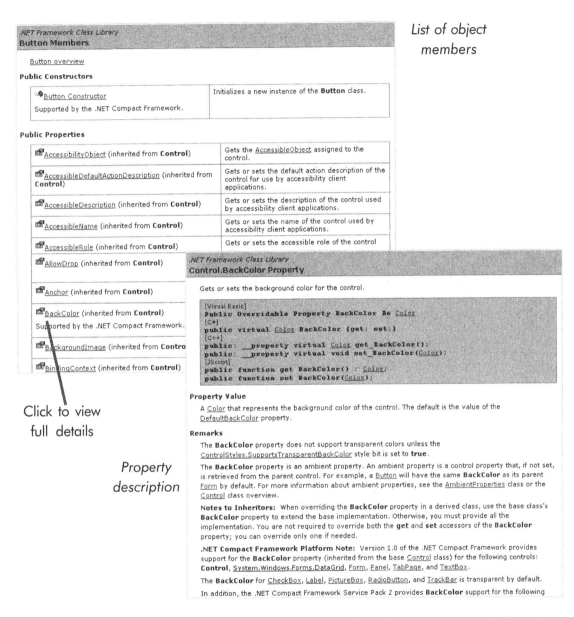

List of object
members

Click to view
full details

Property
description

The **Click** event is generated when the user clicks the mouse button with the pointer over the object; **DoubleClick** occurs when the user double-clicks. For a button or radio button, the Click event is also generated if you set the Value property to True within the program; for a check box, the Click event occurs if the program makes any change to the Value property. The DoubleClick event is not available for buttons.

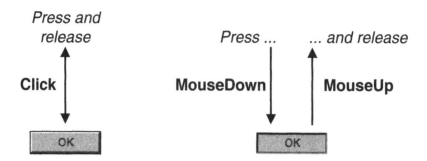

Press and release

Click

OK

Press ...

MouseDown

... and release

MouseUp

OK

Sometimes, you may want to split the Click event into its two component parts: **MouseDown** and **MouseUp**. For instance, you may want to change the appearance of a control when the button is pressed and restore it when the button is released. You also need to use these events to find out which mouse button was pressed and whether the **[Shift]**, **[Ctrl]** or **[Alt]** keys were also pressed. (The Click event provides no extra information.)

The **MouseMove** event occurs when the pointer passes over the top of the object (useful for changing the appearance of the pointer at different places on the screen). **DragOver** occurs when an item is being dragged over the object and the **DragDrop** event is generated at the end of a drag operation when the mouse button is released. For these drag operations you can determine what object was being dragged, and take the appropriate action.

GotFocus and **LostFocus** occur when a control gets or loses the focus, respectively. GotFocus can be used to set initial values, while LostFocus is useful for checking the user's input. For example, you might use GotFocus to give an empty text box a default value and then test the user input with LostFocus; if the entry is invalid, the cursor can be put back into the text box by giving the text box the focus again (but make sure the user does not get stuck in a loop!)

In some circumstances you may want to test for keyboard activity. **KeyPress** occurs when a key is pressed; this may be split into the **KeyDown** and **KeyUp** events.

You can also find out what the user has been doing by writing a procedure for an object's **TextChanged** event. This event occurs whenever the value of a label or text box changes. Similarly, **CheckedChanged** is generated wherever there is a change to a check box or radio button.

Creating a procedure

Procedures are created in a tab on the Visual Studio window. This tab is displayed either by clicking on the View Code button in the Solution Explorer window or, more simply, by double-clicking on either a control or a blank part of the form. The Code window has two list boxes below the title bar:

● The **Object** box on the left shows the current object (the form or a control).

● The **Procedure** box on the right shows the event being coded.

You can choose a new object and event at any time; when you do so, the procedure code for that object and event is displayed.

Every procedure must have a name that is unique within the form. Event-driven procedures are named for you, the name consisting of the object name, an underscore and the event name. For instance, the procedure corresponding to the Click event for a command button called 'btnExit' will be named 'btnExit_Click'.

The procedure is written in the format:

> Private Sub *object_event(parameters)* Handles *object.event*
> > *statements*
> End Sub

The first and last lines are provided for you; all you have to do is fill in the statements in the middle. When the event occurs, the procedure statements will be executed. For example, when the user clicks on the Exit button the btnExit_Click procedure is executed.

Object box:
current object

Enter
code here

Procedure
name

Procedure box:
current event

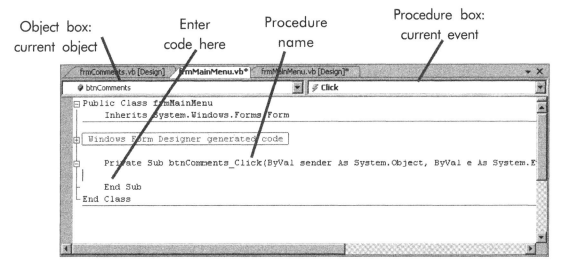

85

Do not change the *parameters* for event procedures. The **Handles** part of the statement tells you the object and event to which the procedure applies; if you rename the object the Handles part is updated so that the procedure still works, even though the procedure name (*object_event*) no longer describes the object accurately.

There is a block of code at the top of the tab that defines the form itself. You can view this code by clicking on the ⊞ button on the left but you must not make any changes to it. Looking through the code, you should be able to identify the instructions that correspond to the changes you have made to the form and control properties. You should also see the lines of code that add the buttons to the form.

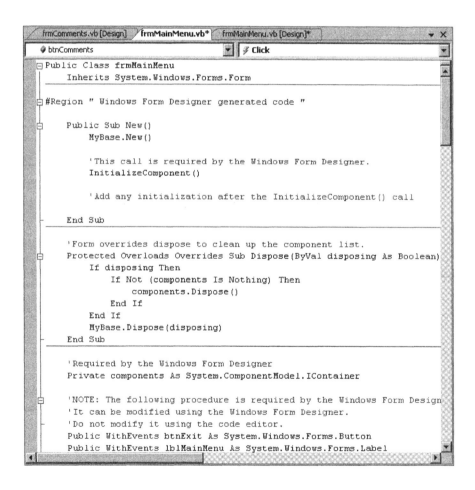

This demonstrates the principles of object-oriented programming. The form you have created is a new class, based on the standard Windows form class. The new class inherits all the behaviour of the original class. The instructions in this block extend the standard form by adding controls. These controls are themselves based on the standard controls and therefore inherit their behaviour: the changes to the properties then modify the new controls.

Displaying a form

The following example demonstrates the code needed to display a form. The code assumes that one form contains a button named btnDisplayCompanyDetails and that there is a second form named frmCompanyDetails. Clicking on the button displays the second form.

To do this you need add only two statements to the btnDisplayCompanyDetails_Click procedure:

1   Display the first form and double-click on the DisplayCompanyDetails button, so that the code tab is displayed.

2   In the blank line in the middle of the procedure type:

```
Dim frmvCompanyDetails As New frmCompanyDetails
frmvCompanyDetails.Show()
```

Press **[Enter]** at the end of each line. Visual Studio tidies up whatever you have written, capitalising words as needed and standardising the spacing. The meaning of these statements is given below.

Tip

As you type a line Visual Studio tries to help by displaying a pop-up box with possible ways to complete the statement. You can accept one of them by clicking on it and pressing [Tab].

Take note

The Click event is generated by clicking the button; tabbing to the button and pressing the spacebar; or pressing [Enter] (when this is the form's AcceptButton).

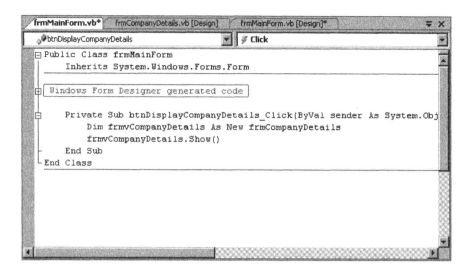

3   Press **[Ctrl-S]** to save the changes.

4   Press **[F5]** to run the application and then click on the Display Company Details button. The Details form is displayed.

5   Select Stop Debugging from the Visual Studio Debug menu to close down the application.

You can switch between the design page and code page for a form at any time; simply click on the appropriate tab at the top of the Visual Studio window. The design page is identified by [Design] in the tab name. Forms and code pages that have not been saved have an asterisk after the name in the tab.

Form display statements

When you create a form in Visual Studio, you are actually defining a new **class** rather than an object. The new class is based on the standard Windows form class. The window **object** is created at run time from inside your program.

The first statement above defines a **variable** to represent the new window. (Variables are described in Chapter 5.) The variable is of type frmCompanyDetails, indicating that it represents a new window object of that class. (The new window is an **instance** of the class.)

The second statement uses the Show **method** to display the window. (Methods are described below.) The method is defined in the standard Windows form class and therefore **inherited** by frmCompanyDetails.

Using and changing properties

You can make use of a control's properties when writing a procedure. You can also change most of them. The instructions to change a property must be in the format:

> control.property = expression

Control is the name you have given to the object, *property* is the Visual Basic property name and *expression* is any valid Visual Basic expression (such as a piece of text or an arithmetic calculation – see page 120).

Text properties

Properties such as Text and PasswordChar can only be assigned text expressions. The expression must consist of a text **string** (an actual piece of text in double quotes), another text property or a combination of the two. Items of text are combined using the '&' symbol.

For example, the text for a label called lblMessage can be changed with a statement such as:

> lblMessage.Text = "Please enter a value"

Any piece of text must be enclosed in a pair of double quotes. Similarly, the same message can be cleared by assigning the **null string** to the Text:

> lblMessage.Text = ""

A text box can be given a default value with a statement such as:

> lblCountry.Text = "UK"

You can refer to an existing property by including it in the expression. For example, if a name is entered in a text box, the LostFocus event for the text box could be used for displaying the name in a label as follows:

> Private Sub txtName_LostFocus(*parameters*)_
>   Handles txtName.LostFocus
>   lblAnswer.Text = "Your company name is " & txtName.Text
> End Sub

When the user tabs to another field, the label is updated.

You don't need to worry about what the text looks like as you type it. The code editor indents the code for you and puts spaces around the = sign; it also capitalises the names to match those specified in the Name properties. You may want to insert a blank line above and below the code statements to make the code easier to read (e.g. below the Private Sub line and above End Sub).

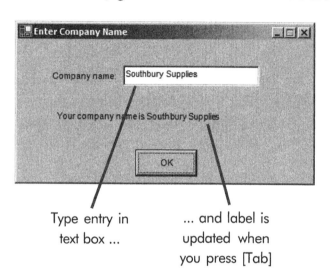

Type entry in
text box ...

... and label is
updated when
you press [Tab]

Tip

To add the procedure, double-click on the text box, then select LostFocus in the Procedure box.

Numeric properties

Most properties have numeric values; for instance, Height, Width, Left, Right, MaxLength and SmallChange are all numeric properties. These must be assigned numeric expressions, consisting of numbers and other numeric properties.

For example, the following statement changes the size of a command button:

```
btnOK.Height = 40
btnOK.Width = 100
```

(Sizes are in pixels – see page 31.)

A text box can be expanded or contracted to fit the inside of a resizable form as follows:

```
txtCoDesc.Top = 0
txtCoDesc.Left = 0
txtCoDesc.Height = Me.Height – 64
txtCoDesc.Width = MeWidth - 8
```

90

The Height and Width properties give the total dimensions of the form, including the title bar and borders; when setting the height of a control you should always allow for the depth of the title bar. (In the example above, 24 pixels have been allowed for the title bar and 8 pixels for the vertical borders of the window.)

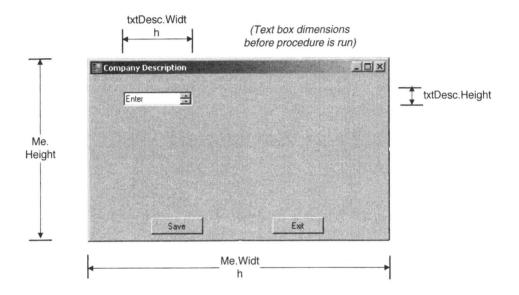

The word 'Me' is a shorthand way of referring to the current form. Although you could specify the variable that holds the form (e.g. frmvCompanyDescription) it is quicker to use just 'Me'. This also has a number of other advantages:

● The code is easier to read.

● If you change the form name, the code will still be right.

● You can copy a set of instructions from one form to another without having to revise the form name in each instruction.

If the statements above are included in the frmCompanyDescription_Resize procedure, the text box will always fill the full width of the window, leaving an area at the bottom for the two buttons.

```
frmCompanyDescription.vb*    frmMainForm.vb [Design]    frmCompanyDetails.vb [Design]         ≑ ✕

⚡ (frmCompanyDescription Events)              ▼  ⚡ Resize                                      ▼

☐ Public Class frmCompanyDescription
        Inherits System.Windows.Forms.Form

  ⊞  Windows Form Designer generated code

  ☐     Private Sub frmCompanyDescription_Resize(ByVal sender As Object, ByVa

            txtCoDesc.Top = 0
            txtCoDesc.Left = 0
            txtCoDesc.Height = Me.Height - 64
            txtCoDesc.Width = Me.Width - 8

            btnSave.Top = Me.Height - 56
            btnExit.Top = btnSave.Top
            btnSave.Left = Me.Width / 2 - 55 - btnSave.Width
            btnExit.Left = Me.Width / 2 + 55

        End Sub
```

If you add buttons to the form, you can ensure that they always stay in the same relative position even when the form is resized. For example, suppose that you have two buttons named btnSave and btnExit. Their positions and sizes are determined by the Top, Left, Height and Width properties.

The position of the buttons can be maintained, relative to the bottom of the form, with the statements:

$$btnSave.Top = Me.Height - 56$$
$$btnExit.Top = btnSave.Top$$

The horizontal positions of the buttons can be kept constant relative to the centre of the form with the statements:

$$btnSave.Left = Me.Width / 2 - 55 - btnSave.Width$$
$$btnExit.Left = Me.Width / 2 + 55$$

The use of the '/' symbol for division is explained on page 121.

Using statements such as these, you can keep full control over the appearance of the form regardless of the user's actions.

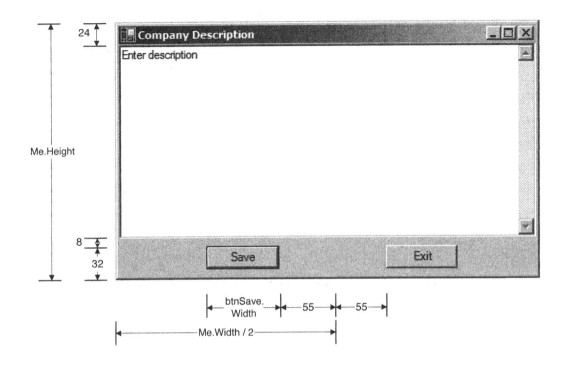

Tip

The position of a window is not usually important, as the user is free to move it around at any time. However, it is worth setting the position of the opening screen so that it gives the right impression when first loaded. You also want to ensure that the window stays on the screen. Remember that screen size will vary from one computer to another, and some screens may have a smaller display than the machine on which the program is being developed.

Boolean properties

A number of properties can take a **Boolean** value: True or False. In such cases you can either assign values of 'True' or 'False' (without quotes) to the properties, or give them numeric values. A value of 0 (zero) is treated as False; any other value is regarded as True. (True and False are Visual Basic constants, whose numeric values are fixed. In a numeric expression, True is evaluated as –1.)

For instance, a button can be greyed out with the statement:

```
btnPostcode.Enabled  =  False
```

When this statement has been executed, the button's caption will be greyed out and clicking on it will not generate a Click event.

Property references

Although most references to properties are in the form *control.property*, there are some variations.

As shown in the example above, you can use the word 'Me' to refer to the current form, rather than a specific control.

Within a form's procedures, you can omit the object name completely when referring to the form. For instance, the following two statements are identical:

```
Me.Height  =  100
Height  =  100
```

However, it is less likely to lead to confusion if you always use 'Me' when referring to the current form's properties.

All objects are assumed to be on the current form unless specified otherwise. You can refer to objects on other forms by prefacing the control name with the form name.

For instance, the following statement disables a button on a frmvSaveData form:

```
frmvSaveData.btnSave.Enabled  =  False
```

(This instruction must appear in a procedure in which the form variable, frmvSaveData, has been defined.)

Using the full name you can access the properties for any controls or forms included in the project.

Methods

Each object has a number of **methods** available. These are internal procedures, which can be executed from within a normal procedure. The methods are used for performing some action on the object. For instance, a text box has a Focus method, which moves the focus to the text box.

The methods are part of the definition of the class from which the object is created. Therefore all objects from the same class have the same set of methods. Some methods are inherited from classes higher up the class structure and therefore appear in several classes; for example, the Focus method applies to all selectable controls but not to non-selectable controls (such as Label and GroupBox).

To execute one of these methods, it must be specified in the format:

object.method

For example, if a value is required for a particular text box you can force the user to make an entry with an instruction such as:

txtCompanyName.Focus()

As for properties and events, the methods available depend on the type of object.

An object's methods, properties and events make up the object's **members**.

Take note

It is important to make the distinction between properties, methods and events:

— Properties are items of information that describe an object (e.g. txtName.TabStop determines whether pressing the [Tab] key can give the text box the focus).

— Methods are built-in procedures that take some action on an object (e.g. txtName.Focus gives the focus to the text box).

— Events are user actions for which customised procedures may be written (e.g. txtName_GotFocus is executed when the text box gets the focus).

TabStop, Focus and GotFocus are all members of TextBox.

The start-up form

You can change the first form that is displayed when the application is run by right-clicking on the project and selecting Properties. Click on the Application tab and select a new Startup form from the drop-down list.

Click on Application tab,
if necessary

Click to display list of forms,
then select start-up form

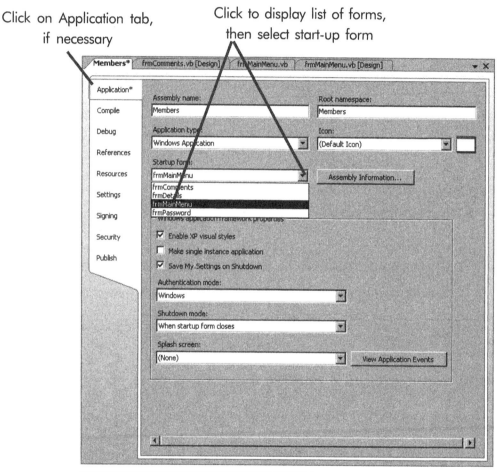

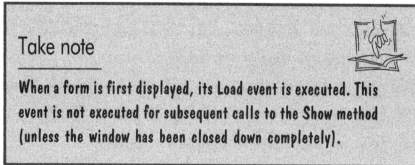

Take note

When a form is first displayed, its Load event is executed. This
event is not executed for subsequent calls to the Show method
(unless the window has been closed down completely).

Displaying other forms

When you run an application, the form specified as the Startup Object is loaded into memory and displayed as a window. Other forms can be loaded and displayed using the **Show** method. For example, the following procedure loads the Details form when the Member Details button is clicked:

```
Private Sub btnDetails_Click()
    Dim frmvCompanyDetails As New frmCompanyDetails
    frmvCoDetails.Show()
End Sub
```

Remember that when you design a form you are creating a **class**. Running the procedure above results in an **object** (the window) being created from that class. On the other hand, when you add a control to a form at the design stage, you are adding a specific object (based on the control's class).

The statement containing 'New' loads a window into memory but does not display it. Therefore when the new window has been created, you can carry out other instructions on it before you use the Show instruction. For example, you may want to set the size of the window or decide which of its controls will be visible and enabled.

Note that the Show method has the same effect as setting the Visible property to True.

Hiding and unloading forms

A form can be hidden again with the **Hide** method; for example:

```
Me.Hide
```

This is the same as setting the Visible property to False.

After a form has been hidden, it is still held in memory. To free the memory used by the form, use the Close method; for example:

```
Me.Close()
```

This statement removes the form from the screen, then deletes the form's data from memory. Just before a form is unloaded, its **Unload** event is executed. The Unload event is also executed when the window is closed in any other way: double-clicking on the Control-menu box, clicking on the Close button or selecting the Visual Studio Debug|Stop Debugging option.

Collections

Visual Basic makes extensive use of **collections**. A collection is simply a set of objects. For example, when you add a list box to a form, the items in the box make up a collection.

Similarly, you can have a collection of objects. For instance, every form has a Controls collection that contains all the controls you have added to the form. This provides you with a means of inspecting and changing the objects on the form.

Collections have properties themselves and these tell you about the collection as a whole. Most importantly, a collection's **Count** property tells you how many objects there are in the list.

For example, collections are used for storing the items are shown on a list box, as descibed below.

Lists

Several types of control are used for selecting an item from a list. The choice of control depends on the options you want the user to have.

List boxes

The list box allows the user to select from a list of options. The box consists of a rectangle containing a list of items, with a vertical scroll bar on the right-hand side (if the list is too long to fit in the box). The size of the box is specified when you add it to the form (though you can change this by varying the Height and Width properties while the program is running).

You can specify the contents of a list box at design time using the **Items** property. This property holds the Items **collection**. The collection is a list of items that appear in the list box.

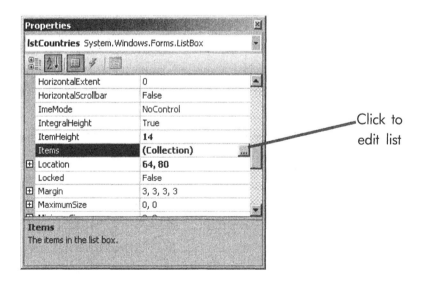

Click to edit list

Clicking on the button on the right of the Items property allows you to edit the list in the String Collection Editor. Type the items to be included in the list, pressing **[Enter]** after each one.

Note that the collection has its own properties and methods.

Items in list collection will
appear in list box at run-time

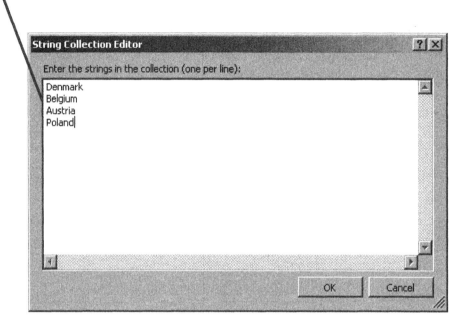

Alternatively, items can be added to the list at run-time (for example, in the form's Load procedure) using the **Add** or **Insert** methods of the **Items** collection. These take the forms:

> *listbox.Items.Add(listitem)*
> *listbox.Items.Insert(index, listitem)*

The *listitem* is the text item to be added to the list; *index* specifies the position for the new item in the list (starting at 0 for the item at the top of the list).

For example:

> lstTypes.Items.Add("France")
> lstTypes.Items.Add(3, "Germany")

The first statement adds the item 'France' to the bottom of the list; the second statement adds 'Germany' as the fourth item in the list.

As an alternative to specifying the index number, setting the list box's **Sorted** property to True sorts the list items in alphabetical order.

When a list box has been filled:

- The **SelectedIndex** property returns the index number of the item that is currently highlighted. If no item is currently selected, SelectedIndex is –1.

- The **Text** property contains the text of the selected item.

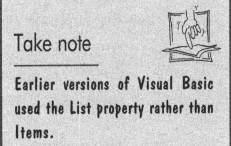

- The **Items.Count** property gives you the number of items in the list.

- The **Items.Item(*index*)** property returns the item with the given index number.

These properties are available only at run-time.

An item can be removed from the list using the **Items.Remove** and **Items.RemoveAt** methods, which take the forms:

> *listbox.Items.Remove.listitem*
> *listbox.Items.RemoveAt(index)*

For example, the first statement below deletes 'Italy' from a list box (named lstTypes) and the second deletes the fourth item in the list:

> lstTypes.Items.Remove("Italy")
> lstTypes.Items.RemoveAt(3)

SelectionMode allows you to select more than one item in the list. The property can take the following settings:

None   No items can be selected.

One   Only a single item can be selected (the default setting).

MultiSimple   Several items can be selected. Clicking on an item selects or deselects it.

MultiExtended   A series of items can be selected by clicking on the first item, holding down **[Shift]** and clicking on the last item. Individual items can be selected by holding down **[Ctrl]** while clicking.

The **MultiColumn** property determines whether the list appears in a single column with a vertical scroll bar (False) or is divided into as many columns as are necessary to fit all the entries into the height available (True). For multi-column lists, you may need to set the **HorizontalScrollbar** property to True. The width of each column is determined by the **ColumnWidth** property; leave this as 0 if you want the columns to be given the default width.

If you want the list to display only whole items, set **IntegralHeight** to True; the box will be resized vertically so that it fits an exact number of items.

The procedures below illustrate the selection of a country from a list.

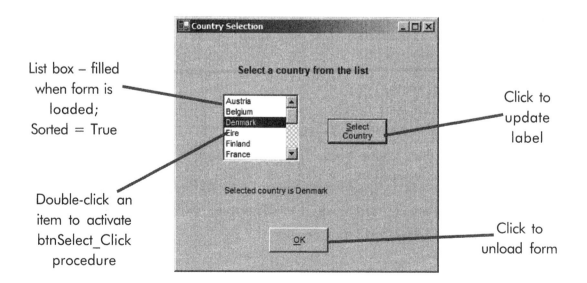

List box – filled when form is loaded; Sorted = True

Double-click an item to activate btnSelect_Click procedure

Click to update label

Click to unload form

Country selection

```
Private Sub frmCountry_Load(...)_
        Handles MyBase.Load
    lstCountries.Items.Add("France")
    lstCountries.Items.Add("Germany")
    lstCountries.Items.Add("Holland")
    lstCountries.Items.Add("Italy")
    lstCountries.Items.Add("Sweden")
    lstCountries.Items.Add("Denmark")
    lstCountries.Items.Add("Belgium")
    lstCountries.Items.Add("Luxembourg")
    lstCountries.Items.Add("Greece")
    lstCountries.Items.Add("Spain")
    lstCountries.Items.Add("Portugal")
    lstCountries.Items.Add("Eire")
    lstCountries.Items.Add("Austria")
    lstCountries.Items.Add("Finland")
    lstCountries.Items.Add("UK")
End Sub

Private Sub lstCountries_DoubleClick(...)_
        Handles lstCountries.DoubleClick
    btnSelect_Click(btnSelect, New System.EventArgs)
End Sub

Private Sub btnSelect_Click(...)_
        Handles btnSelect.Click
    lblChosenCountry.Text = "Selected country is " &_
                            lstCountries.Text
End Sub
```

> Procedure names are highlighted in bold text for ease of identification. Parameters omitted from event procedure headers to save space.

> The underscore character is used to split a single statement over two or more lines.

In the example, an item can be selected either by double-clicking on the item or by clicking on the item and a button. The use of a button provides a useful alternative to double-clicking. It is not a good idea to select an item with a single click, as it is very easy to click on the wrong line in a list box.

Combo boxes

A **combo box** is a combination of a text box and a list box. An item can be selected from the list either by clicking on an item or by typing an item name in the text box at the top of the control. Depending on how the combo box is set up, the user may also be able to type new values in the text box; these are then added to the list. Visual Basic uses combo boxes in a number of places: for example, the object and procedure boxes on the code tab are combo boxes.

The operation of a combo box is controlled by the **DropDownStyle** property, which may take the following settings:

DropDown   Clicking on the arrow makes the list drop down. An item can be selected by clicking or typing in the text box. New items can be inserted in the text box.

Simple   Similar to **DropDown** but the list is displayed at all times.

DropDownList   Clicking on the arrow makes the list drop down. An item can only be selected by clicking on it.

The properties for combo boxes are similar to those for list boxes but the following points should be noted:

● For the **DropDown** and **Simple** styles, a **TextChanged** event is generated when the entry in the text box is edited. The **ListIndex** property is set to −1 for new entries.

● When you click on an item in the list, the **Click**, **TextChanged** and **SelectedIndexChanged** events are generated (in that order).

Combo boxes are useful where you want to give the user the option of extending the list. They also take up less space on the form than a simple list box.

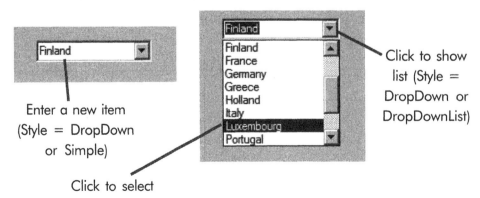

Enter a new item
(Style = DropDown
or Simple)

Click to select

Click to show list (Style = DropDown or DropDownList)

Checked list boxes

The **checked list box** is a combination of the list box and the check box. The list is always visible and each item in the list has a check box next to it.

The list items are held in the **Items** collection and, as for list boxes, you can use the methods that apply to that collection: Add, Insert, Remove, RemoveAt.

The check boxes can take values of Checked, Unchecked and Indeterminate, as for normal check boxes.

The list items that are currently Checked or Indeterminate are held in the **CheckedItems** collection, with the corresponding index numbers in the **CheckedIndices** collection. These collections are both members of the checked list box.

You can determine the state of a particular item with the **GetItemCheckState** property, specifying the index number in brackets. For example, to see if the third item in a checked list box named clbDays has been selected, refer to clbDays.GetItemCheckState(2).

The example below transfers the contents of a checked list box (clbCountries) to a normal list box (lstCountries)

Variables are explained in Chapter 5; 'For' loops are discussed in Chapter 6.

lstSelectedCountries

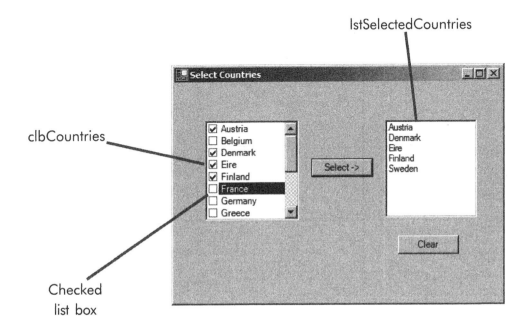

clbCountries

Checked
list box

105

Country selection 2

```
Private Sub btnSelect_Click(...)_
        Handles btnSelect.Click

    'Use variable intIndex to count through collection
    Dim intIndex As Integer
    'Use variable strCheckedItem to hold
    'a specific index number
    Dim strCheckedItem As String

    'Select index of each checked item in turn
    For Each intIndex In clbCountries.CheckedIndices
        'Get item for selected index number
        strCheckedItem = clbCountries.Items.Item(intIndex)
        'Add item to list box
        lstSelectedCountries.Items.Add(strCheckedItem)
    Next

End Sub


Private Sub btnClear_Click(...)_
        Handles btnClear.Click

    'Use variable intIndex to count through collection
    Dim intI As Integer

    'Repeat for number of items in list box
    For intI = 1 To lstSelectedCountries.Items.Count
        'Delete first item in list
        lstSelectedCountries.Items.RemoveAt(0)
    Next

End Sub
```

> Get each item in checked list and copy across to ordinary list those that have been selected.

> After deleting each item from the list, next item becomes item 0. Other items shuffle up

Dealing with errors

Various errors may occur while you are creating procedures and running the application.

● If you make a mistake while typing one of the program statements, so that Visual Studio cannot interpret it, the offending text will be marked with a wavy blue line. This may be because you have typed something incorrectly, referred to something that has not yet been defined or tried to use an invalid object, method or property. You can either make a correction or – if you want to leave it as it is for the moment – just move out of the line. In this way, many of your typing errors will be picked up as soon as you make them; you will also discover many of the errors in your code.

Error while typing an instruction

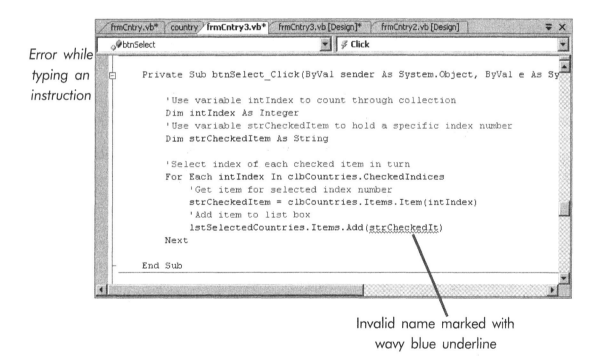

Invalid name marked with wavy blue underline

● If you attempt to run the application before the error has been fixed, a warning message is displayed; click on No to stop the application. The Output window shows that the build failed; click on the Task List tab to see what the problem is. The line number given relates to the number shown on the Visual Studio status bar when you are editing the code.

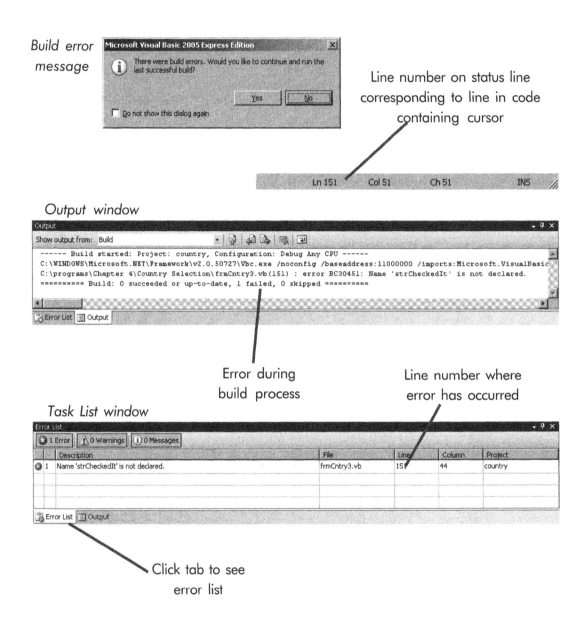

Build error message

Microsoft Visual Basic 2005 Express Edition

There were build errors. Would you like to continue and run the last successful build?

Yes   No

☐ Do not show this dialog again

Line number on status line corresponding to line in code containing cursor

Ln 151   Col 51   Ch 51   INS

Output window

Output

Show output from: Build

```
------ Build started: Project: country, Configuration: Debug Any CPU ------
C:\WINDOWS\Microsoft.NET\Framework\v2.0.50727\Vbc.exe /noconfig /baseaddress:11000000 /imports:Microsoft.VisualBasic
C:\programs\Chapter 4\Country Selection\frmCntry3.vb(151) : error BC30451: Name 'strCheckedIt' is not declared.
========== Build: 0 succeeded or up-to-date, 1 failed, 0 skipped ==========
```

Error List   Output

Error during build process

Line number where error has occurred

Task List window

Error List

⊗ 1 Error   ⚠ 0 Warnings   ① 0 Messages

		Description	File	Line	Column	Project
⊗	1	Name 'strCheckedIt' is not declared.	frmCntry3.vb	151	44	country

Error List   Output

Click tab to see error list

- If you run the application and an error is found – for example, a statement contains a reference to a file that doesn't exist – then a message box will be overlaid, specifying the nature of the error. Click on Break; the code window will be displayed, with a shaded box around the error. Select Debug|Stop Debugging to correct the error.

For more information on handling errors, see Chapter 7.

Shaded box
around line
causing error

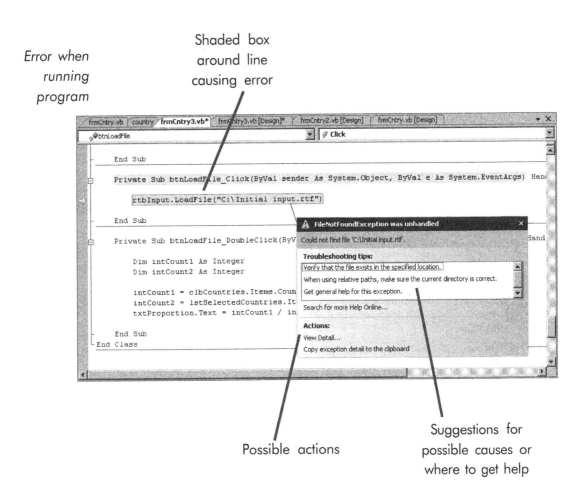

Possible actions

Suggestions for
possible causes or
where to get help

Take note

Visual Studio finds all the obvious errors but if you type an incorrect instruction that is valid, Visual Basic will attempt to execute it. For instance, if you give an instruction to show the wrong form, that form will be displayed. Visual Studio has no way of identifying errors in your logic or in the assumptions you make.

Executable files

Up until this point, the program has been run from within Visual Studio by pressing **[F5]**. As your program begins to develop, you can also test it as a standalone EXE program (which can be run directly from Windows).

When you run the program (with **[F5]**), Visual Studio compiles the various components – forms, procedures etc. – into a single executable file. This .EXE file is held in the **bin** folder in your project directory. It is a completely standalone file, which can be copied to any other folder and can be run without having Visual Studio running at the same time.

Unless you specify otherwise, the file will be given the default program icon. To change the icon (before building the application):

1   Right-click on the project name in the Solution Explorer and select Properties.

2   In the list on the left of the Property Pages, check that the Application tab is selected.

3   Select a new icon (with an ICO extension) and click on OK.

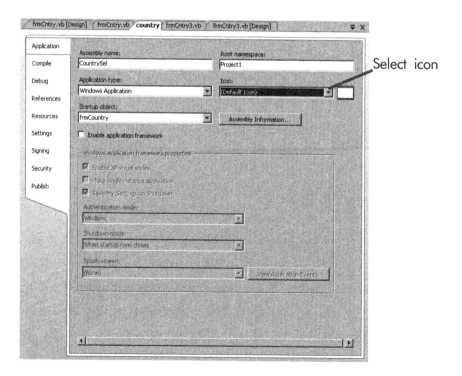

Select icon

The name of the EXE file is taken from the project name. However, if you change the project name the EXE file is not renamed. To create an EXE file with the new name (or a name that is different to that of the project), open the Application tab on the properties dialog and type the name in the **Assembly name** box.

Enter new
project name
to create new
EXE name

Click on
Application
tab

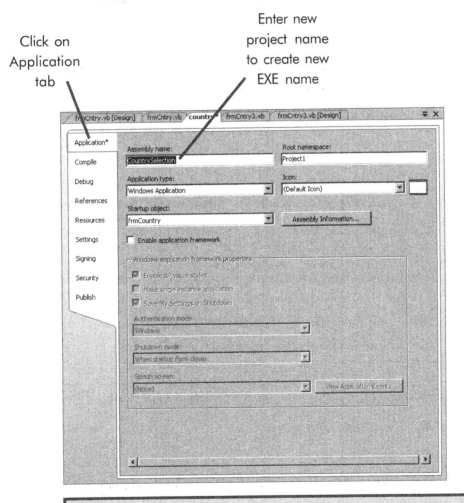

Take note

Every time you make changes to the application and run it by pressing [F5], the executable version in the 'bin' folder will be updated.

Version numbers

Each time you build an application it is given a version number, consisting of up to four parts:

- **Major number**: This is the main version number. When you completely rewrite an application you should increment the major version number. Two applications with different major numbers will not necessarily be compatible.

- **Minor number**: This number is used to indicate that there have been significant changes to the application but that it is still compatible with earlier versions that have the same major version number.

- **Build number**: This number indicates the way in which the application has been built. For example, versions of an application for use with different processors would have different build numbers.

- **Revision number**: This number is used for small changes to the application, such as bug fixes, testing and continuing development.

Every application must have major and minor numbers; the other two parts of the version number are optional.

The version number is held as part of the assembly information in AssemblyInfo.vb. Click on this file in the Solution Explorer and scroll to the bottom of the AssemblyInfo.vb tab to view or change the version number.

The version number is given in the form:

major.minor.build.revision

By default, the version number is 1.0.*. The meaning of this number is as follows:

- The major version is 1.

- The minor version is 0.

- The '*' tells the compiler to apply the build number itself.

- There is no revision number.

It is up to you what system you choose for numbering versions of your software but you should ensure that the system is logical and that it is not too difficult to maintain. The system you use should be consistent between different applications.

AssemblyInfo.vb
code

Click on AssemblyInfo.vb
to view or change version
numbers

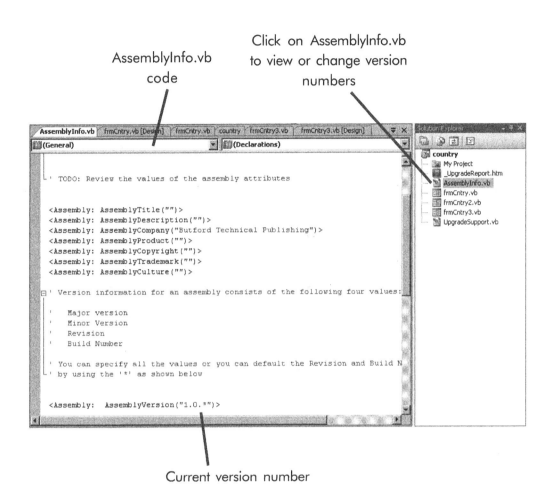

Current version number

Tip

By this stage, as well as saving the project, you should
be taking regular backups of everything in the project
directory; copy all files to a CD or another directory.
Alternatively, use SourceSafe to maintain archive copies
for you.

Exercises

1   Using the example from the Chapter 3 Exercises, modify the Click procedure for the Member Details button on the front-end form so that it displays the Details window.

2   Modify the Click procedure for the Comments button so that it displays the Comments window.

3   Add the necessary code so that the Exit button ends the program.

4   Amend the front-end form so that it is centered when it is first loaded.

5   Add a combo box to the Details form so that the region can be selected from North, South, East and West.

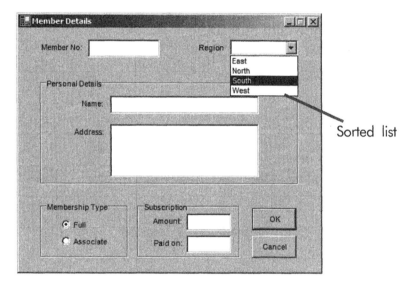

Sorted list

6   Adapt the OK and Cancel buttons on the Details form so that both return the focus to the front-end form (and close the Details form).

7   Modify the Comments form so that the text box fills the full width of the window, leaving enough space at the bottom for the buttons.

8   Adapt the OK and Cancel buttons so that they close the Comments form and return you to the front-end form.

For solutions to these exercises, see page 299.

5 Variables

Using variables

While an application is running, you will want to store information temporarily. For example, if a set of statements is to be processed a number of times you need to hold the repeat number and update a count each time the loop is completed; when users enter information in text boxes, this new data may have to be kept somewhere until you use it. All this information is stored in **variables**.

A variable is simply a named location in memory where a single item of data is held. Variables are created by being **declared** within a procedure or form. They can then be given values and these values can be retrieved or changed.

In the same way as for properties, variables fall into two categories:

● **Numeric variables** hold numbers (whole numbers, decimals, percentages, currency amounts and date values) and the settings for numeric properties.

● **String variables** hold items of text and the settings for text properties.

You cannot mix these two types; for instance, a numeric variable cannot hold a text string unless the string has first been converted to a number.

Variable names

Variable names must follow these rules:

● A variable name can be up to 255 characters long, consisting of letters, numbers and the underscore character.

● The name must start with a letter.

● There must be no spaces or other symbols in the name.

● Upper and lower case letters are treated as being the same.

● You must not use reserved words (names that have a special meaning within Visual Basic, such as If and Left). These are listed in the various topics under 'keywords' in the Visual Basic on-line help.

You should choose sensible names for your variables; programs are much more readable if names are meaningful. The aim should be to create a set of names whose content is reasonably obvious: for example, CurrentDate and AddressLine1. The use of capitals helps distinguish separate words within the name; for example, 'LastTypeToProcess' is more quickly and easily understood than the equivalent 'lasttypetoprocess'.

It is a good idea to start each name with a three-letter prefix to identify the type of data being stored.

Declaring variables

Before you can use a variable it should be **declared**. A declaration is a statement specifying the name of a variable and its type.

The point at which a variable is declared determines its **scope**: the scope of a variable affects where else in the project it may be used:

● **Local variables**, declared at the start of a procedure, are available only within that procedure.

● **Form-level variables**, declared at the top of the form class (immediately below the 'Inherits' statement), are available to all procedures in the form.

Local variables are declared using the **Dim** keyword as follows:

Dim *variable* As *type*

For example:

Dim BoxWidth As Integer

Take note

Properties can be thought of as predefined variables attached to particular objects; the property names are equivalent to the variable names and the property settings are the variable values.

Take note

You can use the Static keyword as an alternative to Dim. The values of Static variables are remembered after you leave a procedure and will be the same when the procedure is called again; the values of variables declared with the Dim keyword are cleared (to zero for numeric variables or the null string for string variables) every time the procedure is called.

The *type* can be any of the following:

Type	Bytes	Use
Boolean	2	Values that can be either True or False
Byte	1	Whole numbers in the range 0 to 255
Integer	2	Whole numbers in the range –32,768 to +32,767
Long	4	Very large whole numbers (±2,000,000,000)
Currency	8	Numbers with an exact number of decimal places (depending on your Country settings in Windows Control Panel)
Single	4	Floating-point (decimal) numbers with up to 7 significant figures
Double	8	Floating-point numbers, up to 14 sig. figs.
Date	8	Floating-point numbers representing a combined date and time
String	*	Text values
Object	**	Capable of holding any type of value, including objects
*		Strings require 1 byte per character
**		Object values require 4 bytes plus 1 extra byte per character

When declaring a numeric variable, use a type from as high in this list as possible. For instance, if you know that a value will always be a whole number, choose Integer rather than Single; if the value will always be in the range 1–100, choose Byte. The types higher in the list use less memory and programs run faster.

Form-level variables are declared immediately below the Inherits statement, using the **Private** keyword:

> Private *variable* As *type*

These variables can be used by any procedure in the form. You can also use Dim instead of Private; the effect is the same.

Constants

Some variables have fixed values that cannot be changed, either by the user or a procedure. These can be declared as **constants** using the **Const** keyword.

●   Constants declared in a procedure are local to that procedure.

●   Constants declared at the top of a form are available throughout the form.

Constant declarations take the form:

> Const *variable* As *type* = *value*

Constants help to make your program easier to understand. They also reduce the risk of things going wrong, since the value of a constant cannot be changed inadvertently.

(Declarations) section

Form-level variable declarations

Constant declarations

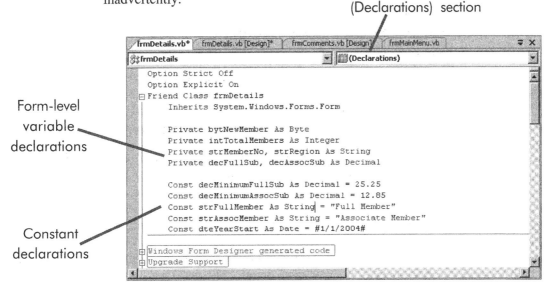

```
Option Strict Off
Option Explicit On
Friend Class frmDetails
    Inherits System.Windows.Forms.Form

    Private bytNewMember As Byte
    Private intTotalMembers As Integer
    Private strMemberNo, strRegion As String
    Private decFullSub, decAssocSub As Decimal

    Const decMinimumFullSub As Decimal = 25.25
    Const decMinimumAssocSub As Decimal = 12.85
    Const strFullMember As String = "Full Member"
    Const strAssocMember As String = "Associate Member"
    Const dteYearStart As Date = #1/1/2004#

Windows Form Designer generated code
Upgrade Support
```

Tip

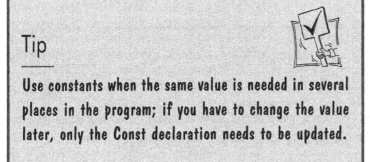

Use constants when the same value is needed in several places in the program; if you have to change the value later, only the Const declaration needs to be updated.

Take note

Dates must be enclosed in # signs when given specific values.

Expressions

Values are assigned to variables using **expressions**. Such statements take the form:

> *variable* = *expression*

The expression can be either a specific value or a combination of variables and values, linked together by **operators**. For example:

> intStartPos = 5
> intEndPos = intStartPos + 37

In the first case, the variable intStartPos is given an explicit value of 5. In the second case, 37 is added to the value of intStartPos and the result is stored in intEndPos; so if intStartPos is 5, intEndPos will be 42. The value of the variable on the left of the expression is always changed by the statement; any variables in the expression itself are never changed.

Variables can also refer to themselves, as in this example:

> intStockIn = 32
> intCurrentStock = intCurrentStock + intStockIn

The value of intStockIn (32) is added to the existing value of intCurrentStock. So, if intCurrentStock was originally 68, its value is now 100.

This statement can be abbreviated using '+ =':

> intCurrentStock += intStockIn

The effect is the same as before, increasing the value of intCurrentStock by the value of intStockIn.

You can do the same thing with the other arithmetic symbols; for example, use '*=' to multiply the variable on the left by the amount on the right.

Take note

When declaring variables, you can put several variables of the same type on a single line (as demonstrated on the previous page).

Numeric operators

For numeric expressions, you can combine variables and values using the following operators:

- ∧ Raising to the power (e.g. $5 \wedge 2$ is 5 squared, or 25)

- * Multiplication (e.g. $6 * 7$ is 42)

- / Division (e.g. $14 / 5$ is 2.8)

- \\ Integer division (e.g. $14 \backslash 5$ is 2)

- **Mod** Remainder (e.g. 14 Mod 5 is 4)

- + Addition

- – Subtraction

Where an expression contains more than one operator, the calculation is not done from left to right but according to the following **order of precedence**:

- ∧ Raising to the power

- – Negation (when the operator starts the expression; e.g. –2)

- * / Multiplication and division

- \\ Integer division

- **Mod** Remainder

- + – Addition and subtraction

For example:

$$137 - 6 \wedge 2 * 3 = 137 - 36 * 3 = 137 - 108 = 29$$

However, to avoid confusion, it is better to use brackets.

Take note

For very large or very small numbers, values are displayed in exponential form, *n.nn*E±*pp* where *n.nn* is in the range 1.00 to 9.99 and *pp* is a power of ten; e.g. 8,750 is represented by 8.75E+03 (i.e. 8.75 x 1000) and 0.000875 is 8.75E–04 (i.e. 8.75 / 10,000).

Brackets

Inserting brackets in an expression changes the order of calculation. Anything inside a pair of brackets is calculated first. Brackets must always be in matching pairs. Use only round brackets ( ), not square brackets [] or braces {}.

If brackets are nested – one pair inside another – the calculations start with the innermost pair of brackets and work outwards. For example:

$$8 + (3 * (10 / 2 - 3)) \wedge 2$$
$$= 8 + (3 * 2) \wedge 2$$
$$= 8 + 6 \wedge 2$$
$$= 44$$

However, it is usually better to split complex expressions over two or more lines.

The following program demonstrates the use of some simple expressions.

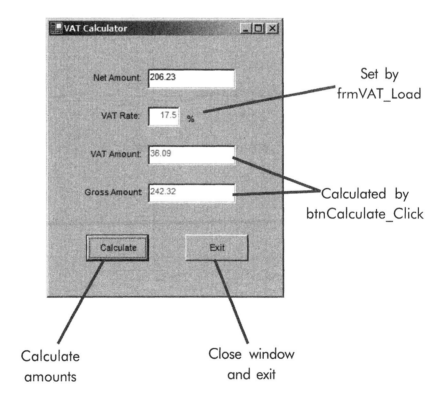

Set by frmVAT_Load

Calculated by btnCalculate_Click

Calculate amounts

Close window and exit

VAT calculation

```vbnet
Public Class frmVAT
    Inherits System.Windows.Forms.Form

#Region " Windows Form Designer generated code "
#End Region

    'Declare constants for use in whole form
    Const dblVatPercentage As Decimal = 17.5
    Const dblVatRate As Decimal = dblVatPercentage / 100

    Private Sub btnCalculate_Click(...)_
            Handles btnCalculate.Click
        'Declare local variables
        Dim decNetAmount, decVAT As Decimal
        Dim decGrossAmount As Decimal

        'Get amount for calculations
        decNetAmount = Val(txtNet.Text)
        'Calculate values
        decVAT = decNetAmount * dblVatRate
        decGrossAmount = decNetAmount + decVAT
        'Put results in text boxes
        txtVAT.Text = Format(decVAT, "F")
        txtGross.Text = Format(decGrossAmount, "F")
    End Sub

    Private Sub btnExit_Click(...) Handles btnExit.Click
        Me.Close()
    End Sub

    Private Sub frmVAT_Load(...) Handles MyBase.Load
        'Put constant VAT percentage in VAT % box
        txtRate.Text = Str(dblVatPercentage)
    End Sub

    Private Sub txtNet_Leave(...) Handles txtNet.Leave
        btnCalculate_Click(btnCalculate, New System.EventArgs)
    End Sub
End Class
```

Anything after a single quote is a comment and is ignored by Visual Basic

Val converts a string value to a number – see page 132.

Format specifies format for numbers – see on-line help.

Str converts a numeric value to a string – see page 132.

Non-numeric variables

As well as numeric variables and values, expressions can also include string variables (for handling text) and properties (both string and numeric). However, you cannot usually mix numeric and string variables.

You will also need to define variables for handling objects and data where the type is not known in advance.

String variables

String variables are much simpler to use than numeric variables. You can assign a particular item of text to a string variable by enclosing it in double quotes:

        strHomeCountry = "UK"

You can also combine strings. (This is called **concatenation**.) The & operator adds one string to another. For instance:

        strFullName = strFirstName & " " & strSurname

Here, the two parts of the name are added together with a space in the middle.

Tip

Unlike other operators, it is essential to put a space on either side of the & symbol; otherwise, it will not be recognised.

Take note

You can use + instead of &; the effect is the same. However, it is better to use & to avoid ambiguity.

Properties

You can use properties in expressions in the same way as you would variables. The following statements place a text box in the middle of a form, the height of the box being provided by a variable, intHistHt:

        txtHistory.Height = intHistHt
        txtHistory.Top = (frmHist.ScaleHeight – intHistHt) / 2

The text box can be filled by the value of a string variable, strHistText, as follows:

        txtHistory.Text = strHistText

Numeric expressions can only include numeric properties and string expressions can only include text properties.

However, you can put a numeric value in a text property or copy the contents of a text box into a numeric variable. For example:

```
txtNewDist.Text  =  decMiles
txtTotalDist.Text  =  txtNewDist.Text  +  txtOldDist.Text
decMPG  =  txtTotalDist.Text  /  decGallons
```

All the conversions between text and numeric values are carried out for you when dealing with properties.

Object variables

If you define a variable as type **Object**, it can hold data of any type (text or numeric). Such variables can then be included in either numeric or string expressions without causing errors. This can be useful if you are not certain what type of data you will be dealing with (for example, when using the contents of a text box where the user can enter either numbers or text).

However, these general-purpose variables should be used sparingly, as they take up a large amount of memory. The variable itself holds a pointer to the data, which is stored at another location in memory and is as large as is needed for each particular occasion.

A more common use of the Object variable is to create a specific instance of a particular class. An Object variable was used in Chapter 4 to create and display an instance of a form class:

```
Dim frmvCompanyDetails As New frmCompanyDetails
frmvCompanyDetails.Show()
```

The first statement creates a specific instance of the form class, resulting in a new object of that type (a window). Since the object type was specified when the variable was declared, the new object (frmvCompanyDetails) inherits all the properties and methods of the class (frmCompanyDetails). Thus the Show method can be invoked to display the new window.

There are many uses for Object variables in Visual Basic 2005, for example when selecting fonts, drawing lines and printing. Other examples are given later.

Numeric functions

Visual Basic incorporates a number of built-in **functions**. These are routines that carry out specific operations on one or more values and return a result.

The values supplied to a function are called **arguments** and are enclosed in brackets, following the function name. Multiple arguments are separated by commas. (If you do not put spaces after the commas, Visual Studio will insert them for you.)

Each argument can be a specific value or an expression. For example, the **Int** function returns the integer part of a floating-point number:

```
intLengthMetres = Int(decTotalLength)
intNearestInt = Int(sngX + 0.5)
```

In the first example, the value of decTotalLength is rounded down to the nearest whole number, with the answer stored in intLengthMetres. In the second case, the argument is an expression and has the effect of rounding sngX to the nearest whole number. The **Fix** function truncates the value. This produces the same effect as Int for positive numbers; for negative numbers, the value is rounded up.

Mathematical functions

Visual Basic provides many numeric functions as part of the Math class, including:

Abs	Absolute (positive value)
Sign	Sign of value (returns 1 if positive, −1 if negative and 0 if zero)
Round	Rounds to nearest whole number
Min	Smaller of two numbers
Max	Larger of two numbers
Sqrt	Square root
Log	Natural logarithm
Exp	Exponential value
Sin	Sine of angle in radians
Cos	Cosine of angle in radians
Tan	Tangent of angle in radians
Atan	Arctangent (angle whose tangent is given)

> **Take note**
>
> In VB6, the Sign, Sqrt and Atan functions appear as Sgn, Sqr and Atn respectively.

Random number functions

The **Rnd** function generates a random number between 0 and 1. If a negative number is given as the argument for the first call to the function, the same sequence is generated each time; the argument is the 'seed' for the random number sequence.

If you want a different sequence each time, use the Randomize statement to initialise the random number sequence. If no argument is given for **Randomize**, the system timer is used to generate the seed, giving a genuinely random starting point.

An example of the use of the random number generator is given below.

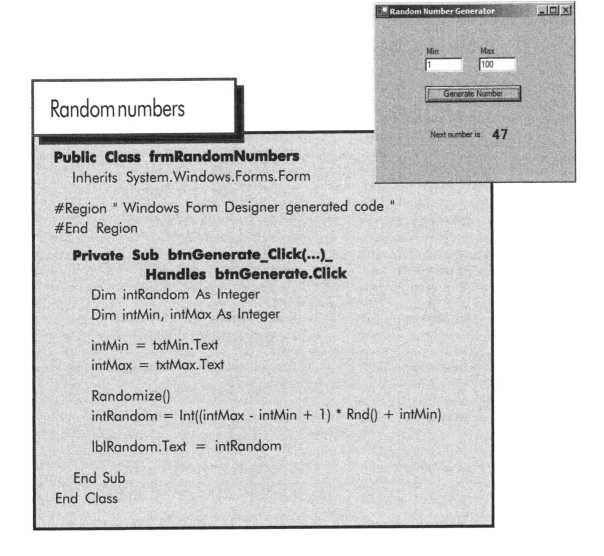

Random numbers

```
Public Class frmRandomNumbers
    Inherits System.Windows.Forms.Form

#Region " Windows Form Designer generated code "
#End Region
    Private Sub btnGenerate_Click(...)_
            Handles btnGenerate.Click
        Dim intRandom As Integer
        Dim intMin, intMax As Integer

        intMin = txtMin.Text
        intMax = txtMax.Text

        Randomize()
        intRandom = Int((intMax - intMin + 1) * Rnd() + intMin)

        lblRandom.Text = intRandom

    End Sub
End Class
```

String functions

Visual Basic provides a number of ways for manipulating text. In addition to a variety of built-in functions that allow you to change or extract text, there is a string class that has methods for every type of operation imaginable.

Built-in functions

There are many built-in string functions. Some of the most useful functions are those that act on one string to produce another. These include:

Left(*string, length*)

Returns a string of given *length* from the left-hand side of the *string*

e.g. Left("South", 2) returns 'So'

Right(*string, length*)

Returns a string of given *length* from the right-hand side of the *string*

e.g. Right("South", 2) returns 'th'

Mid(*string, start, length*)

Returns a string of given *length* for the specified *string*, beginning at the *start* character position; if no *length* is given, the text returned continues to the end of the string

e.g. Mid("South", 2, 3) returns 'out'

Len(*string*)

Returns the length of the *string*

e.g. Len("South") is 5

LTrim(*string*)

Removes leading spaces from *string*

e.g. LTrim(" South") is 'South'

RTrim(*string*)

Removes trailing spaces from *string*

e.g. RTrim("South ") is 'South'

Trim(*string*)

Removes spaces at both ends of the *string*

e.g. Trim(" South ") is 'South'

UCase(*string*)

Converts the *string* to capitals

e.g. UCase("South") returns 'SOUTH'

LCase(*string*)

Converts the *string* to lower case

e.g. LCase("South") returns 'south'

The programs later in this book contain many examples of these functions.

Visual Basic functions

In some cases, where there could be confusion between a function and a property with the same name, you need to specify that it is a Visual Basic internal function by preceding the function with Microsoft.VisualBasic.

For example:

```
Microsoft.VisualBasic.Left(strName, 1)
```

This avoids any confusion with the form's Left property.

To make things easier, you can include the following line at the top of the form code:

```
Imports VB = Microsoft.VisualBasic
```

You now need only refer to 'VB' when specifying the function. For example:

```
VB.Left(strName, 1)
```

String searches

The **InStr** function allows you to search for one string within another. There may be up to three arguments for the function, which takes the form:

```
InStr(start, main, search)
```

The function searches the *main* string for the first occurrence of the *search* string, beginning the search at the *start* position. (Characters in the main string are numbered from 1 on the left-hand side.)

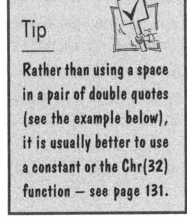

Tip

Rather than using a space in a pair of double quotes (see the example below), it is usually better to use a constant or the Chr(32) function — see page 131.

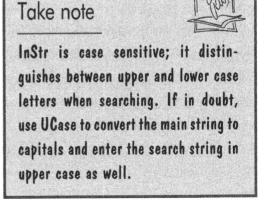

Take note

InStr is case sensitive; it distinguishes between upper and lower case letters when searching. If in doubt, use UCase to convert the main string to capitals and enter the search string in upper case as well.

If no *start* value is given, the whole string is searched. For example, the following code extracts the surname from a text box:

```
Dim strSurname As String
Dim intSpacePos As Integer
intSpacePos = InStr(txtFullName.Text, " ")
strSurname = Mid(txtFullName.Text, intSpacePos + 1)
```

The first two lines declare the variables that are used in the routine. The third line searches a text box (named txtFullName) for a space, putting the position of the space in the intSpacePos variable. The final line extracts from the text box the text starting from the character after the space to the end, putting it in the string variable strSurname.

Make sure that you put exactly one space between the double quotes; otherwise, the search will not be successful. If the search string is not found, the function returns a value of 0.

String class

You can also use the methods provided by the **String** class to perform all the operations described above, along with several others. In some cases, the methods work in the same way as built-in functions. For example, the **Concat** method combines two or more strings in a string variable:

```
strName = String.Concat(strFName, " ", strSName)
```

Here, the contents of the two variables strFName and strSName are combined into a single variable, strName, with the two items of text separated by a space.

Since any string variable is derived from the String class, the methods of the class can be applied directly to the string variable. For instance:

```
chrInitial = strSName.Chars(1)
```

In this case the **Chars** method of the String class extracts a specified number of characters from the left-hand side of the string. Therefore this statement has the same effect as:

```
chrInitial = Microsoft.VisualBasic.Left(strSName, 1)
```

You can create a string containing a given number of characters by initialising a new instance of the String class. For example:

strFilledS = new String("S", 4)

This statement creates the string variable strFilledS and gives it an initial value of 'SSSS'.

Character conversions

Each character in a string is represented in memory by a numeric code in the range 0 to 255. The codes used are from the **ASCII character set**. In this system, A is represented by 65, B by 66 and so on; lower-case letters start at 97, numeric digits at 48; the space character is 32. If you specify one of these codes in a string, the required character will be displayed on screen or printed.

Take note

Two characters that may cause problems are 35 (which can appear as # or £, depending on the device selected) and 127 (the Delete control character).

The first 128 ASCII codes are mostly standard and should produce the same result in any character font. Codes 0–31 are used for control characters, which are often found embedded in files. The most useful control characters are 9 (tab character), 10 (line feed), 11 (form feed) and 13 (carriage return). Codes between 32 and 126 are all printable characters.

The codes for 128 onwards are rather more variable and their interpretation depends on how the computer or printer is set up and the fonts being used. These are the **extended ASCII codes**. For example, if you create a string of Greek characters on one computer they may appear as a completely different set of characters on another screen or when printed.

For this reason, the extended characters are best avoided unless you are contolling the fonts that are used. Remember that you may have to supply users with any unusual fonts you are using.

The **Chr** function returns the character whose ASCII code is given; for example, Chr(32) returns a space. The reverse of this is the **Asc** function, which converts a character to its ASCII code. So Chr(74) is 'J' and Asc("J") is 74. Examples are given below.

String conversions

As we have seen, Visual Basic makes a very clear distinction between numeric and string variables. The only time you may be able to mix numbers and text in an expression is when using Object variables or properties. Two functions, Str and Val, convert values from one format to the other.

Str converts a number (or the contents of a numeric variable or expression) to a string. The first character of the string is a space if the value is positive or zero; the string starts with '–' if the value is negative.

Most data types also have a **ToString** method that converts the value into a string.

The following code assumes that intHouseNum is a numeric variable and strStreetName is a string:

```
Dim strHouseNumS As String, strFullAddress As String
strHouseNumS = Trim(Str(intHouseNum))
strFullAddress = strHouseNumS & Chr(32) & strStreetName
```

If intHouseNum has the value 23 and strStreetName is 'High Street', the contents of strFullAddress will be '23 High Street'.

The **Val** function reverses this process, converting a string to a numeric value. The function uses as much of the string as it can, up to the first non-numeric character, ignoring spaces. Using the example above, Val(strFullAddress) would return 23.

There are also a number of functions for converting values to each of the Visual Basic data types. For instance, **CInt** converts a number to an integer, **CStr** converts a number or text value to a string and **CDate** converts a number or string to a date (see below). Other functions include **CBool**, **CByte**, **CChar**, **CDbl**, **CDec**, **CLng**, **CObj**, **CShort** and **CSng**.

As an alternative, you can use the **Convert** class. This includes methods such as **ToDouble**, **ToString** and **ToDateTime**.

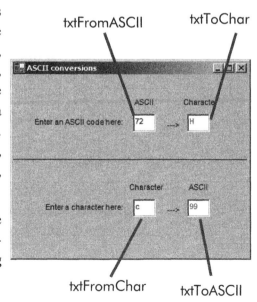

txtFromASCII   txtToChar

txtFromChar   txtToASCII

The program below demonstrates the use of functions to convert between characters and their ASCII equivalents. The dialog for the program is illustrated above.

ASCII conversions

```
Public Class frmASCII
    Inherits System.Windows.Forms.Form

#Region " Windows Form Designer generated code "
#End Region

    Private Sub txtFromASCII_TextChanged(...)_
            Handles txtFromASCII.TextChanged
        'Event triggered every time change is made in text box

        Dim shoASCIINum As Short

        'Convert text entry to number
        shoASCIINum = Val(txtFromASCII.Text)

        'Convert ASCII value to text equivalent
        txtToChar.Text = Chr(shoASCIINum)
    End Sub

    Private Sub txtFromChar_TextChanged(...)_
            Handles txtFromChar.TextChanged
        Dim shoASCIINum As Short

        'Convert text entry to ASCII
        '(Add space to prevent error when text box empty)
        shoASCIINum = Asc(txtFromChar.Text & Chr(32))

        'Convert ASCII result to string for display
        txtToASCII.Text = CStr(shoASCIINum)
    End Sub
End Class
```

Dates and times

The **DateTime** structure holds a floating-point number that represents a combined date and time. The integer part of the number returns the date, representing the number of days since 30-Dec-1899. Therefore 1 represents 31-Dec-1899, 2 is 1-Jan-1900 and 36526 is 1-Jan-2000. Negative numbers give you dates before 30-Dec-1899. (The dates are accurate back to 1752, when the Gregorian calendar was introduced but theoritically go back as far as 1-Jan-0001.)

Take note

This is the same system that is used on Excel and other spreadsheet programs. However, some versions of Excel are inaccurate for dates before 1-Mar-1900 and will produce different results to Visual Basic.

Excel and Lotus do not allow negative dates. Excel 95 stops at 31-Dec-2078 (65380) while Lotus continues to 31-Dec-2099 (73050); dates in Visual Basic and later versions of Excel go on to the year 9999.

The decimal part of the date/time value represents the time as a proportion of the day. For instance, 6 a.m. is represented by 0.25, midday is 0.5 and midnight is 0.

The combination of the two numbers gives a complete date and time; so 36526.25 represents 1-Jan-2000 6:00 a.m.

You can define a variable as being of type DateTime, in which case the various properties and methods of the structure are available to you.

For example, the **Day**, **Month** and **Year** properties extract appropriate values from a date/time value. Similarly, **Hour**, **Minute**, **Second** and **Millisecond** extract the relevant time values.

Date returns just the date part of the value, while **TimeOfDay** gives you the time portion. **DayOfWeek** returns a number representing the day of the week (by default, 1 for Sunday, 2 for Monday etc.) and **DayOfYear** gives the day number as measured from 1st January. **WeekdayName** converts the day of the week to the corresponding string.

Time spans

You can also use the **TimeSpan** structure for dates and times; variables of this type are used to represent time intervals (in terms of days and parts of a day). Thus a TimeSpan variable can hold the number of days between two dates or the time that has elapsed since a specific date/time value.

The properties for the TimeSpan structure include **Days**, **Hours**, **Minutes**, **Seconds** and **Milliseconds**; these return the number of whole days, hours etc. included in the TimeSpan value. The **TotalDays** property returns the number of days as a decimal value, **TotalHours** gives the total number of hours (and parts of an hour), and so on.

Current time

For the DateTime structure, the **Today** property returns a date/time value representing the current system date; **Now** returns a value representing both date and time. Today and Now are expressed as properties of the general DateTime class, rather than specific date/time variables: i.e. DateTime.Today and DateTime.Now.

To get the current time, use DateTime.Now.TimeOfDay. You can convert this value to a string using the **ToString** method.

Date and time methods

The DateTime structure has a number of methods that let you manipulate date/time values. For example, the **Add** method adds a TimeSpan value, **AddYears** adds a specific number of years and there are similar methods for the other time units. The **Subtract** method subtracts either a DateTime value or a TimeSpan value.

The **Compare** method returns the difference (in days) between two specified DateTime values. The **DaysInMonth** method returns the number of days in the month for the specified DateTime value and **IsLeapYear** returns a True or False value to tell you whether the DateTime value falls in a leap year.

The TimeSpan structure also has **Add**, **Subtract** and **Compare** methods.

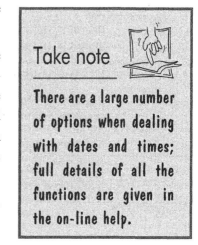

Take note

There are a large number of options when dealing with dates and times; full details of all the functions are given in the on-line help.

Visual Basic dates and times

The DateTime structure is part of the .NET framework. Visual Basic includes an equivalent **Date** data type. Variables of this type represent a date and time in the same way as DateTime variables.

There are several Visual Basic functions for manipulating such dates:

● **DateAdd** adds a specific value to part of a date.

● **DateDiff** returns the difference between two dates (for a specific part of the date or time).

● **DatePart** returns just one unit (days, hours etc.) from the date.

● **Format** returns the date as a string with a specified layout.

For full details of these functions, see the on-line help.

Date/time conversions

DateValue converts a string to a date value; for example, DateValue ("31 Dec, 2005") returns the date '31/12/05'. Similarly, **TimeValue** converts a string to a time value; for instance, TimeValue ("6:00 PM") and TimeValue ("18:00") both return the time '18:00:00'.

In both cases, the functions return date/time variables. If you display these in text boxes, their string representations are shown. However, in calculations they are treated as numbers.

DateSerial and **TimeSerial** return similar values but take three arguments: year, month and day for DateSerial, or hour, minute and second for TimeSerial. To get the same values as the examples above you could use DateSerial(2005, 12, 31) and TimeSerial(18, 0, 0).

Use DateValue and TimeValue when dealing with text strings entered by the user or derived from some other source; use DateSerial and TimeSerial where the separate date/time components are available.

The following program converts a date/time value to a real date and gives the day of the week; it also calculates the date/time value for a real date and adds or subtracts a given number of days to give a second date.

Enter date/time value; date and time calculated

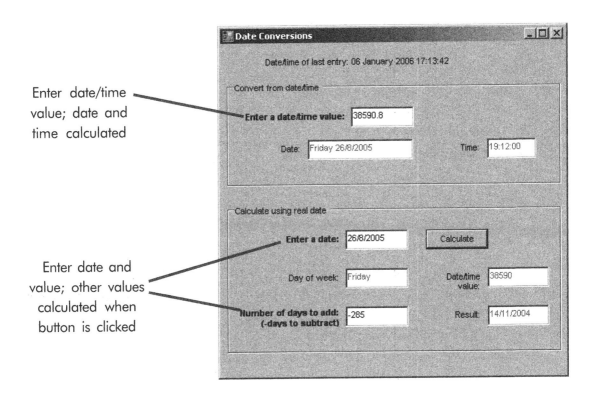

Enter date and value; other values calculated when button is clicked

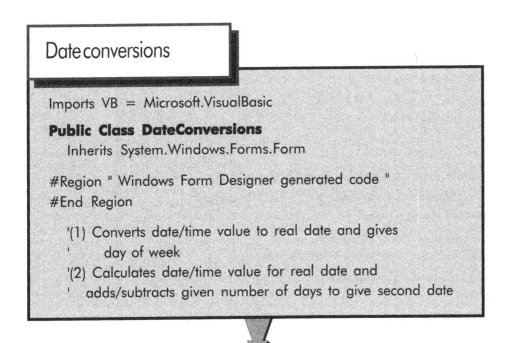

Date conversions

```
Imports VB = Microsoft.VisualBasic

Public Class DateConversions
    Inherits System.Windows.Forms.Form

#Region " Windows Form Designer generated code "
#End Region

    '(1) Converts date/time value to real date and gives
    '        day of week
    '(2) Calculates date/time value for real date and
    '    adds/subtracts given number of days to give second date
```

```vbnet
Private Sub btnCalculate_Click(...)_
        Handles btnCalculate.Click
    Dim dteDateNumber, dteResultDateNumber As DateTime
    Dim intNumberOfDays As Integer
    Dim shoDayNumber As Short
    'Constants for creating strings
    Const sp As String = " "

    'Calculate date/time value
    dteDateNumber = DateValue(txtDateIn.Text)
    intNumberOfDays = dteDateNumber.ToOADate
    txtDateTime.Text = intNumberOfDays

    'Calculate day of week
    'DayOfWeek is 0 (Sunday) to 6 (Saturday)
    shoDayNumber = dteDateNumber.DayOfWeek
    'Use WeekdayName with Sunday (1) to Saturday (7)
    txtDayOfWeek.Text = WeekdayName(shoDayNumber_
            + 1, , FirstDayOfWeek.Sunday)

    'Calculate value for Result box
    dteResultDateNumber =_
        dteDateNumber.AddDays(Val(txtAddDays.Text))
    txtResult.Text = dteResultDateNumber

    'Update date/time label
    lblNow.Text = "Date/time of last entry: " &_
        Now.ToLongDateString & sp & Now.ToLongTimeString

End Sub

Private Sub txtDateTimeIn_TextChanged(...)_
        Handles txtDateTimeIn.TextChanged
    Dim dteDateIn As DateTime
    Dim shoDayNumber As Short
    Dim strDateString, strDayOfWeek As String
    Dim strSecString, strHourString, strMinString
    Dim strTimeString As String
```

> Continue statement on next line.

```vbnet
'Constants for creating strings
Const sl As String = "/"
Const sp As String = " "
Const zr As String = "00"
Const cn As String = ":"

'Get day of week
dteDateIn = DateTime.FromOADate(Val(txtDateTimeIn.Text))
'DayOfWeek is 0 (Sunday) to 6 (Saturday)
shoDayNumber = dteDateIn.DayOfWeek
'WeekdayName default is Monday (1) to Sunday (7)
'Change so that it is Sunday (1) to Saturday (7)
strDayOfWeek = WeekdayName(shoDayNumber + 1, _
                    FirstDayOfWeek.Sunday)

'Extract date components and create date string
strDateString = dteDateIn.Day & sl & dteDateIn.Month & sl_
                    & dteDateIn.Year
txtDate.Text = strDayOfWeek & sp & strDateString

'Extract time components and create time string
'Pad with leading zeroes
strHourString = VB.Right(zr & Hour(dteDateIn), 2)
strMinString = VB.Right(zr & Minute(dteDateIn), 2)
strSecString = VB.Right(zr & Second(dteDateIn), 2)
strTimeString = strHourString & cn & strMinString & cn_
                    & strSecString

txtTime.Text = strTimeString

'Update date/time label
lblNow.Text = "Date/time of last entry: " &_
Now.ToLongDateString & sp & Now.ToLongTimeString

    End Sub
End Class
```

Arrays

When handling many values or strings, the use of simple variables can be rather cumbersome. For instance, if you want to hold the values to fill a large list box you do not want a separate variable for each item, nor do you want a separate statement for adding each item to the list. You can overcome these problems by the use of arrays.

An **array** is a set of variables, represented by a single name. The individual values are called **elements** and are identified by **index numbers**. The index number is given in brackets after the name. The first index number is always 0.

For example, the array MonthDays could hold the number of days in the month; MonthDays(1) would hold the number of days in January, MonthDays(2) is for February and so on to MonthDays(12), which would represent the number of days in December.

Arrays are declared in the same way as for variables. You must declare the type of the array and, within the brackets, specify the largest index number. For example:

        Dim MonthDays(12) As Integer

This statement declares an array of 13 elements (numbered from 0 to 12), each of which can hold an integer value.

An array may have more than one **dimension**. For example:

        Dim MaxTemp(12, 31) As Single

Each possible combination of the two index numbers identifies a different element. In this case there are 416 single-precision values in the array, which can be used for storing the maximum temperature in each day of the year. For instance, MaxTemp(4, 17) could hold the value for 17 April. Some elements, such as MaxTemp(11, 31) and all those with an index number of 0, will never be used.

Arrays can consume a considerable amount of memory. To save space, you may need to calculate the index number from a 'real-world' number. For example, an AnnualSales array may be set up to hold a value for each year from 1980 to 2009:

        Dim AnnualSales(29) As Double

If the variable intCurrentYear holds a year, the corresponding array value can be derived from AnnualSales(intCurrentYear − 1980).

Any element in the array can be used in an expression in the same way as for a normal variable.

The example below adds text to a string array, depending on the day of the week (selected from a combo box). The code also retrieves any existing text from the array when the same day is selected a second time.

Select day from the list

Enter reminder

Program displays corresponding information from array

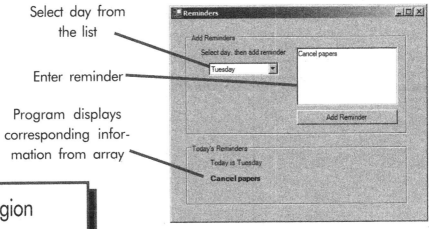

Selecting a region

```
Public Class Reminders
    Inherits System.Windows.Forms.Form

    Private strReminder(6) As String

    'Add reminders for each day of the week and
    'display the reminder for today.
    'To be useful, need to save the reminders to file
    '(see Chapter 10).

#Region " Windows Form Designer generated code "
#End Region

    Private Sub Reminders_Load(...) Handles MyBase.Load
        Dim i As Integer

        'For each day of week, add weekday to list,
        'starting with Sunday
        For i = 0 To 6
```

```
        cboDaySelection.Items.Add(WeekdayName(i + 1, ,_
                FirstDayOfWeek.Sunday))
    Next
    cboDaySelection.SelectedIndex = 0    'Select first day of week
    'Display current day
    lblToday.Text = "Today is " &_
                WeekdayName(Now.DayOfWeek)
End Sub

Private Sub btnAdd_Click(...) Handles btnAdd.Click
    Dim bytSelectedDay, bytToday As Byte
    'Get index number (0 to 6) of selected day
    bytSelectedDay = cboDaySelection.SelectedIndex
    'Store reminder text in array
    strReminder(bytSelectedDay) = txtDayReminder.Text
    'Display reminder for today
    bytToday = Now.DayOfWeek
    lblReminder.Text = strReminder(bytToday)
End Sub

Private Sub cboDaySelection_SelectedIndexChanged(...)
    Handles cboDaySelection.SelectedIndexChanged
    'Display existing reminder (if any) when different day selected
    txtDayReminder.Text = strReminder(cboDaySelection._
                SelectedIndex)
    End Sub
End Class
```

Tip

In previous versions of Visual Basic you could specify the lowest index number; in VB 2005 the first index number is always 0.

Take note

You can also define dynamic arrays, where the maximum index number is not specified in the original declaration but is given later in the program by a ReDim statement.

Message boxes

A particularly useful function, **MessageBox.Show**, displays a temporary dialog box. The box contains a line of text and one or more command buttons. The function is invoked with a statement in the following format:

variable = MessageBox.Show(*message, title, buttons, icon, default*)

The *message* is any line of text; *title* is the text to be displayed in the title bar; *buttons* is a code indicating the buttons to be included; *icon* specifies the symbol to be shown to the left of the message; and *default* is another code for the default button (the one that is activated when you press **[Enter]**).

The *buttons* and *icon* values are inserted as standard Visual Basic constants; for example, a *buttons* value of MessageBoxButtons.YesNoCancel places three buttons on the dialog box. The *variable* indicates the button that was pressed.

As you type the statement, the parameters are shown in a pop-up box. Note that there are 12 versions of this function, depending on the parameters you enter; the function is said to be **overloaded**. Although you can select the version you want, Visual Basic knows which version you are using from the parameters you enter.

When you reach the parameters for the buttons and icons, further pop-up boxes appear. These list the possible values available to you; select one by clicking on it and pressing **[Tab]**. For example:

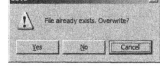

```
Dim bytButtonVal As Byte
bytButtonVal = MessageBox.Show("File already exists._
    Overwrite?", "Save", MessageBoxButtons.YesNoCancel,_
    MessageBoxIcon.Warning, MessageBoxDefaultButton.Button3)
```

A dialog box is displayed, with a warning icon and three buttons (Cancel is the default). The variable bytButtonVal is returned with a value indicating the button that was pressed (e.g. DialogResult.Cancel if the Cancel button was pressed).

Alternatively, if the key press is unimportant, you can omit the return variable:

```
MessageBox.Show("File saved successfully", "Save Done",_
    MessageBoxButtons.OK, MessageBoxIcon.Information,_
    MessageBoxDefaultButton.Button1)
```

This version of the statement is only really useful if there is only one button on the message box.

Exercises

1   Create the unit conversion form below. When one of the buttons is clicked the value in the left-hand box should be converted into the new units and shown in the right-hand box, to two decimal places.

The labels to the right of the boxes should be changed to show the two conversion units. When a new entry is started, the labels should be blanked out and the right-hand box should be cleared.

The Exit button should end the program.

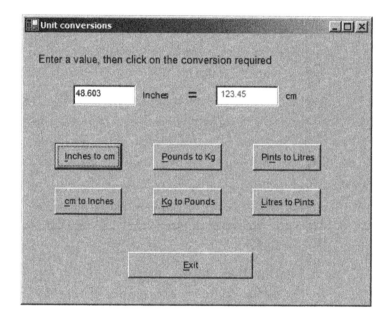

2   Add a Rep label to the Member Details form with code to display a representative name depending on the Region selected.

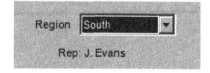

3   Write a program to calculate the number of weeks and days between any two dates.

For solutions to these exercises, see page 302.

6 Basic instructions

Modules

Much of the work done by an application is performed by event-driven procedures; these provide the responses to the user's actions. However, some code will be needed for more general-purpose actions, such as reading data from a file or checking that a date is valid. This code is put in a code **module**.

A module is a separate file that contains a collection of general-purpose procedures, which are available throughout the application. Procedures within modules are called **module-level** procedures; those in forms are **form-level**. There is no particular order to a module's procedures and they will be listed alphabetically in the Procedure box.

Most applications will have at least one code module, containing procedures for performing frequently-used tasks. These procedures are called as and when needed. This has a number of advantages:

- The code has to be written only once; when it has been tested satisfactorily you will be able to use it elsewhere in the application without having to go through the coding process again.

- Since there is only one copy of the code, there is no danger that the same process somewhere else in the application will work in a slightly different way.

- If you need to make a change to the way a procedure works, this has to be done only once; there is no need to search through your program looking for other occurrences of the same code.

- Code modules can be re-used by other applications; when you have developed a set of general-purpose procedures, these can be incorporated in other projects, helping to give all your applications the same 'look and feel'.

You can have any number of code modules in your project so it is a good idea to split up your general-purpose procedures. For instance, you may have one module for text-handling procedures, another for date routines and a third for dealing with graphics.

If you decide that part of a form procedure will be useful elsewhere, you can move it to a code module using cut-and-paste operations.

Scope

When designing the overall structure of your application it is essential to have an understanding of the **scope** of procedures. This determines what procedures are available in any part of the application. The rules are as follows:

● Any module-level procedure can call any other module-level procedure, from any module in the project (but cannot call any form-level procedures).

● Any form-level procedure can call any procedure in the same form or any module-level procedure (but not any procedures in other forms).

This is illustrated below.

You can declare a module-level procedure as **Private**, rather than Public, in which case it is available only to other procedures within that module.

Note that procedures in forms and modules can refer to any control property providing you specify the form name. See page 147 for more information on the scope of variables.

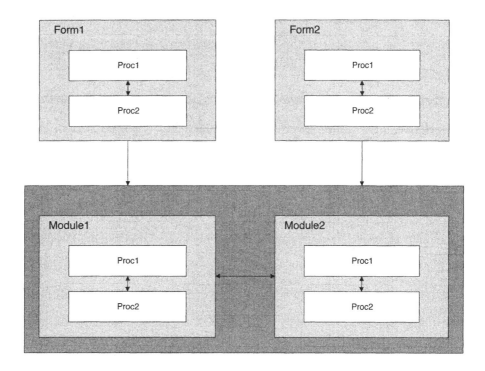

Creating modules and procedures

New modules and procedures are created with a few simple commands.

Creating modules

To create a new code module:

1   Select Project|Add Module. The Add New Item dialog is displayed, with the
       Module template selected.

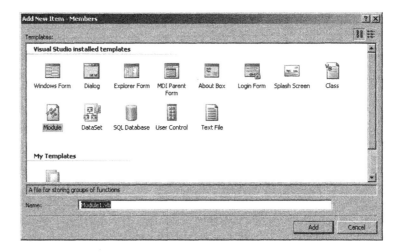

2   Type a name for the module (the vb extention will be added for you) and click
       on Open. A code window is displayed.

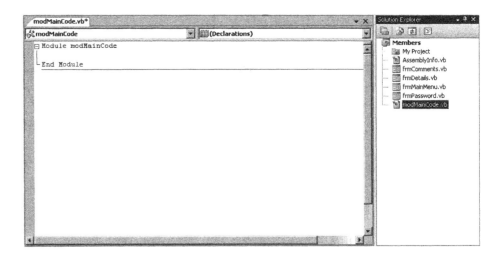

3 The new module is included in the Solution Explorer window. Click on the module name to see the module's properties.

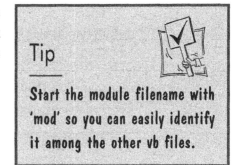

If you close the code window you can redisplay it at any time by highlighting the module name in the Solution Explorer window and then clicking on the View Code button.

Changing modules

You can add an existing module to the project with Project|Add Existing Item. Select a file with a vb extension to add either a form or a module.

To remove a module, click on its name in the Project Explorer window and then select Project|Exclude From Project.

Creating procedures in modules

To add a general-purpose procedure to a code module:

1 Double-click on the module name in the Project Explorer window (or click on the module and then on the View Code button). The Code window is displayed.

Initially, the only 'objects' for a code module are '(General)' and the module name. This is because there are no visible objects for the module (such as buttons and list boxes) and therefore no events.

2 In between the Module and End Module statements type the procedure declaration, in the form:

Sub procedurename()

When you press **[Enter]** an End Sub statement is added for you. Make the code more readable by inserting blank lines above and below the procedure.

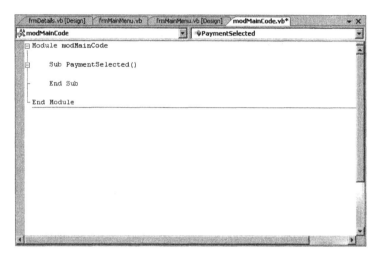

3 Type the code for the procedure between the Sub and End Sub lines.

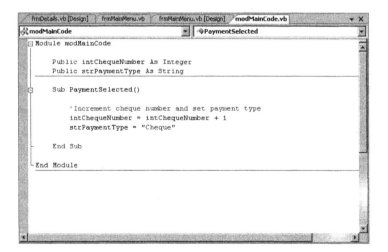

You can view or edit this code at any time.

Take note

In earlier versions of Visual Basic procedures were added using a menu option, rather than by directly typing them into the code window.

Take note

You can place a keyword in front of the Sub statement to limit the availability of the procedure. By default, procedures are assumed to be 'Public', so are available throughout the application. If you put 'Private' in front of the Sub statement, the procedure is available only within the module.

Creating procedures in forms

You can also add a general-purpose procedure to a form. This is achieved in a similar way to that for module-level procedures:

1 Click on the form name in the ProjectExplorer window, then on the View Code button.

2 Make some space above the first event-handling procedure (below the Windows Form Designer generated code).

3 Type the Sub procedure declaration. When you press **[Enter]** the End Sub is added for you.

4 Type the code for the procedure.

Form-level procedures are useful for routines that may be used more than once in a form but cannot be used by any other form or code module.

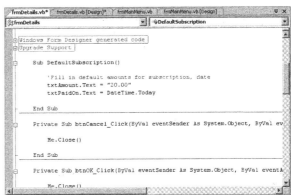

151

Procedure names

Event procedures are automatically named for you. Their names are not necessarily unique in the project as a whole; for example, if two forms each have a btnOK button, then both will have a btnOK_Click procedure. However, this is not a problem, since the procedures can only be called from within their own forms.

On the other hand, each general-purpose procedure in a project must be given a unique name.

The rules for naming procedures are the same as those for variables: no more than 255 characters; starting with a letter; no spaces or symbols apart from the underscore.

Use capital letters to identify individual words within the name; this helps to make the name meaningful.

Tip

For modules that will be used in several projects, you can avoid clashes in procedure names by starting each name with the same word. For instance, all procedures in a date-handling module could begin 'Date', while text-manipulation procedures in another module could all start 'Text'.

Take note

If you change the name of a control, its event procedures will not be renamed. However, the procedures will still work in the same way as before as the Handles part of the procedure declaration is updated to reflect the new name.

Calling procedures

A general-purpose procedure is executed by **calling** it from another procedure. The procedure is called by entering the name on a line on its own in the code.

The empty brackets at the end of the procedure name will be added for you when you move out of the statement line.

For example, a module procedure called FillWithDefaults may be used to fill the boxes on a form with default values:

```
Sub  FillWithDefaults()
    frmMain.txtDiscountRate.Text  =  "0.10"
    'Use  global  variable,  intNextInvoiceNumber
    frmMain.txtInvoiceNumber.Text  =  intNextInvoiceNumber
End  Sub
```

This procedure could be called either as part of the form's Load event or when a Defaults button is pressed on the form.

The event procedures would be as follows:

```
Private  Sub  Form_Load()
    FillWithDefaults()
End  Sub

PrivateSub  btnDefaults_Click()
    FillWithDefaults()
End  Sub
```

In both cases, the effect is the same.

In the same way, you can call a general-purpose procedure that has been added to a form within any other procedure in the form.

Procedure call

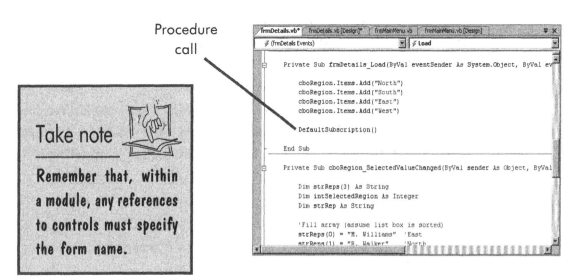

Take note

Remember that, within a module, any references to controls must specify the form name.

Public and passed variables

When you call an event-driven procedure, no other information is needed for the procedure to be executed. However, for general-purpose procedures, you usually need to make further details available to it and the procedure will often need to pass back some result. For instance, a procedure to calculate the number of days between two dates needs to know the dates to be used in the calculation and must be able to return the answer; if a procedure is used for setting up an array, the contents of the array must be made available to other procedures. All this is handled by the use of public variables and by passing the contents of variables to and from procedures.

Private and public variables

Variables declared in a procedure (with a Dim statement) are local to that procedure – they have no meaning elsewhere in the project. Form-level variables declared in the Declarations section (with a Private statement) are available throughout the form – but not in other forms or modules.

Modules also have a Declarations section where variables can be declared. The declarations take the following forms:

> Private *variable* As *type*
>
> Public *variable* As *type*

The **private** variables are available throughout the module but not in other modules or forms.

The **public** variables are available throughout the whole project. The value of a public variable can be used by any procedure, in any form or module. For example, a user name entered on one window may be needed elsewhere in the program, so its value must not be lost.

As a general rule, you should make variables as local as possible; use local variables in preference to private (form-level or module-level) variables, and private variables in preference to public variables. This reduces memory requirements and helps you to keep track of your variables and their values.

To add module-level variables, make some space at the top of the module (just above the first Sub statement) and type them in the usual way.

(After declaring the variables, any statements that use them will no longer have errors highlighted.)

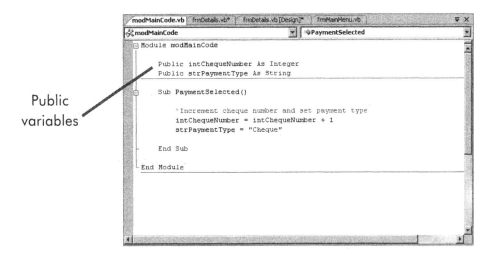

Public
variables

```
modMainCode.vb    frmDetails.vb*    frmDetails.vb [Design]*    frmMainMenu.vb

modMainCode                                    PaymentSelected

Module modMainCode

    Public intChequeNumber As Integer
    Public strPaymentType As String

    Sub PaymentSelected()

        'Increment cheque number and set payment type
        intChequeNumber = intChequeNumber + 1
        strPaymentType = "Cheque"

    End Sub

End Module
```

Private and public constants

Constants can also be declared in the Declarations section of a module. By default, constants are private and therefore available to all procedures in the module but not to other modules or forms.

You can also make constants **public**, making their values accessible to all procedures in the project:

> Public Const *variable* As *type* = *value*

For example:

> Public Const strProgVersion As String = "1.4"
> Public Const intStartYear As Integer = 1997

These statements can be included in the Declarations section of any module.

Passing variables to procedures

One way of exchanging information with procedures would be to hold the values in public module-level variables. However, it is more efficient to **pass** the values across when the procedure is called. The variables that are passed to the procedure must be declared in the Sub statement, in the brackets following the procedure name. The first line of the procedure will be as follows:

> Sub *procname*(*variable* As *type*, ...)

The brackets can contain more than one variable (when more than one value is passed). If no variables are passed, the brackets are empty. The brackets should also contain any variables that are to be passed back to the calling procedure.

When the procedure is called the variable values are listed in the brackets following the procedure name. For example, the following procedure extracts the house name or number from the first line of an address:

```
Sub ExtractHouse(ByRef strHouseName As String, ByRef_
                              strStreetName As String)
    Dim intCommaPos As Integer

    'Find comma
    intCommaPos = InStr(strStreetName, ",")

    'Get house name/no. from left of street name
    strHouseName = Left(strStreetName, intCommaPos - 1)

    'Remove house from street
    strStreetName = Trim(Mid(strStreetName,intCommaPos + 1))
End Sub
```

There is no need to specify that 'Left' is a VB function, as this code is in a module, rather than a form (and therefore there is no 'Left' property to cause confusion).

Here, strStreetName is used for passing a value to the procedure; the procedure uses strHouseName for passing a value back and it also changes strStreetName, passing back a different value.

The **ByRef** keyword specifies that the procedure may change the values of the variables. The variable intCommaPos is a local variable, which exists only while the procedure is running.

If you want to stop a variable being changed when passed back from a procedure, include the **ByVal** keyword before the variable name in the procedure definition: e.g. FillArray(ByVal intCount As Integer). Here, any change to intCount will not be passed back to the calling procedure. By including ByVal in the Sub line you are effectively declaring the variables as local for that procedure.

If you don't place any keyword in front of the variable name, then the variable is assumed to be of type ByVal and changes to its value will not be passed back to the calling procedure.

The following procedure, which is invoked by clicking on a button, gets the contents of a text box and calls the ExtractHouse procedure. The returned values are copied into two text boxes.

```
Private Sub btnExtract_Click(...) Handles btnExtract.Click

    Dim strHouse As String
    Dim strStreet As String

    'Get first line of address
    strStreet = txtAddressLine1.Text

    'Call procedure to extract house and street
    ExtractHouse(strHouse, strStreet)

    'Put results back into boxes
    txtHouse.Text = strHouse
    txtStreet.Text = strStreet

End Sub
```

The variables that appear on the line calling the procedure do not have to have the same names as those used within the procedure itself (though they may be the same, if you wish). In the example above, the original value is passed across in the strStreet variable; the procedure transfers this into the corresponding strStreetName local variable, which is then changed; the new value of strStreetName is passed back into the strStreet variable. Similarly, strHouseName is passed back as strHouse.

Comments and spacing

You can make your programs more readable by adding **comments**. Although you may understand now what your program does, a few reminders might be helpful when you come to look at it again in a few months' time. On a line, any text following a single quote is treated as a comment and is ignored by Visual Basic. Therefore, you can add comments on lines of their own or at the ends of lines.

Programs are also easier to understand if they are well spaced out. Visual Basic adds spaces within each line for you but extra blank lines between sections of code help to make it clearer.

User-defined functions

Visual Basic provides many built-in functions for handling text and numbers but there will be others that you must create yourself. One way of doing this would be to use a procedure. For example, the following procedure converts inches to centimetres:

```
Sub InchesToCmP(ByRef sngInches As Single,_
                                ByRef sngCm As Single)
    Const sngCmPerInch = 2.54
    sngCm = (Int((sngInches * sngCmPerInch * 100) + 0.5)) / 100
End Sub
```

The converted value can be displayed in a text box with the following code:

```
Dim sngInches As Single, sngCm As Single

sngInches = txtEntry.Text
InchesToCmP(sngInches, sngCm)
txtResult.Text = sngCm
```

However, it is often simpler to define your own function.

User-defined functions are created in a similar way to procedures:

1   Display the Code window for the module or form where you need the function. (If the function is to be called entirely from within a form's procedures, add it to the form; otherwise, insert it in a module.)

2   At some point above the first procedure to call the function, create a blank line and type the function declaration in the form:

```
Function functionname(ByVal argument1 As type, ...) As type
```

The *functionname* follows the same rules as procedure names. The arguments are the variables being passed to the function and each must be given a *type*. You must also specify the *type* of the function itself (i.e. the type of the returned value).

3   When you press **[Enter]** the End Function statement will be added for you. Insert the function code in the space above End Function.

The function returns a single value, calculated in the function code using a variable that has the same name and type as the function itself.

In order to use the function, include it in a statement in the same way as for a built-in function.

For example, the following function converts inches to centimetres:

```
Function InchesToCm(ByVal sngInches As Single) As Single

    Const sngCmPerInch = 2.54
    InchesToCm = (Int((sngInches * sngCmPerInch * 100)_
                                        + 0.5)) / 100

    End Function
```

This function could be used to supply the value for a text box, named txtResult, as follows:

```
txtResult.Text = InchesToCm(txtEntry.Text)
```

When this statement is executed, the InchesToCm function is called and the value in the txEntry text box is passed to it. The function calculates the value in centimetres using the passed value and the sngCmPerInch constant, defined in the function. The calculated value is held in the InchesToCm variable (defined as Single in the function header).

The calculated value is then slotted back into the original expression and hence into the text box's Text property.

Rather than place the result of the function in a variable, you can use the Return keyword as an alternative. Whatever follows the 'Return' is the value passed back.

Tip

Use a function when just one value is to be returned to the calling procedures; use a procedure when two or more values are returned, or when there are no return values.

Take note

In the same way as for procedures, several variables can be passed to a function. The types of the variables passed to the function must be an exact match for those defined in the function header.

Conditional statements

So far, the statements in a procedure have followed a linear, unbroken path; the program starts at the first line and works down through each line in turn until the last line has been completed.

Procedures are rarely like this, however. Most of the time there are choices to be made and, as a result, statements to be executed only **if** a condition is true. For example, if a value entered in a text box exceeds some limit you may want to display an error message.

Such decisions are made using the **If...Then...End If** set of statements, which take the form:

```
If condition Then
    statements
End If
```

The *statements* are executed only if the *condition* is true. The condition usually takes the form:

```
expression operator expression
```

Any valid *expressions* can be used, with the restriction that both must be numeric or both text; you cannot mix the two types.

The *operator* is one of the following:

=	Equal to
<>	Not equal to
<	Less than
<=	Less than or equal to
>	Greater than
>=	Greater than or equal to

For example, the following procedure tests the value of an entry in a text box when the focus is moved to another control. If the value is too high when you try to Tab out of the text box, it is replaced by the maximum allowed, a warning message is displayed and the cursor is put back in the text box.

```
Private Sub txtMinutes_LostFocus(...)_
                              Handles txtMinutes.LostFocus
    If Val(txtMinutes.Text) > 59 Then
        lblWarning.Text = "Minutes cannot exceed 59"
        txtMinutes.Text = "59"
    End If
End Sub
```

Visual Studio inserts the End If statement for you as soon as you finish entering the If statement. It also indents the statements between If and End If, making the code more readable. This becomes particularly important when you start putting one condition inside another.

Take note

If you are only executing one statement, this can be put immediately after 'Then', on the same line. For example:

If intTotalTime < 30 Then intPayRate = 1

There is no need for an End If statement in such cases.

For numeric conditions, the tests are carried out on the relative numeric values of the expressions. For string expressions, the comparisons are performed character-by-character, according to the ASCII code of the characters. The following conditions are all true:

Numeric	String
-4 < 21	"B" < "Ba"
5 < 2^3	"B" < "a"
2.1 < 20	"2" < "B"
3 < 21	"21" < "3"

Tip

To sort strings containing numbers into numerical order, pad the numbers with leading zeroes or spaces.

Logical operators

You can combine conditions with the following **logical operators**:

And   Both conditions must be true for the combined condition to be true

Or   One (or both) of the conditions must be true

Xor   One of the conditions must be true but not both (Exclusive Or)

The two sets of conditions can be either numeric or text, independently of each other.

For example:

```
intDaysInFeb = 28
If intNumMonth = 2 And booLeapYear = True Then
    intDaysInFeb = 29
End If
```

In this case, if intNumMonth is not equal to 2 or booLeapYear is 'False', the value of DaysInFeb would remain at 28. If both conditions are true (intNumMonth equals 2 *and* booLeapYear has a 'True' value) the statement below the If statement is executed and the value of intDaysInFeb is changed to 29.

You can also negate a condition by putting **Not** in front of it. The Not operator is applied first, followed by the other logical operators in the order given above (for example, And operators are implemented before Or).

Tip

Using brackets, you can combine as many conditions as you like into a single If statement. However, to avoid any possibility of confusion, it is better to break up complex conditions using brackets or split them into a series of related If statements.

162

The Else statement

The conditional statements can provide alternatives for when the condition is false by including an **Else** statement, as follows:

```
If condition Then
    true_statements
Else
    false_statements
End If
```

If the *condition* is true, the *true_statements* are executed; otherwise, the *false_statements* are performed. For example:

```
If booLeapYear = True Then
    intDaysInFeb = 29
Else
    intDaysInFeb = 28
End If
```

The use of Else allows you to provide two alternative sets of statements, only one of which will ever be executed.

Nested Ifs

For complex conditions you can **nest** the If statements. For instance:

```
If intNumMonth >= 1 And intNumMonth <= 12 Then
    lblMonth.Text = strMonthName(intNumMonth)
    lblDays.Text = intDaysInMonth(intNumMonth)
    If intNumMonth = 2 And booLeapYear = True Then
        lblDays.Text = 29
    End If
Else
    lblMonth.Text = "ERROR"
    lblDays.Text = ""
End If
```

This illustrates the importance of indenting within If statements. It is clear from the indents that the statement lblDays.Text = 29 will only be executed if both sets of conditions are true.

Case statements

When you are choosing between a number of alternatives, the **Case** statement is more appropriate than the If statement. The structure for a Case statement is as follows:

```
Select Case  expression
      Case test1
            statements1
      Case test2
            statements2
      ...
      Case Else
            statementsN
End Select
```

Take note

The Case Else section is not essential, but it lets you mop up any missing values. The End Select statement must always be included, however.

The *expression* is evaluated and the result is compared against the various test values. If the expression evaluates to *test1*, then *statements1* are executed; if it is *test2*, *statements2* are executed; and so on. If none of the tests matches the expression, the final set of statements (*statementsN*) is executed.

The tests for each case can be any of the following:

● A number or numeric expression (e.g. 7, sqr(intA))

● A string or string expression (e.g. "Yes", strUserName)

● A range of values (e.g. 2 To 6, "A" To "AZ")

● A comparative value (e.g. Is > 6, Is < "M")

You can also combine any of these, separating them with commas; for example:

```
Case 3, 6 To 8, Is > 12
```

Here, the corresponding code is executed if the expression evaluates to 3, 6, 7, 8 or a value greater than 12.

The most important thing to remember is that the expression and the tests must be all numeric or all string.

An example is given below. (Include the 'Imports VB = Microsoft.VisualBasic' statement at the top of the class.)

Identify call type

```vb
Private Sub txtTelNum_LostFocus(...)_
          Handles txtTelNum.LostFocus
    Dim strDialCode As String

    'Get first five characters of telephone number
    'Remove leading spaces, pad to at least 5 characters
    strDialCode = VB.Left(Trim(txtTelNum.Text) & "XXXXX", 5)

    '(Other checking is needed to remove spaces
    'and non-numeric characters)

    Select Case strDialCode

        Case "001" To "00199"
            lblCallType.Text = "USA/Canada"

        Case "002" To "00999"
            lblCallType.Text = "International (not USA/Can)"

        Case "01386", "01905", "550000" To "751999"
            lblCallType.Text = "Local"

        Case "001100" To "09999"
            lblCallType.Text = "National"

        Case "100" To "199XX"
            If VB.Right(strDialCode, 2) = "XX" Then
                lblCallType.Text = "Operator service"
            Else
                lblCallType.Text = "Invalid number"
            End If

        Case "999XX"
            lblCallType.Text = "Emergency"

        Case Else
            lblCallType.Text = "Invalid number"

    End Select
End Sub
```

Loops

The conditional statements give you the opportunity to decide whether or not some piece of code is to be executed but this still restricts you to a linear flow down through a procedure, from top to bottom. There are occasions when you also need to repeat a set of statements. Visual Basic provides looping instructions for every occasion:

- Repeating a section of code a number of times

- Repeating while a condition is true

- Repeating until a condition becomes true

- Repeating indefinitely

Each of these alternatives has its own set of Visual Basic instructions.

For...Next loops

The simplest approach to looping is to repeat a group of statements a given number of times. This is achieved with the **For...Next** statements, which have the following structure:

```
For variable = start To end Step step
    statements
Next  variable
```

The loop begins with the *variable* set to the *start* value and the *statements* are executed. When the Next statement is reached the variable is increased by the *step* amount. If this is greater than the *end* value, the loop ends and execution continues with the statement below Next. Otherwise, the *statements* are executed again. This continues until the *end* value is exceeded.

The Step can be omitted, in which case the *variable* increases by 1 each time. The *step* may also be negative, reducing the variable value each time: in this case, the *end* should be less than the *start*.

For example:

```
For i = Len(strTextIn) To 1 Step –1
    strTextOut = strTextOut & Mid(strTextIn, i, 1)
Next
```

This loop is repeated for each character in the string, strTextIn, starting from the end and working forwards. Each time, the character is added to the output string, strTextOut. The effect is to put the contents of the original string into reverse order.

You can **nest** one loop inside another. The inner loop must be completely enclosed; its For and Next statements must be between the outer loop's For and Next lines. Similarly, you can nest one type of structure inside another: for example, a For...Next loop inside an If...End If structure or vice versa.

The example below demonstrates a number of uses of For loops. The first three loops have If...End If structures nested inside them. There is also an example of a For loop nested inside another For loop. The inner loop is executed the required number of times every time the outer loop is processed. For example, if intNumWords is 4, the outer loop will be executed for values of i equal to 3, 2 and 1. When i is 3, the inner loop is processed three times (for j equal to 1, 2 and 3); when i is 2, j takes values of 1 and 2; and when i is 1 (on the last time through), the j loop is executed just once.

Note that when you type a For statement, the 'Next' statement is added for you. No variable is specified on the Next line as this isn't strictly necessary; the level of indent shows you which For statement the Next is paired with. However, it is worth adding the variable yourself as it increases the clarity of the code and makes it easy to see which loop is ending without having to compare indents; this is particularly helpful when there is a large amount of code in the loop.

The example program takes a text string and splits it into its individual words; these are stored in a string array, which is displayed in a text box. The array is then sorted into order using a bubble sort (this is the part with the nested loops), with the sorted array being displayed in another text box. The words are combined again and the sorted text is displayed in the final text box.

The case of the text is ignored when comparing words to be sorted; this is done by converting the words to capitals.

When the array is displayed, the words are forced onto separate lines by adding a carriage return/line feed sequence after each one (CR is ASCII code 13, LF is code 10).

Take note

If the *end* value is less than the *start* value when the loop is first entered (for a positive *step*), the *statements* will never be executed. Similarly, if the *end* is greater than the *start* for a negative *step*, the loop is omitted.

Enter text to be sorted, then click button

Bubble Sort

Enter text to sort:

Sunday Monday Tuesday Wednesday Thursday
Friday Saturday

Process

Unsorted	Sorted
Sunday	Friday
Monday	Monday
Tuesday	Saturday
Wednesday	Sunday
Thursday	Thursday
Friday	Tuesday

Sorted phrase

Friday Monday Saturday Sunday Thursday
Tuesday Wednesday

Bubble sort

```
Private Sub btnProcess_Click(...)_
        Handles btnProcess.Click
    Dim strTextArray(20) As String
    Dim strTextIn As String
    Dim strTextOut As String
    Dim intNumSpaces As Integer
    Dim intNumWords As Integer
    Dim intSpacePos As Integer
    Dim i As Integer, j As Integer
    Dim strTemp As String

    'CR/LF characters
    Const CR As String= Chr(13) & Chr(10)

    'Remove unwanted spaces at either end
    strTextIn = Trim(txtTextIn.Text)
```

Include the 'ImportsVB = Microsoft.VisualBasic' statement at the top of the class

```
'Remove multiple spaces
For i = Len(strTextIn) - 1 To 1 Step -1
    If Mid(strTextIn, i, 2) = " " Then
        strTextIn = VB.Left(strTextIn, i) & Mid(strTextIn, i + 2,_
                            Len(strTextIn) - i - 1)
    End If
Next i

'Count number of spaces
intNumSpaces = 0
For i = 1 To Len(strTextIn)
    If Mid(strTextIn, i, 1) = " " Then
        intNumSpaces += 1
    End If
Next i

'Calculate number of words
If intNumSpaces > 0 Then
    intNumWords = intNumSpaces + 1
Else
    intNumWords = 0
End If

'Max number of words = 20 (because of array size specified)
'Extra words will be ignored
If intNumWords > 20 Then intNumWords = 20

'Split input text into array of separate words
For i = 1 To intNumWords
    'Find space, move first word into array
    intSpacePos = InStr(strTextIn, " ")
    If intSpacePos > 0 Then
        'Word found - add to array and delete from input text
        strTextArray(i) = Microsoft.VisualBasic.Left(strTextIn,_
                            intSpacePos - 1)
        strTextIn = Mid(strTextIn, intSpacePos + 1)
    Else
```

```
            'Last word
            strTextArray(i) = strTextIn
        End If
    Next i

    'Display unsorted array
    txtUnsortedArray.Text = strTextArray(1)
    For i = 2 To intNumWords
        txtUnsortedArray.Text = txtUnsortedArray.Text & CR_
                                    & strTextArray(i)
    Next i
    'Sort array into order
    For i = intNumWords - 1 To 1 Step -1
        For j = 1 To i
            If UCase(strTextArray(j)) > UCase(strTextArray(j + 1)) Then
                strTemp = strTextArray(j)
                strTextArray(j) = strTextArray(j + 1)
                strTextArray(j + 1) = strTemp
            End If
        Next j
    Next i

    'Display sorted array
    txtSortedArray.Text = strTextArray(1)
    For i = 2 To intNumWords
        txtSortedArray.Text = txtSortedArray.Text & CR &_
                                        strTextArray(i)
    Next i

    'Combine words into single string and display
    strTextOut = strTextArray(1)
    For i = 2 To intNumWords
        strTextOut = strTextOut & " " & strTextArray(i)
    Next i
    txtSortedText.Text = strTextOut

End Sub
```

Do loops

The **Do...Loop** group of statements provides an alternative to For...Next loops, repeating the loop until some condition is either true or false. There are five varieties of this loop:

Do *statements* Loop	Repeats until an Exit Do statement is encountered or the user presses **[Ctrl-Break]**
Do While *condition* *statements* Loop	Repeats as long as the condition is true; loop is never executed if the condition is false initially
Do *statements* Loop While *condition*	Repeats as long as the condition is true; loop is always executed at least once
Do Until *condition* *statements* Loop	Repeats until the condition is true; loop is never executed if the condition is true initially
Do *statements* Loop Until *condition*	Repeats until the condition is true; loop is always executed at least once

Each of these is useful in particular circumstances. The most important decision is whether to place the While/Until part of the structure at the top or bottom of the loop; this depends on whether or not you want the loop to be executed at least once, regardless of the initial state of the condition.

Choose between Until and While depending on which makes the condition easier to understand. An Until statement can be converted into a While statement by putting Not in front of the condition: for example, While A > 0 is the same as Until Not A > 0 or Until A <= 0.

You can use Exit Do to jump out of any loop but, where possible, this statement should be avoided; it is neater to exit via the Loop statement. The program below demonstrates the use of these loops.

This program has two functions: the function to put a piece of text into reverse order (described earlier) and a function to extract a valid postcode from a line of text.

The main procedure is activated when the Process Address button is clicked. The first loop in this procedure extracts the text up to the first comma in the address that has been entered in the text box. Note that the procedure needs to find a comma before entering the loop for the first time; if there is no comma the loop will never be executed. At the end of the loop, after the text (and following comma) have been removed, the next comma is found. The loop is exited when there are no commas left.

The second loop adds the separate lines of the address (which have been stored in an array) to a multi-line text box. The loop is repeated for each non-blank element in the array. Again, the test is at the start of the loop, so if the first element of the array is empty the loop will never be executed. The line number is incremented at the end of the loop, so the 'Until' statement tests to see if the next address line is blank before the loop is executed.

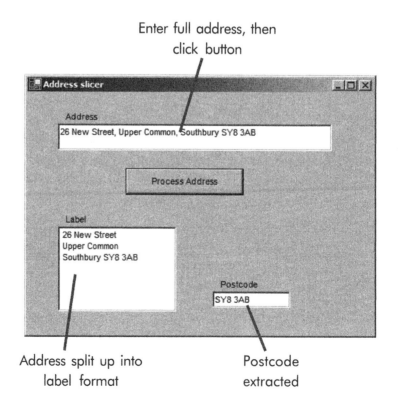

Enter full address, then click button

Address split up into label format

Postcode extracted

Address slicer

```vb
Imports VB = Microsoft.VisualBasic

Public Class frmAddSlice
    Inherits System.Windows.Forms.Form

#Region "Windows Form Designer generated code "
#End Region

    Function ReverseText(ByVal strTextIn As String)_
                                    As String

        Dim i As Integer
        Dim strTextOut As String

        strTextOut = ""
        For i = Len(strTextIn) To 1 Step -1
            strTextOut = strTextOut & Mid(strTextIn, i, 1)
        Next i

        Return strTextOut

    End Function

    Function ExtractPostcode(ByVal strTextIn As String)_
                                    As String
        'Extracts complete postcodes from end of input string

        'First part of postcode must be 2-4 chars, ending in numeric
        'Second part must be 3 chars, starting with numeric

        Dim strRevText As String
        Dim shoSpacePos As Short
        Dim strPostcode As String
        Dim chrNumeric As Char
        Dim booPostcodeFound As Boolean

        Const Sp As String= " "

        booPostcodeFound = True     'Set initial value

        'Reverse input text and find first space (from end)
```

```
strRevText = ReverseText(strTextIn)
shoSpacePos = InStr(strRevText, Sp)
strPostcode = ""

'Extract first word from reversed text if exactly 3 chars
If shoSpacePos = 4 Then
    strPostcode = VB.Left(strRevText, shoSpacePos - 1)
    strRevText = Mid(strRevText, shoSpacePos + 1)
Else
    booPostcodeFound = False
End If

'Check for starting numeric (postcode is currently
If booPostcodeFound Then
    chrNumeric = Mid(strPostcode, 3, 1)
    If chrNumeric < "0" Or chrNumeric > "9" Then
        booPostcodeFound = False
    End If
End If

If booPostcodeFound Then
    'Find next word
    'Add space at end to allow for case where there is nothing
    'but the postcode on the line
    strRevText = strRevText & Sp
    shoSpacePos = InStr(strRevText, Sp)
    'Extract word if between 2 and 4 chars
    If shoSpacePos >= 3 And shoSpacePos <= 5 Then
        strPostcode = strPostcode & Sp & VB.Left(strRevText,_
                            shoSpacePos - 1)
        strRevText = Mid(strRevText, shoSpacePos + 1)
    Else
        booPostcodeFound = False
    End If
End If

'Check for numeric
```

If there is no operator, the expression is calculated as either True (non-zero) or False.

```vb
    If booPostcodeFound Then
        chrNumeric = Mid(strPostcode, 5, 1)
        If chrNumeric < "0" Or chrNumeric > "9" Then
            booPostcodeFound = False
        End If
    End If

    'Reverse postcode if found, otherwise return error
    If booPostcodeFound Then
        strPostcode = ReverseText(strPostcode)
    Else
        strPostcode = "*Missing*"
    End If

    Return strPostcode

End Function

Private Sub btnProcessAddress_Click(...)_
            Handles btnProcessAddress.Click
    'Takes a full address from a single-line text box and displays
    'it in a multi-line text box, splitting it at the commas.
    'Takes account of address starting with number and comma.
    'Extracts postcode from last line.

    Dim strFullAddress As String
    Dim strNextLine As String
    Dim booFollowingHouseNumber As Boolean
    Dim shoLineNumber As Short
    Dim strAddress(10) As String
    Dim shoCommaPos As Short

    Const Comma As String = ","
    Const CR As String = Chr(13) & Chr(10)    'CR/LF characters

    'Get full address from text box
    strFullAddress = txtFullAddress.Text
    'Point to first line of address array
```

```
        shoLineNumber = 1
        'Initialise indicator
        booFollowingHouseNumber = False

        'Find first comma in address
        shoCommaPos = InStr(strFullAddress, Comma)

        'Loop as long as a comma has been found
        Do While shoCommaPos > 0

            strNextLine = VB.Left(strFullAddress, shoCommaPos - 1)

            If booFollowingHouseNumber Then
                'Add to first address line
                strAddress(1) = strAddress(1) & ", " & strNextLine
                booFollowingHouseNumber = False
            Else
                'Put into next address line
                strAddress(shoLineNumber) = VB.Left(strFullAddress,_
                                shoCommaPos - 1)
            End If

            If shoLineNumber = 1 And Len(strNextLine) < 5 And_
                            Val(strNextLine) > 0 Then
                'First part of address is a house number
                'so next time round loop add rest of line 1
                'Stay on line 1
                booFollowingHouseNumber = True
            Else
                'Beyond house number so move to next line
                shoLineNumber += 1
            End If

            'Cut out text that has been dealt with
            strFullAddress = LTrim(Mid(strFullAddress,_
                                shoCommaPos + 1))

            'Find next comma
```

```
        shoCommaPos = InStr(strFullAddress, Comma)

Loop
'Put rest of text in array
strAddress(shoLineNumber) = strFullAddress

'Now build up text in multi-line box (txtAddressLabel)
'Reset pointer
shoLineNumber = 1

'Clear multi-line box
txtAddressLabel.Text = ""

'Loop as long as there is something in the array
Do Until strAddress(shoLineNumber) = ""

    'Add each new line to existing text,
    'with CR/LF characters to start new line
    txtAddressLabel.Text = txtAddressLabel.Text &_
            strAddress(shoLineNumber) & CR
    shoLineNumber = shoLineNumber + 1

Loop

'Extract postcode and display
If shoLineNumber > 1 Then
    txtPostcode.Text =_
        ExtractPostcode(strAddress(shoLineNumber - 1))
End If

End Sub

End Class
```

Exercises

1 Write a function to check whether a password is valid. The function should return a value of True or False.

2 Write a single procedure to add a given number of days, weeks, calendar months or years to a given date, returning the calculated date and its day of the week (as a number). Create a form that uses the procedure to display the results for entered numbers.

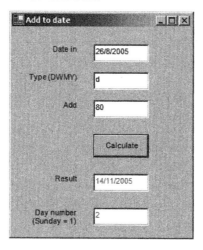

3 Write a function to remove all non-alphabetical characters from a string, converting the first letter of each word to a capital. Use a Do loop in the function.

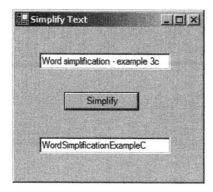

For solutions to these exercises, see page 306.

178

7 Classes

Creating classes

Visual Basic is supplied with an impressive range of ready-made classes, allowing you to add dozens of different controls and specialised dialog boxes to your applications. In addition, there are many third-party controls available. However, there are occasions when you need to create classes of your own. This task is much simpler than you might expect.

Adding a class

The example below demonstrates the creation of a class for a new control: a read-only text box that displays negative values in red. The first stage is to create the class itself:

1   In the application where the new control is needed, select Project|Add Class.

2   The Add New Items dialog is displayed, defaulting to the Class template. Type a name for your class.

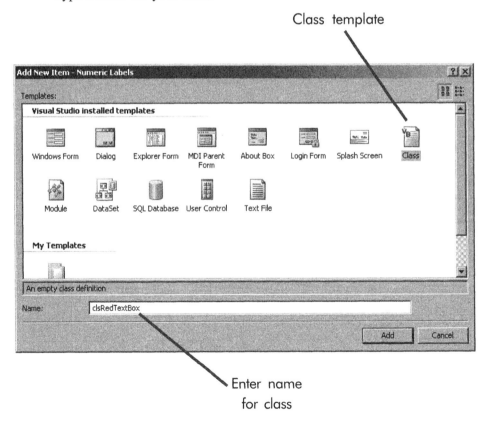

Class template

Enter name
for class

3 Click on Open. You now have an empty class and a vb file has been added to the Solution Explorer.

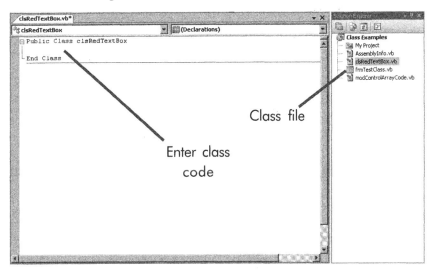

Class file

Enter class code

4 Finally, specify that the new type of control is to be based on the standard Windows text box by adding an Inherits statement.

Inherits statement identifies base class for the new class

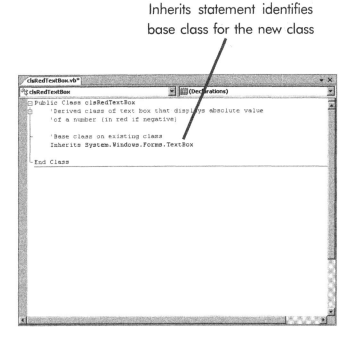

Instantiating an object

You can now add the new text box to a form. At present, this text box is identical to any other text box but this demonstrates that the new class is working; the code below shows you how to create an instance of the object based on the new class:

1   The new object must be visible to all the procedures in the form. Display the code window for the form and add the following statement immediately below the Inherits statement:

Public RedTextBox1 As New clsRedTextBox

Using the Public keyword to declare the variable ensures that the control that is created is available to all procedures. Inserting the keyword 'New' before the class name means that this statement also creates a new instance of the class, resulting in the new object (RedTextBox1).

Take note

Declaring and instantiating an object in a single statement is the most efficient way but only if you are certain that the object is needed. If there is a chance that it will not be required, you can save resources by using two separate statements:

Dim RedTextBox1 As clsRedTextBox

RedTextBox1 = New clsRedTextBox

2   Double-click on Form1 to show the Load event and add the following code:

Me.Controls.Add(RedTextBox1)

RedTextBox1.Left = 24
RedTextBox1.Top = 192
RedTextBox1.Text = "Red!"

The first statement adds the text box to the form's list of controls, resulting in the box being displayed on the form. The other statements change the position of the box (its size will be the default for normal text boxes) and insert some text.

3   Run the program. The window is displayed and includes the text box, which acts like any other text box. (At this stage, of course, the text won't be red!) Close the program.

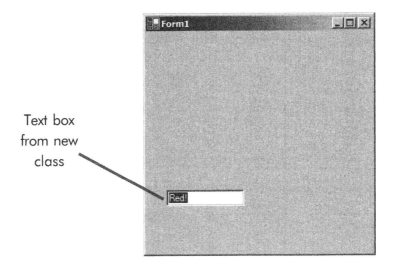

Text box from new class

Adding methods and properties

You can now add the features that will make this class different to the standard text box class. Start by adding a procedure to the class to set the default properties for any new control based on this class. This is done with a **New** procedure. Whenever you instantiate an object, the corresponding class's New procedure (if any) is called.

Make sure the procedure is above the 'End Class' statement and include a statement to set the colour of the text to red. Add two further statements to make the text box read-only and then set the background colour to white. (By default, read-only text boxes turn grey and the red text would not show up.)

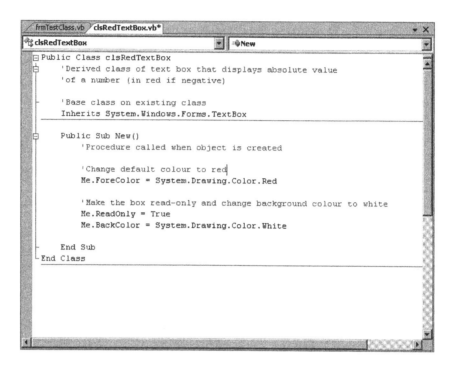

```
frmTestClass.vb   clsRedTextBox.vb*
clsRedTextBox                                    New
Public Class clsRedTextBox
    'Derived class of text box that displays absolute value
    'of a number (in red if negative)

    'Base class on existing class
    Inherits System.Windows.Forms.TextBox

    Public Sub New()
        'Procedure called when object is created

        'Change default colour to red
        Me.ForeColor = System.Drawing.Color.Red

        'Make the box read-only and change background colour to white
        Me.ReadOnly = True
        Me.BackColor = System.Drawing.Color.White

    End Sub
End Class
```

If you run the program again, the text box will default to red text.

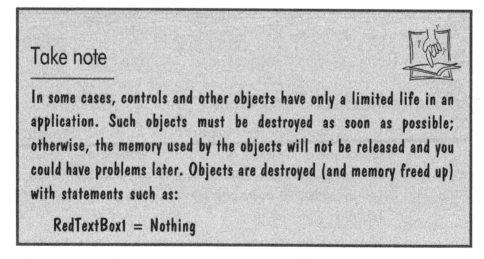

Take note

In some cases, controls and other objects have only a limited life in an application. Such objects must be destroyed as soon as possible; otherwise, the memory used by the objects will not be released and you could have problems later. Objects are destroyed (and memory freed up) with statements such as:

RedTextBox1 = Nothing

The example text box needs an extra property to hold the numeric value of the text. Properties are added by inserting a special type of function in the class code. The header for these functions takes the form:

Public Property *propertyname*() As *type*

In this case, you need to add a property called NumberValue of type Double:

```
Public Property NumberValue() As Double
```

As soon as you enter this statement, Visual Studio creates the framework for the property.

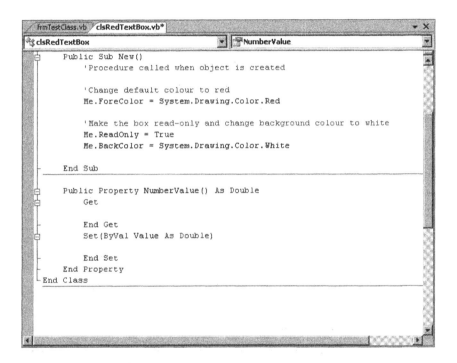

There are two sections to the code:

● The **Get** section returns the current value of the property.

● The **Set** section changes the value of the property. The **Value** variable referred to in the Set statement is the value passed to the property from the main code.

You now have a NumberValue property that can be used like any other property (although it will not do anything until you fill in the gaps below Get and Set).

The actual numeric value of the property must be stored in a class-level variable (below the Inherits statement):

```
Private dblNumberValue As Double
```

You can now fill in the property code.

```
frmTestClass.vb  clsRedTextBox.vb                                    ▾ ✕
clsRedTextBox                          ▾  NumberValue                    ▾

    Public Property NumberValue() As Double
        'Create property to hold original numeric value

    Get
        'Return stored value of property
        Return dblNumberValue
    End Get

    Set(ByVal Value As Double)
        'Store new value of property
        dblNumberValue = Value

        'Copy absolute value to Text property
        Me.Text = Math.Abs(Value)

        'Set text colour to black or red for positive/negative number
        If Value >= 0 Then
            Me.ForeColor() = System.Drawing.Color.Black
        Else
            Me.ForeColor() = System.Drawing.Color.Red
        End If
    End Set

    End Property
```

In most cases, all that the Get and Set sections will do is return the current value
of the property and store the incoming value respectively. In this example, the
property is doing quite a lot of work:

● The Get section returns to the calling procedure the current value, as held in
  dblNumberValue. (The Return statement is used in the same way as for a
  standard function.)

Tip

Use Private rather than Public when declaring a property if you don't want
it to be available to the rest of the application. Private properties can
only be accessed within the class itself.

● The Set section stores the passed value in the class-level variable. It then copies the absolute value (with any minus sign stripped off) to the Text property, so that the value appears in the box. Lastly, the code changes the colour of the text to red or black according to whether the actual value is negative or positive.

Finally, add a Clear method to delete the contents of the text box. Add a Sub procedure and enter a single line of code, changing the value of NumberValue to 0. You don't need to do anything else; when you change the property value, the property's Set code is called and this will tidy up everything else.

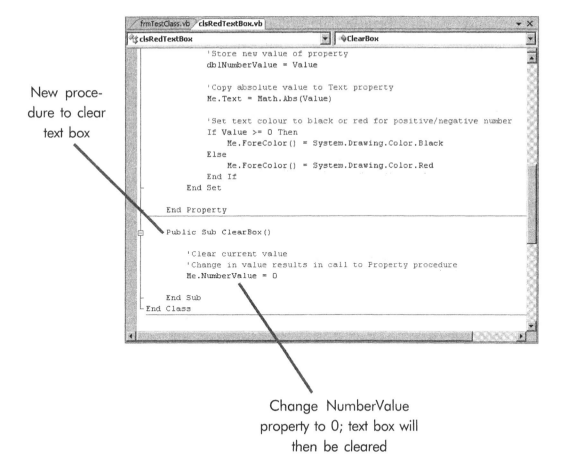

New procedure to clear text box

```
frmTestClass.vb   clsRedTextBox.vb                                    ▼ ✕
clsRedTextBox                              ▼    ClearBox                ▼
              'Store new value of property
              dblNumberValue = Value

              'Copy absolute value to Text property
              Me.Text = Math.Abs(Value)

              'Set text colour to black or red for positive/negative number
              If Value >= 0 Then
                    Me.ForeColor() = System.Drawing.Color.Black
              Else
                    Me.ForeColor() = System.Drawing.Color.Red
              End If
          End Set

      End Property

    Public Sub ClearBox()

          'Clear current value
          'Change in value results in call to Property procedure
          Me.NumberValue = 0

      End Sub
  End Class
```

Change NumberValue property to 0; text box will then be cleared

The completed class, as it now appears, is shown below.

Red Text Box class

```
Public Class clsRedTextBox
    'Derived class of text box that displays absolute value
    'of a number (in red if negative)

    'Base class on existing class
    Inherits System.Windows.Forms.TextBox

    'Use private variable to store property value
    Private dblNumberValue As Double

    Public Sub New()
        'Procedure called when object is created

        'Change default colour to red
        Me.ForeColor = System.Drawing.Color.Red

        'Make the box read-only; make background colour white
        Me.ReadOnly = True
        Me.BackColor = System.Drawing.Color.White

    End Sub

    Public Property NumberValue() As Double
        'Create property to hold original numeric value

        Get

            'Return stored value of property
            Return dblNumberValue

        End Get

        Set(ByVal Value As Double)

            'Store new value of property
            dblNumberValue = Value

            'Copy absolute value to Text property
            Me.Text = Math.Abs(Value)

            'Set text colour to black/red for positive/negative number
```

```
        If Value >= 0 Then
            Me.ForeColor() = System.Drawing.Color.Black
        Else
            Me.ForeColor() = System.Drawing.Color.Red
        End If

    End Set

End Property

Public Sub ClearBox()
    'Clear current value
    'Change in value results in call to Property procedure
    Me.NumberValue = 0

End Sub

End Class
```

You can now test the new class. Rename Form1 (remembering to change the Startup Form in the project properties), delete the line that sets the initial text for RedTextBox1, add text boxes and buttons as shown in the illustration below and add suitable code. The code for the form is shown in full.

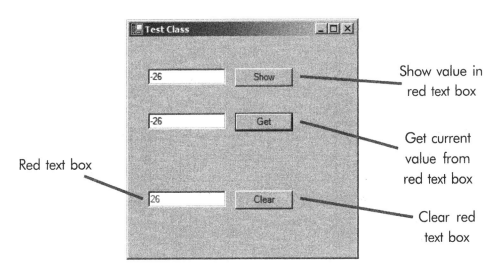

Red text box

Show value in red text box

Get current value from red text box

Clear red text box

Test class form

```
Public Class frmTestClass
    'Form to test new class

    'Form based on existing class
    Inherits System.Windows.Forms.Form

    'Define object variable and create instance of it
    Public RedTextBox1 As New clsRedTextBox

#Region " Windows Form Designer generated code "
#End Region
    Private Sub Form1_Load(...) Handles MyBase.Load
        'When form is loaded, add new text box to it

        'Add text box to list of controls for form
        Me.Controls.Add(RedTextBox1)

        'Set initial position of new text box
        RedTextBox1.Left = 24
        RedTextBox1.Top = 192

    End Sub

    Private Sub btnShow_Click(...) Handles btnShow.Click
        'Update new text box with contents of input box

        'Put any numeric value from the input box into the
        'new text box's NumberValue property

        'The rest of the work is done by the object itself
        RedTextBox1.NumberValue = Val(txtInput.Text)

    End Sub

    Private Sub btnGet_Click(...) Handles btnGet.Click
        'Display the numeric value held by the new text box
        'Copy the value from the text box's NumberValue
        'property to the output box
        txtOutput.Text = RedTextBox1.NumberValue

    End Sub
```

```
Private Sub btnClear_Click(...) Handles btnClear.Click
    'Clear the contents of the new text box

    'Call the text box's ClearBox method to zero the
    'NumberValue property and hence update the display
    RedTextBox1.ClearBox()

End Sub
End Class
```

The effect of the program is as follows:

● Typing a value in the top box and clicking on Show results in the absolute value being shown (in the appropriate colour) in the bottom box (which was created from the red text box class).

● Clicking on the Get button retrieves the original value from the bottom box and displays it in the second box.

● Clicking on Clear deletes the contents of the bottom box and sets the value to 0.

Take note

Creating a new class is not as difficult as it looks, provided you take your time and plan carefully what you want to achieve. The most important thing is to choose a base class that is already close to what you want to do; that way, you will already have most of the functionality and you will only need to add in the extra properties and methods needed to fulfil your requirements.

191

Control arrays

Visual Basic allows you to create control arrays, providing you with the ability to place a number of similar contols on a form. The array is set up and manipulated from within the program, so that you can decide how many controls to add at run time. By using the array, you can change the properties of individual controls as needed; since all the controls share the same name, all you need to know is the index number for a particular control in order to change its properties.

The code for handling such an array is spread throughout the application:

- The creation and manipulation of the controls is handled by a new class (which is created as a separate Visual Basic program within the project).

- The controls are added to the form by inserting the relevant code in the form's procedures; this code calls the methods that are part of the new class.

- You need to keep track of the controls; the variables that do this must be available to both the form's procedures and the new class's methods. Therefore, these variables must be held in a separate code module.

The example below generates a very simple form containing a set of numbered buttons. Also included on the form are standard buttons that allow you to delete or move a selected button, and add further numbered buttons. By itself, this is not a useful program but the code can be copied and amended in other applications, letting you perform a wide range of control-based operations.

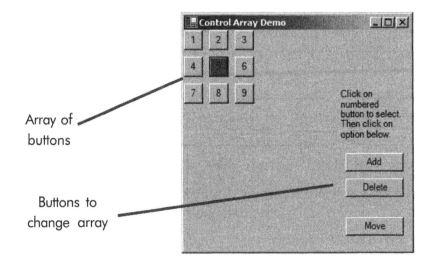

Array of buttons

Buttons to change array

Code module

The first task is to create a code module, modControlArrayCode.vb, which holds the variables that will keep track of the controls in the array.

To create the module, select Project|Add Module, click on the Module template, type the module's name and click on Open. You can then add the necessary code, along with any comments that may be useful later as a reminder of what the variables do.

```
Module ControlArrayCode

    'Latest button to be clicked or created
    Public intCurrentButton As Integer

    'Total number of buttons created so far
    Public intTotalButtons As Integer

End Module
```

In this case, the module contains just two lines of code, defining two variables:

intCurrentButton   The button that was most recently created or the button that has just been added

intTotalButtons   The number of buttons currently included in the array

Array-handling class

The next stage is to create the array-handling class, clsButtonArray.vb. This class will store all the information you need to define and manipulate the controls in the array. The class will also provide all the methods for creating the array, adding or removing controls, and making changes to individual controls' properties.

To create the class, select Project|Add Class, give the class a name and click on Open. You are presented with a completely empty class, to which you can add the array-handling code.

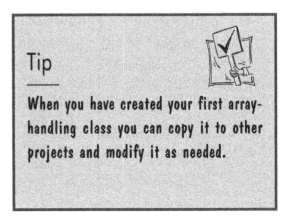

Tip
___

When you have created your first array-handling class you can copy it to other projects and modify it as needed.

```
Public Class clsButtonArray
    'Handles creation and use of array of buttons

    'Button array is held as a collection
    Inherits System.Collections.CollectionBase

    'Variable to identify form containing buttons
    Private ReadOnly ThisForm As System.Windows.Forms.Form

    'Button width and height
    Const intButtonsize As Integer = 25

Public Function AddButton() As_
            System.Windows.Forms.Button
    'Create new instance of Button class
    Dim ibtnNew As New System.Windows.Forms.Button

    'Button co-ordinates
    Dim intX, intY As Integer

    'Add button to collection list
    Me.List.Add(ibtnNew)

    'Add button to the form's controls collection
    ThisForm.Controls.Add(ibtnNew)

    'Calculate button co-ordinates for grid 3 buttons wide
    intX = (Me.Count - 1) Mod 3
    intY = Int((Me.Count - 1) / 3)

    'Set properties for the new button
    ibtnNew.Left = intX * (intButtonsize + 8)
    ibtnNew.Top = intY * (intButtonsize + 8)
    ibtnNew.Width = intButtonsize
    ibtnNew.Height = ibtnNew.Width

    'Store index number in Tag
    ibtnNew.Tag = Me.Count - 1
```

```
        'Display button number in button caption
        intTotalButtons += 1
        ibtnNew.Text = intTotalButtons

        'Set new button as current button
        intCurrentButton = Me.Count - 1

        'Display new button on top
        ibtnNew.BringToFront()

        'Add handler for click event
        AddHandler ibtnNew.Click, AddressOf ButtonClickHandler

        Return ibtnNew

    End Function

    Public Sub Remove(ByVal Index As Integer)
        'Remove current button, providing list is not empty
        If Me.Count > 0 Then

            'Remove button from collection of form controls
            'and from array collection
            ThisForm.Controls.Remove(Me(Index))
            Me.List.RemoveAt(Index)

            'If last button removed, make previous button current
            If intCurrentButton >= Me.Count Then
                intCurrentButton = Me.Count - 1
            End If

        End If

    End Sub

    Public Sub New(ByVal AForm As_
                System.Windows.Forms.Form)
        'When array is created, generate nine buttons

        Dim i As Integer
```

```
        'Identify current form
        ThisForm = AForm

        For i = 1 To 9
            Me.AddButton()
        Next

    End Sub

    Default Public ReadOnly Property Item(ByVal Index_
            As Integer) As System.Windows.Forms.Button
        'Set available properties for list items to standard
        'button properties

        Get
            Return CType(Me.List.Item(Index),_
                        System.Windows.Forms.Button)
        End Get

    End Property

    Public Sub ButtonClickHandler(ByVal sender As_
            Object, ByVal e As System.EventArgs)
        'Store index number of clicked button in global variable
        intCurrentButton = CType(sender,_
                    System.Windows.Forms.Button).Tag

        'Change color of selected button
        CType(sender, System.Windows.Forms.Button).BackColor =_
                        SystemColors.Desktop()

    End Sub
End Class
```

There are three statements at the top of the class code:

- The **Inherits** statement declares that the new class will be based on the standard CollectionBase class. This means that the buttons in the array will be contained in a collection and all the normal collection properties and methods will be available.

- The second statement defines a form variable (ThisForm). The array of buttons will be placed on the form identified by ThisForm.

- The third statement sets the width and height of the new buttons as a constant. Changing the value here alters the size and position of the buttons.

The remainder of the code defines the class's methods, properties and events:

- The **AddButton** method adds a button to the collection and hence to the form. This is declared as a Function rather than a Sub procedure, as it has to return the new button to the calling procedure.

- The **Remove** method deletes a button from the collection (and the form).

- The **New** method generates the initial array of nine buttons.

- There is a default property that returns a reference to a specified button in the array.

- The **ButtonClickHandler** procedure provides the code that is executed when one of the array buttons is clicked.

Each of these is described below.

AddButton method

The AddButton method adds a button to the array and to the form. The method starts by creating an instance of a button (ibtnNew) and adds this to the collection (using the collection's List.Add method); it also adds the button to the form's collection of controls.

Two integers (intX and intY) are used to identify individual buttons on the array; the buttons form a grid three wide. The current button is identified by Me.Count − 1, which gives an index number starting at 0. Therefore for the first button, Me.Count is 1 and the index number is 0; the second button has value 2 for Me.Count and index 1; and so on. The index numbers are then converted into (intX, intY) co-ordinates.

The Left, Top, Width and Height properties for the new button are calculated from the button's co-ordinates and the button size. Most importantly, the button's index number is stored in the button's Tag property; this is essential, as it is the only way that the form can identify which button in the array has been clicked.

The global variables are updated:

```
intTotalButtons += 1
ibtnNew.Text = intTotalButtons
intCurrentButton = Me.Count – 1
```

The first statement increments the number of buttons in the array; the second statement uses this number as the text to be displayed on the button surface; and the third statement stores the new button's index number in the intCurrentButton variable.

The **BringToFront** method (which is available for any standard button) ensures that the new button is displayed on top of any existing controls.

The **AddHandler** statement associates the button's Click event with the ButtonClickHandler procedure; all buttons in the array use the same event procedure for their Click events.

Finally, the function returns the button to the calling procedure.

Remove method

The Remove method deletes a specified button from the array. The argument passed to the method is the index number of the button to be deleted.

The code is executed only if there is a button to be removed. The button was added to both the button collection and the form's control collection and must therefore be removed from both collections. The button is removed from the form's control collection using its Controls.Remove method; similarly, it is removed from the array collection with the List.RemoveAt method. In all these statements 'Me' refers to the class (i.e. the array collection).

If the button being removed is the last one in the array, the button that is now the last one becomes the current button.

New method

The New method is called when the array is created. The argument passed to the method is the name of the form to which the buttons are being added.

The method stores the identity of the form in the class's ThisForm variable (for use in the other methods).

Nine buttons are added to the form by calling the AddButton method nine times.

Default property

The default property returns a reference to a button with a specified index number. This allows you to refer to buttons and their properties using their index number (e.g. arrButtons(index) where arrButtons is a variable of type clsButtonsArray).

ButtonClickHandler procedure

The ButtonClickHandler procedure handles the Click event for all the buttons in the array.

The first statement makes the button that has been clicked the 'current' button by storing its index number in the intCurrentButton global variable. Any actions carried out on the current button will refer to this button. The index number is available in the Tag property of the button that has been clicked.

The second statement changes the background colour of the button.

Control array form

The final stage is to create a form that will display the control array and allow you to perform operations on individual controls.

The main part of the form will be used for displaying the array of buttons. Three further buttons (which are not included in the array) are needed:

● An Add button to add a button to the array

● A Delete button to remove the current button from the array.

● A Move button to shift the current button one space to the right.

You can also add a label to provide instructions for using the program.

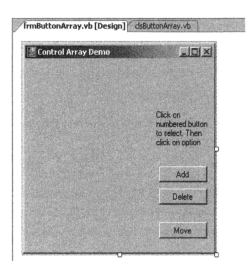

Form to which array of buttons will be added

After creating the form, you need to add procedures for the form's Load event and for each button's Click event.

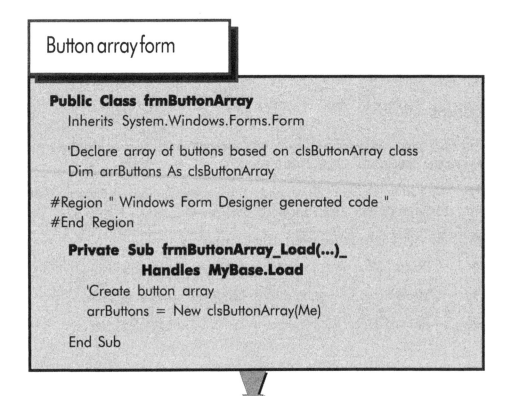

Button array form

```
Public Class frmButtonArray
    Inherits System.Windows.Forms.Form

    'Declare array of buttons based on clsButtonArray class
    Dim arrButtons As clsButtonArray

#Region " Windows Form Designer generated code "
#End Region

    Private Sub frmButtonArray_Load(...)_
            Handles MyBase.Load
        'Create button array
        arrButtons = New clsButtonArray(Me)

    End Sub
```

```
    Private Sub btnMove_Click(...)_
            Handles btnMove.Click
        'Move current button one place to right
        arrButtons(intCurrentButton).Left += 33

        'Change colour back to grey
        arrButtons(intCurrentButton).BackColor =_
                            SystemColors.Control

    End Sub

    Private Sub btnDelete_Click(...)_
            Handles btnDelete.Click
        'Delete current button

        Dim i As Integer

        arrButtons.Remove(intCurrentButton)

        'Renumber all existing buttons (but leave button
        'caption the same)
        For i = 0 To arrButtons.Count - 1
            arrButtons(i).Tag = i
        Next

    End Sub

    Private Sub btnAdd_Click() Handles btnAdd.Click

        'Change colour of currently selected button back to grey
        arrButtons(intCurrentButton).BackColor =_
                                SystemColors.Control

        'Add button to array
        arrButtons.AddButton()

    End Sub
End Class
```

The declaration at the top of the code defines the array variable, arrButtons, as type clsButtonArray. However, this statement only creates the variable; it does not create the array object itself.

The remaining procedures handle the form's events:

- **frmButtonArray_Load** is called when the program is first run and the form is loaded. The single statement in this procedure creates the button array and calls the array class's New procedure (resulting in the first nine buttons being displayed in the top left-hand corner of the window). The parameter passed to the New procedure is 'Me', representing the form name.

- **btnMove_Click** is executed when the Move button is clicked. The first statement increases the value of the current button's Left property by 33 pixels (with the effect that the button moves to the right). The second statement restores the button's colour to the standard Windows control colour.

- **btnDelete_Click** calls the array class's Remove method, deleting the current button from the list and also removing the control from the form. The procedure then renumbers the remaining buttons (so that there are no gaps) by making the value in the Tag property match the index number in the array. (When a control is removed from the array, the gap is closed up and the index numbers of later controls will be reduced.) However, the labels on the surface of the remaining buttons are not changed.

- **btnAdd_Click** starts by changing the colour of the current button back to the default colour. It then adds a button to the array and the form by calling the array class's AddButton method. In the process, the new button becomes the current button (but its colour will not be changed).

When you have set up the event procedures, you can execute the program.

Array of buttons, created when the form is loaded; buttons are added or removed when the appropriate user buttons are clicked; button changes colour to blue when clicked (and all others are set to grey)

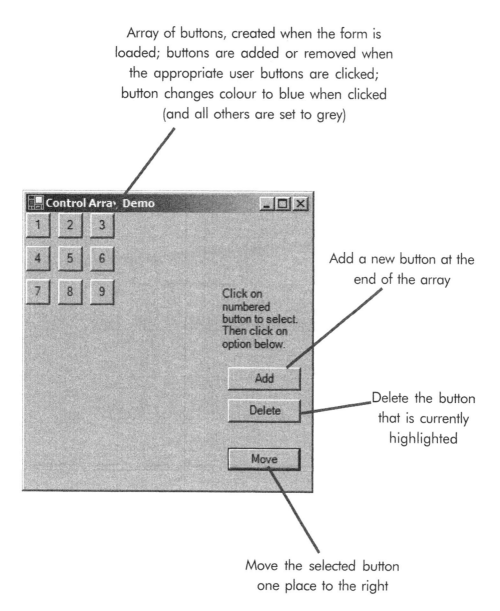

Add a new button at the end of the array

Click on numbered button to select. Then click on option below.

Delete the button that is currently highlighted

Move the selected button one place to the right

Exercises

1 Create a new class of labels that distinguish between text and numeric values. If the contents of the label is numeric, the numeric part should be displayed on the right of the label (with negative numbers in red); otherwise the text should be displayed on the left in blue. The label should have a pale blue background. The class must store the actual value of the label in a new property. Create a form to test the new class.

2 Write a program to display a calendar, as shown below. The display should be updated whenever the month or year is changed. The user should be able to enter values in the blank cells to the right of the numbers.

Selecting new month
updates display

Typing new year and clicking
on button updates display

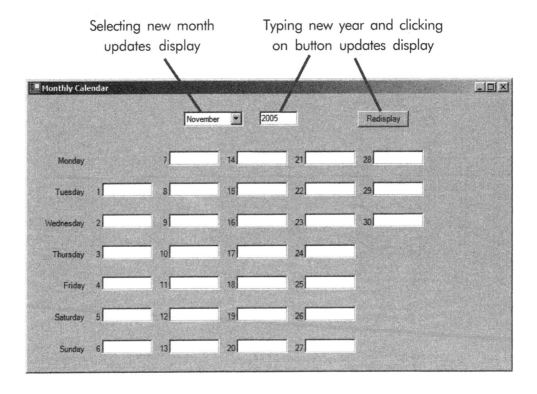

For solutions to these exercises, see page 308.

8 Error handling

Debugging

When the program encounters a problem it cannot handle, it displays an error message and highlights the line in the program that is causing the problem. The program is now in Break mode.

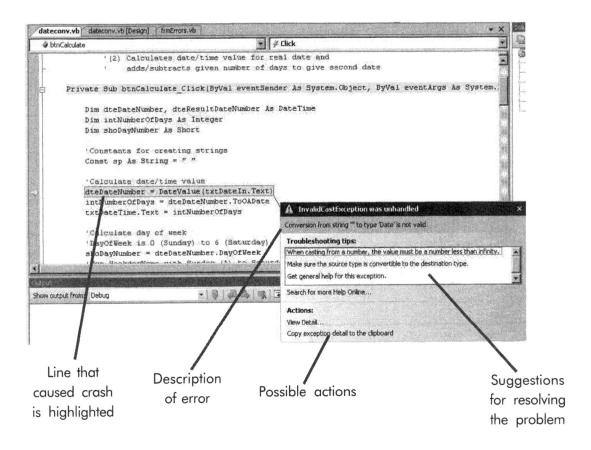

Line that caused crash is highlighted

Description of error

Possible actions

Suggestions for resolving the problem

The Code window is displayed with the line that caused the problem highlighted by a yellow box. The program has not halted; it has only been temporarily suspended. Therefore, if the error is not too serious, you can make a correction and continue running.

The error message box has three sections:

● At the top of the box is a description of the error that has occurred. This will be enough in most cases to tell you what needs to be done to correct the error.

● The middle section points to relevant sections of the on-line help.

- The bottom of the box lets you display more detail relating to the error or copy some of the detail to the clipboard (for pasting into Notepad, for example).

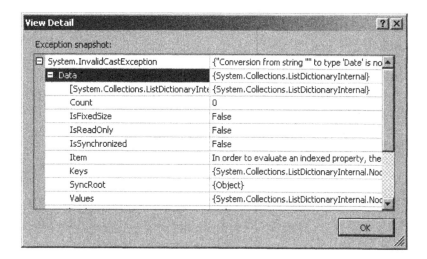

The Debug toolbar is displayed at the top of the window.

Show next statement

Watch

Locals

- Click on the Locals button. The box below the Code window lists the current values of relevant variables. These are the values held by the variables before the line is executed.

Variable name

Current value

Tabs for other debug views

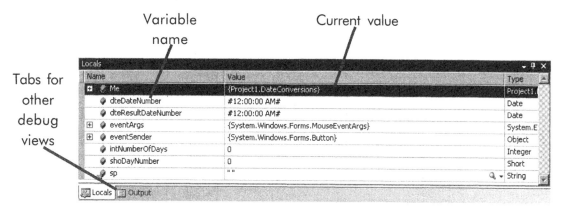

●   Click on the Watch window to see the values of other selected variables.

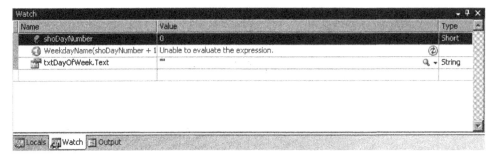

During Break mode, the following options are available:

●   You can inspect the line that caused the problem, and the values of relevant variables; then press **[F5]** (Debug|Continue) to continue running the program. The system will attempt to handle the error.

●   You can close down the program so that you can make changes to the code by pressing **[Ctrl-Alt-Break]** (Debug|Stop Debugging).

●   You can restart the program from a different point in the current procedure by clicking on another line, right-clicking and selecting Set Next Statement; then press **[F5]** (Debug|Continue). This may allow you to skip a troublesome portion of code but is not usually a viable option.

If you lose your place in the program, right-clicking and selecting Show Next Statement displays the procedure containing the next statement to be executed.

While the program is halted, you can also inspect the values of other variables or expressions (see *Watching variables* on page 215).

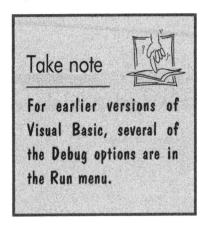

Take note

For earlier versions of Visual Basic, several of the Debug options are in the Run menu.

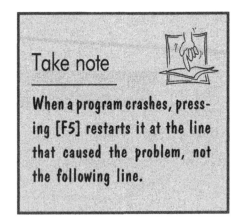

Take note

When a program crashes, pressing [F5] restarts it at the line that caused the problem, not the following line.

Breakpoints

You can force Visual Basic to halt execution at a particular point in the program by setting a **breakpoint**. Put the cursor on the required line and press **[F9]**; alternatively, click on the grey area to the left of the line or right-click on the line and select Insert Breakpoint.

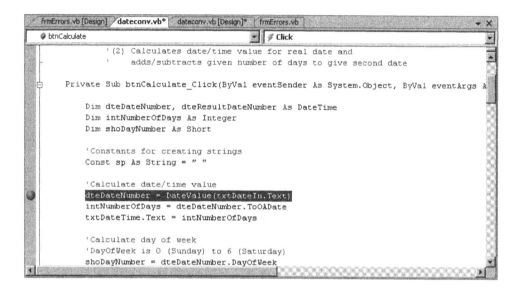

The line is shown with a red background and a circle is displayed in the grey area. When the program is run, it will halt at this point, before the line is executed.

Having interrupted the program in this way, you can inspect the contents of variables, step through the code a line at a time, make minor changes to the code, or continue execution by pressing **[F5]**.

You can set several breakpoints at once; the program halts each time a breakpoint is encountered. A breakpoint can be cancelled by clicking on the breakpoint line and pressing **[F9]** again; all breakpoints can be cancelled with Debug|Delete All Breakpoints.

Take note

You can also break into a program by pressing [Ctrl-Break] or by switching to the Code window and selecting Debug|Break All.

209

Alternatively, you can temporarily deactivate a breakpoint by right-clicking on it and selecting Breakpoint|Disable Breakpoint; the Enable Breakpoint command restores the disabled breakpoint.

Single-stepping

When a program halts because of an error or a breakpoint, the line that is about to be executed is highlighted in yellow and a yellow arrow appears on the left-hand side of the current line.

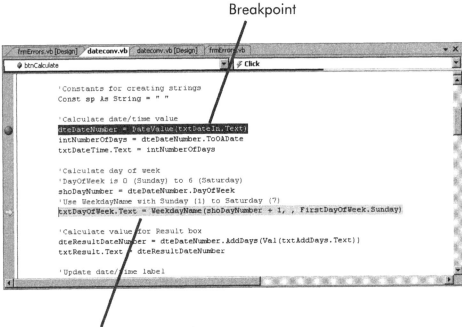

Breakpoint

Line about to be executed

You can now run the program a line at a time using the following options:

- Press **[F8]** (Debug|Step Into) to execute the line; if the line contains a procedure or a function call, the procedure or function is displayed and you can continue to step through it a line at a time. This is called **single-stepping**.

- Press **[Shift-F8]** (Debug|Step Over) to execute the line, including any procedure or function call; the next line in the current procedure is then highlighted.

- Press **[Ctrl-Shift-F8]** (Debug|Step Out) to finish running the current procedure or function and then continue execution until control returns to the procedure or function.

- Move the cursor to some other point in the program, right-click and select Run To Cursor; execution restarts and continues until this point is reached.

When you have finished single-stepping, you can use the Debug options either to continue or to end the program.

Breakpoint options

There are several ways in which you can make more sophisticated use of a breakpoint, rather than stopping the program every time the breakpoint is reached. Note that these options apply to Visual Basic .NET and Visual Basic 2005 Standard Edition and Professional Edition; the breakpoint options are not available in the Express Edition.

Right-click on a breakpoint and select Breakpoint Properties to display a dialog containing the breakpoint options.

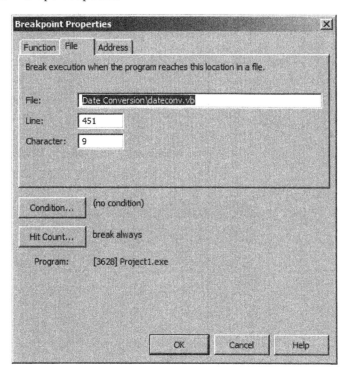

The Breakpoint Properties dialog shows you, on the File tab, the line at which the break occurs. (As an alternative, you can set the breakpoint in terms of its position within a particular function or at a specific memory address.)

Click on the Condition button to set a condition that must be satisfied for a break to occur. For example, you may specify that a variable must equal a particular value or that one expression must be larger than another. This is useful if a program is only going wrong when particular values are encountered.

Breakpoint condition: break
when condition is true

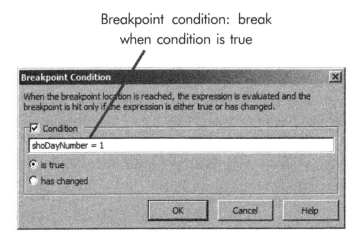

Alternatively, you can enter an expression and specify that the break should occur only when the value of the expression changes. This is a useful option if you are trying to detect the point at which some limit is reached or the status of a variable changes.

Breakpoint condition: break
when value has changed

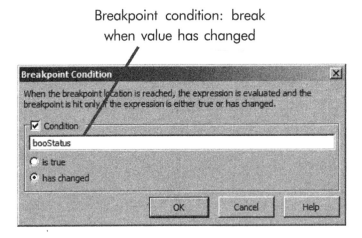

Finally, you can specify that the break occurs when the breakpoint has been reached a specific number of times. For example, you may want to execute a For...Next loop until the last time through, in which case you would specify one less than the final value of the loop counter.

Click on Hit Count and choose from the following options:

- Break every time the breakpoint is reached (the default).

- Break after a specific number of 'hits'.

- Break when the hit count is a multiple of a specified number (for example, break every fifth time through a loop).

Hit Count condition: break when
the hit count is a multiple of 5

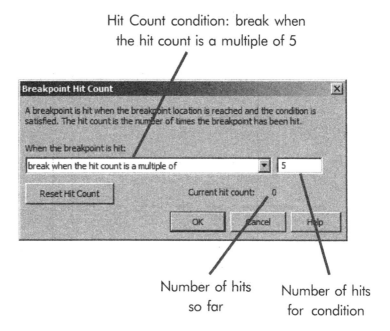

Number of hits
so far

Number of hits
for condition

- Break every time after the hit count has reached a specific number.

These options allow you to set up the most efficient way for reaching a particular point in the program. For example, you may want to break when a particular piece of data has been read from a file or after you have been through a loop a specific number of times.

When the program is in break mode, you can display the Breakpoint Properties dialog and reset the hit counter.

Position in file at which the
break will occur

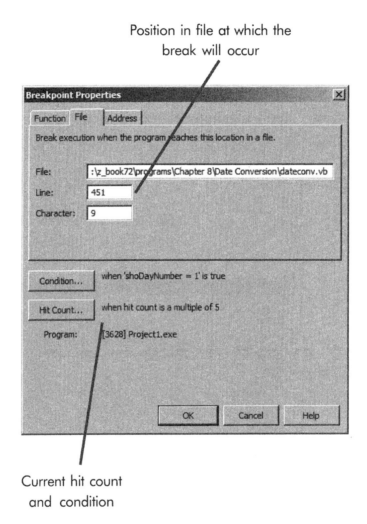

Current hit count
and condition

Note that the current condition and hit count setting are shown on the Breakpoint Properties dialog. You can set a combination of conditions, so that the break occurs only when both the condition and hit count setting are satisfied.

Watching variables

Having broken into a program, you can inspect the values of any variables or expressions. If you put the cursor on a variable name in the code, the current value pops up below the name.

You can also see how the value changes as the program progresses. Click on a variable name or highlight an expression in the code; then right-click and select Add Watch. The Watch window is displayed. This shows the expression and its current value. Each time you use Add Watch, another expression is added to the Watch window. Now, as you single-step through the program, you will be able to see how the values of variables are affected by the code, making it much easier to identify the causes of problems.

Click to calculate
expression

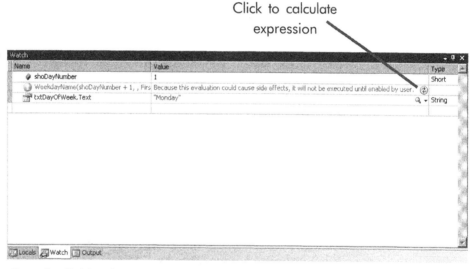

Drag the dividers between the column headers to change the widths of the columns in the Watch window.

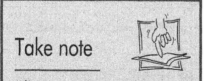

To remove an expression from the Watch window, right-click on it and select Delete Watch.

If you only want to check the value of an expression once, mark the expression, right-click and select Quick Watch. The QuickWatch dialog shows the current value of the expression. You can add this expression to the list in the Watch window by clicking on Add Watch. Alternatively, select another recently-watched expression from the drop-down list and click on Recalculate to see its current value.

Trapping errors

You will have noticed that some of the programs you have been writing crash if an invalid entry is made (for instance, if a text box that is supposed to contain a date is blank when a button is clicked). You can test for some errors – and correct them – using a control's LostFocus event. To be sure of handling all errors, however, you should include error-trapping statements in your code. These statements are activated when an error occurs.

Error-trapping is implemented as follows:

1   Turn error-trapping on with a statement in the form:

> On Error GoTo *label*

When a **trappable** error occurs (one that On Error GoTo can handle), the program jumps to the code pointed to by the *label*.

2   Identify the end of the normal part of the procedure with an Exit Sub statement (just above End Sub).

3   After Exit Sub, enter the *label*, adding a colon (:) to the end of it.

4   Following the *label*, insert the statements that will correct the error (for instance, statements to display a warning message or change the contents of a text box).

5   End the error-handling statements with a Resume statement (see below).

6   If the Resume statement includes a label, insert the label (with a colon) at the appropriate point in the procedure.

The **Resume** statement must be one of the following:

Resume	Re-execute the statement that caused the problem.
Resume Next	Continue with the statement following the one that caused the error.
Resume *label2*	Resume execution on the line following *label2*.

Most errors can be trapped, though only certain types of error are likely to occur in any procedure.

The procedure below demonstrates the use of error-trapping statements.

Error trapping

Sample procedure taken from Date Conversions program on pages 137-139.

```
Private Sub btnCalculate_Click(...)_
        Handles btnCalculate.Click
    Dim dteDateNumber, dteResultDateNumber As DateTime
    Dim intNumberOfDays As Integer
    Dim shoDayNumber As Short
    Const sp As String = " "  'Constants for creating strings

    On Error GoTo BadDate

ErrorRestart:
    'Calculate date/time value
    dteDateNumber = DateValue(txtDateIn.Text)
    intNumberOfDays = dteDateNumber.ToOADate
    txtDateTime.Text = intNumberOfDays

    'Calculate day of week
    shoDayNumber = dteDateNumber.DayOfWeek
    txtDayOfWeek.Text = WeekdayName(shoDayNumber + 1,_
                        , FirstDayOfWeek.Sunday)
    'Calculate value for Result box
    dteResultDateNumber =_
        dteDateNumber.AddDays(Val(txtAddDays.Text))
    txtResult.Text = dteResultDateNumber
    'Update date/time label
    lblNow.Text = "Date/time of last entry: " &_
    Now.ToLongDateString & sp & Now.ToLongTimeString
    Exit Sub

BadDate:
    'This routine is invoked if any error occurs but at
    'this stage handles only one type of error.
    'Insert current date in text box and then continue
    txtDateIn.Text = Today
    'Jump back to start of procedure
    Resume ErrorRestart
End Sub
```

Error messages

Whenever a trappable error occurs, the system generates an error number to identify the type of error. You can use this number in your error-handling code to decide how best to deal with the error.

The error information is returned in the Err object. This object has two particularly important properties:

- The **Number** property holds the error number. This is the value you can use to drive your error-handling code.

- The **Description** property holds a detailed description of the error, including the values of relevant variables.

In addition, the **ErrorToString** function returns a simple, general error message for a given error number.

The following code displays a message box containing the error number, simple message and full description:

```
Dim intError As Integer
Dim strSimpleError As String
Dim strFullError As String
Dim strErrorMsg As String

intError = Err.Number
strSimpleError = ErrorToString(intError)
strFullError = Err.Description

strErrorMsg = "Error" & Str(intError) & ": " & strSimpleError &_
                              " Details: " & strFullError

MsgBox(strErrorMsg)
```

Code such as this can be included in the error-handling section of a procedure.

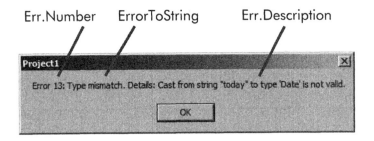

The procedure below lists all the available error messages in a text box.

```
Private Sub frmErrors_Load(...) Handles MyBase.Load

    Dim i As Integer
    Dim strError As String

    Const CRLF = Chr(13) & Chr(10)
    Const TAB = Chr(9)

    txtErrSimple.Text = "1" & TAB & ErrorToString(1)
    For i = 2 To 100
        strError = i & TAB & ErrorToString(i)
        txtErrSimple.Text = txtErrSimple.Text & CRLF & strError
    Next i

End Sub
```

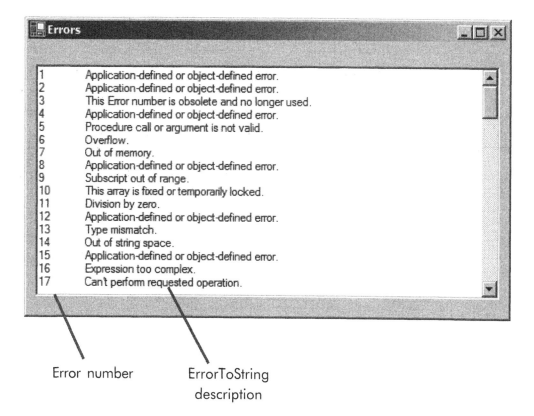

Error number

ErrorToString
description

Structured error handling

The On Error method of error trapping described above provides an *unstructured* approach. When an error occurs, control jumps to the end of the procedure; after dealing with the error, control returns to a point higher up the procedure. As an alternative, you can use the Try...Catch...Finally group of statements to provide *structured* error-handling.

The statements take the following form:

```
Try
    'Statements that may cause an error
Catch  condition1
    'Statements to be executed when condition1 is satisfied
Catch  condition2
    'Statements to be executed when condition2 is satisfied

...

Finally
    'Tidying-up statements
End Try
```

The statements that may cause an error are placed immediately below the Try statement. The *conditions* are tests for various errors that may occur. If an error occurs in the Try section control moves down to the first Catch statement that satisfies the error condition (if any) and the code within that block is executed. The code below the Finally statement is always executed, regardless of whether there is an error or not. Therefore this is a good place to sort out any potential problems: deleting unwanted objects, closing files, freeing up memory etc.

Using the previous example, the On Error statements can be replaced by a much simpler Try...Catch structure. In this procedure, the only statement likely to cause an error is the line that converts the input text to a date value. The only possible error is error 13, Type Mismatch.

Therefore there is just one statement in the Try section and there is only one Catch statement; the code within the Catch block deals with the error in exactly the same way as for the On Error method. There is no tidying up to be done, so the Finally block is omitted.

Sample procedure taken from Date Conversions program on pages 137-139.

```
Private Sub btnCalculate_Click(...)_
          Handles btnCalculate.Click
    Dim dteDateNumber, dteResultDateNumber As DateTime
    Dim intNumberOfDays As Integer
    Dim shoDayNumber As Short
    'Constants for creating strings
    Const sp As String = " "
    'Calculate date/time value

    Try
       dteDateNumber = DateValue(txtDateIn.Text)
    Catch When Err.Number = 13
       'Deal with invalid date in input box
       txtDateIn.Text = Today
       dteDateNumber = DateValue(Today)
       MsgBox("Invalid date")
    End Try

    intNumberOfDays = dteDateNumber.ToOADate
    txtDateTime.Text = intNumberOfDays
    'Calculate day of week
    'DayOfWeek is 0 (Sunday) to 6 (Saturday)
    shoDayNumber = dteDateNumber.DayOfWeek
    'Use WeekdayName with Sunday (1) to Saturday (7)
    txtDayOfWeek.Text = WeekdayName(shoDayNumber + 1,_
                    , FirstDayOfWeek.Sunday)

    'Calculate value for Result box
    dteResultDateNumber =_
         dteDateNumber.AddDays(Val(txtAddDays.Text))
    txtResult.Text = dteResultDateNumber

    'Update date/time label
    lblNow.Text = "Date/time of last entry: " &_
    Now.ToLongDateString & sp & Now.ToLongTimeString
End Sub
```

Exercises

1 Use the debugging options to interrupt the Membership Database program when the Region is changed; watch the values for lblRep.Text and cboRegion.Text as they are changed.

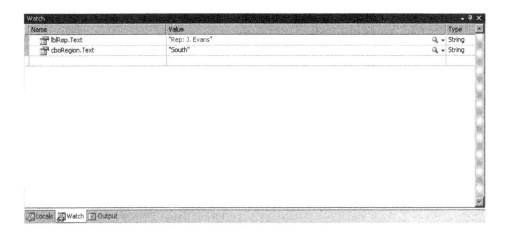

2 Add error-handling statements to the Calendar program so that it deals with an entry in the Year box of more than 9999.

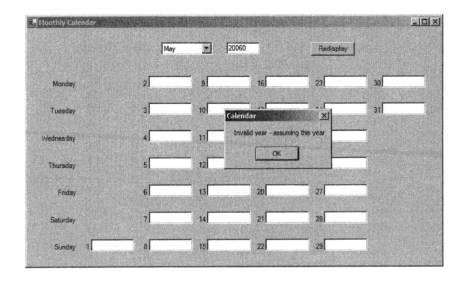

For solutions to these exercises, see page 319.

9 Menus

The MenuStrip control

You can add a drop-down menu to a form using the **MenuStrip** control. Display
the form to which you want to add a menu and double-click on the MenuStrip control
in the Menus & Toolbars section of the toolbox. A box with the text 'Type Here'
is added at the top of the form and the MenuStrip1 object is shown in an area below
the form (called the **component tray**).

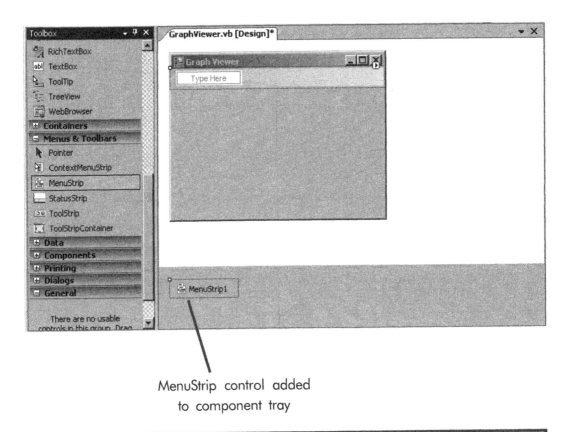

MenuStrip control added
to component tray

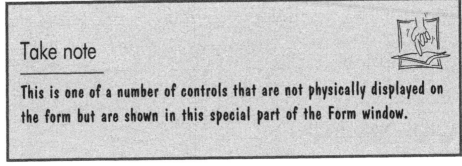

Take note

This is one of a number of controls that are not physically displayed on
the form but are shown in this special part of the Form window.

Adding options

To add the first menu name to the menu system, click on the 'Type Here' box and type the menu name. Include an & in front of the character that is to be used as an **access key**: this is the letter that, when pressed in combination with **[Alt]**, will invoke the menu. For example, type '&File' for a File menu that is accessed by pressing **[Alt F]**.

As you type the menu name, further 'Type Here' boxes are added to the right and below.

Include & in front of access key

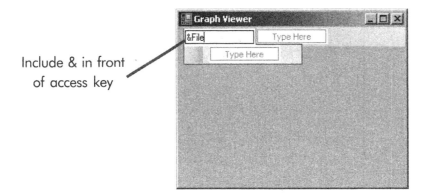

When you press **[Enter]** or click away from the menu name the menu is displayed as it will appear on the form.

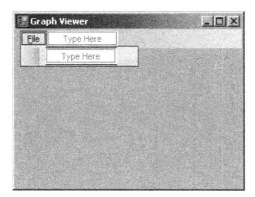

Click on the 'Type Here' box below the menu name to add the first menu option. Again, include an access key, if required. Further 'Type Here' boxes are added the right and below.

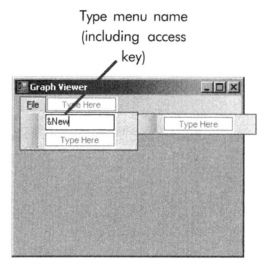

You can now extend the menu system in every direction:

● Add further options below the latest entry to extend the menu.

● Add another menu by typing in the box to the right of the first menu name.

● Add sub-menu options by typing on the right of an existing menu option.

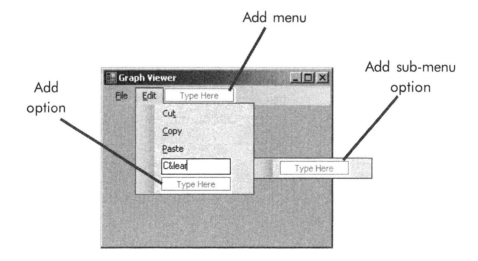

As a general rule, you should give each menu, sub-menu and option an access key with no two menus or options in a menu having the same key. By convention, any option that leads to a dialog box should have three dots (...) at the end of its name. Options that lead to sub-menus will be given an arrow on the right of the name. You can edit any part of the menu by clicking on it.

Sub-menus

Sub-menus are created by adding options at a second level of indent, so that the first-level option effectively becomes a sub-menu name.

The sub-menu options can themselves become a further level of sub-menu by indenting the next set of items to a third level. In all, you can have up to four levels of sub-menus, though it is unusual to go beyond the first sub-menu.

Adding sub-menus

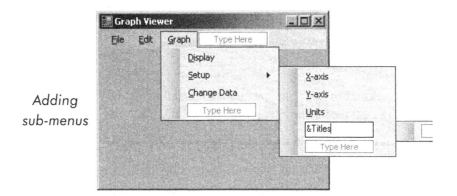

Tip

Don't get too carried away with sub-menus. Keep the menu structure as simple as possible so that users can navigate with ease.

Separator bars

For long menus, it is useful to split the options into groups. This is done by inserting a separator bar.

To add a separator bar above a particular option, right-click on the option and select Insert|Separator. The bar can be moved around in the same way as any other menu item and right-clicking on it results in the same pop-up menu.

Adding separator bars

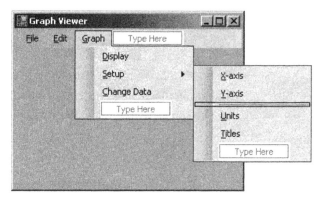

Editing the menus

You can select any menu item by clicking on it. When an item is highlighted, you have the following options:

- Click on the item again to edit the text.

- Right-click and select Insert|MenuItem to add another option above the current option or another menu to the left of the selected menu.

- Right-click and select Delete to remove the option or menu.

- Drag an option up or down the list to change the order within the menu. You can also drag separator bars to new positions.

- Drag a menu name to the left or right to change the order of the menus.

- Use the Cut and Paste options from the pop-up menu to move any option, sub-menu or menu to another menu or to a point on the row of menu names to change its status. For example, you can make a sub-menu into a top-level menu or vice versa. Any options within a menu or sub-menu will follow it to the new location.

Menu properties

Each menu, sub-menu and option within the menu system is a separate object, with its own set of properties. Separator bars are also independent objects, with their own properties.

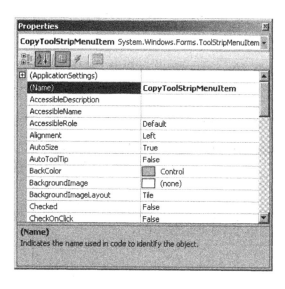

Menu item names

Like all other objects, each menu item (whether it's a menu name, sub-menu, menu option or separator bar) must have a unique name. By default, these names are allocated as the items are created. However, to make life easier when coding menu events you should change these names to something easier to handle. The convention is to give the items names consisting of 'mnu' followed by the sequence of options (e.g. mnuFile for the File menu and mnuFileSave for the File|Save option).

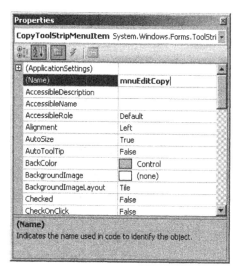

You can change the Name for each individual item by clicking on the item and then editing the name in the Properties window. Alternatively, you can change all the names for a whole menu by right-clicking on any item and selecting Edit DropDownItems. The Items Collection Editor is displayed. Clicking on an item on the left results in the item's properties being shown on the right.

Click on each item in turn and replace the default name with a meaningful alternative. You can also use the editor to add or delete menu items or move existing items up and down in the menu.

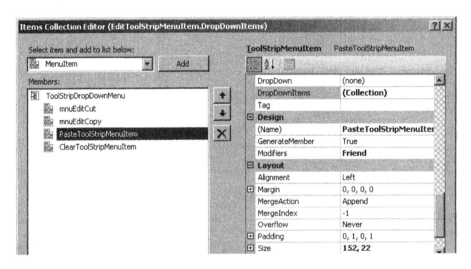

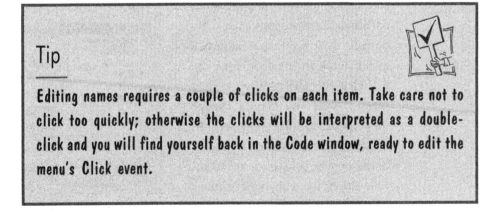

Tip

Editing names requires a couple of clicks on each item. Take care not to click too quickly; otherwise the clicks will be interpreted as a double-click and you will find yourself back in the Code window, ready to edit the menu's Click event.

After you have edited the names, right-click on a menu item and select Edit Names again to hide the display of object names.

Boolean properties

Each menu item has three useful Boolean properties:

- The **Checked** property, when True, places a tick on the left of the menu option.

- The **Enabled** property, when False, greys out the menu or option; clicking on the menu or option has no effect.

- The **Visible** property, when False, hides the option when the menu is displayed (or hides the menu).

Usually, you will want to leave the properties as they are when developing the menu system but change them while the program is running. For instance, an option may be used for switching some feature of the program on or off. Clicking on the option will set Enabled to True (and place a tick against it); clicking on it again will set Enabled to False (and remove the tick). As another example, after saving a file the File|Save option may have its Enabled property set to False; as soon as further changes are made to the data the Enabled property can be set to True again. The Visible property can be used for restricting options: for instance, some menu options may be visible only to users with certain passwords.

Shortcut keys

You can attach a **shortcut key** to any option in any of the menus. This is a key combination that the user can press to activate the menu option without having to click on the option itself. For example, it is usual for the File|Save option to have a **[Ctrl-S]** shortcut, so that the save routine is invoked when the user presses **[Ctrl-S]**.

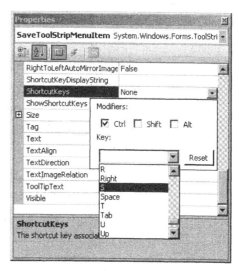

A shortcut is attached to an item by clicking on the ShortcutKeys property and then choosing a modifier key and shortcut key. When you run the program and display the menu, the shortcut is shown to the right of the option name.

Whether or not the shortcut is shown on the menu is determined by the ShowShortcut property.

All menu items should have an *access key* (a key used in combination with **[Alt]** to activate the option). Only the most frequently-used options should have *shortcuts* (which use keys other than **[Alt]**).

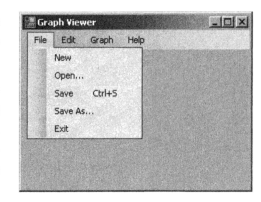

Other properties

When you have created a menu system for a form, you can alter other properties using the Properties window. Select the menu item from the drop-down list at the top of the window or click on the menu item on the form and then change the properties in the usual way.

In Visual Basic .NET, four other properties may be useful in more complex applications:

● The **Index** property sets the position of the menu on the menu bar or an option within a menu. The position is numbered from 0 on the extreme left or top of the menu. When you change the index for one item all the rest are renumbered accordingly.

● The **DefaultItem** property, when True, indicates that the option is the default option in the menu or sub-menu. The item is displayed in bold and double-clicking the menu or sub-menu results in the default item being selected.

● The **MdiList** property, when True, results in a list of all subsidiary windows currently open in the main window being added to the menu.

● The **RadioCheck** property, when True, replaces the tick for checked items with a radio button.

These properties are not available in Visual Basic 2005.

For more information on menu properties, search the Visual Basic on-line help for the MenuItem class.

Menu events

Menu controls respond to a Click event, which is activated either by clicking on the menu option or by pressing the access key or shortcut.

For menus and sub-menus, the Click event results in the list of options dropping down. For menu options, you need to supply a Click procedure. The code for

Take note

You can set up a Click event for a menu or sub-menu; for example, you may want to change the contents of a menu each time it is displayed.

this is added in exactly the same way as for any other event. (You can either select the menu item object and event name in the boxes at the top of the Code window or double-click on the item in the form.)

The Edit menu

Most applications have an Edit menu with the following options:

Cut	Deletes highlighted text and copies to clipboard
Copy	Copies highlighted text to clipboard
Paste	Pastes text from clipboard at cursor position (replacing any highlighted text)
Clear	Deletes highlighted text

The implementation of these options, shown below, will be very similar in most applications.

The clipboard

The **clipboard** is an object that is supplied with every Windows application. It does not have any physical appearance or events but it does two useful methods:

SetDataObject	Copies the specified text to the clipboard
GetDataObject	Returns the contents of the clipboard

The clipboard can hold data in a number of formats – not just text. Therefore the retrieval of data from the clipboard is not entirely straightforward. The GetDataObject method returns data as an object of type **IDataObject**. In order to retrieve the data from IDataObject you must use the object's **GetData** method and specify the format of the data (which will be one of the standard formats specified by the **DataFormats** class).

The Edit menu example below illustrates the usual way of doing this for the mnuEditPaste_Click procedure. (It is usually only the Paste operation that requires you to retrieve data from the clipboard.) The procedure consists of two statements:

● The Dim statement performs two operations: defining a variable of type IDataObject and giving it the current clipboard value.

● The second statement uses the new variable's GetData method to retrieve the data in the Text format, converting the result into a string that is placed in the text box's Text property.

The clipboard methods can be used in conjunction with the following text box properties:

SelectedText   String of highlighted characters (blank if none selected)

SelectionLength Length of highlighted string

SelectionStart   Current cursor position (0 if in front of first character)

The procedures below show how the Edit menu options are usually implemented.

Edit menu

```
Private Sub mnuEditCut_Click(...)_
          Handles mnuEditCut.Click
    'Assumes text being edited is in a text box called txtEntry

    'Copy highlighted text to clipboard
    Clipboard.SetDataObject(txtEntry.SelectedText)

    'Delete highlighted text
    txtComments.SelectedText = ""

End Sub
```

```vb
Private Sub mnuEditCopy_Click(...)_
        Handles mnuEditCopy.Click
    'Copy highlighted text to clipboard
    Clipboard.SetDataObject(txtComments.SelectedText)
End Sub

Private Sub mnuEditPaste_Click(...)_
        Handles mnuEditPaste.Click
    'Define object to hold clipboard data
    'and fill with current clipboard contents
    Dim iData As IDataObject = Clipboard.GetDataObject()

    'Replace current selection with clipboard contents
    'or insert at cursor position (if nothing selected)
    txtComments.SelectedText =_
        CType(iData.GetData(DataFormats.Text), String)

End Sub

Private Sub mnuEditClear_Click(...)_
        Handles mnuEditClear.Click
    Dim bytButtonVal As Byte

    'Display warning message, returning button
    'press (OK or Cancel)
    bytButtonVal = MessageBox.Show("All text in Comments_
                box will be deleted!", "Delete all text",_
                MessageBoxButtons.OKCancel)

    If bytButtonVal = DialogResult.OK Then

    'Clear contents of text box if OK pressed
        txtComments.Text = ""

    End If

End Sub
```

Adding menus at run-time

You can add menus, sub-menus and menu options while a program is running and change the properties of existing menu items.

The following code adds a main menu object to a form:

```
Dim MainMenu2 As New MenuStrip
Me.Controls.Add(MainMenu2)
Me.MainMenuStrip = MainMenu2
```

This code creates the object (MainMenu2) and makes it the main menu for the current form.

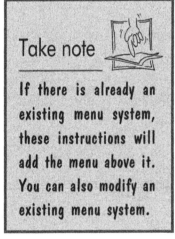

Take note

If there is already an existing menu system, these instructions will add the menu above it. You can also modify an existing menu system.

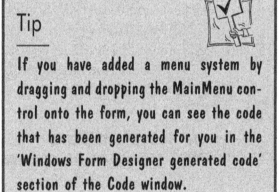

Tip

If you have added a menu system by dragging and dropping the MainMenu control onto the form, you can see the code that has been generated for you in the 'Windows Form Designer generated code' section of the Code window.

To add a menu to your menu system, use code in the following form:

```
Dim mnuMenu1 As New ToolStripMenuItem("&Menu1 name")
MainMenu2.Items.AddRange(New ToolStripItem() {mnuMenu1})
```

The following code adds an item to an existing menu:

```
Dim mnuMenu1Option1 As New _
                ToolStripMenuItem("&Option1 name")
mnuMenu1.DropDownItems.AddRange(New _
                ToolStripItem() {mnuMenu1Option1})
```

Finally, you can change the properties for a menu or menu item:

```
mnuMenu1.Name = "&Save"
mnuMenu1Option1.Visible = False
```

The following procedure adds a Tools menu, with three options, to an existing menu system (with the default name, MenuStrip1).

```
Public Sub AddToolsMenu()

    'Define menu items
    Dim mnuTools As New ToolStripMenuItem("&Tools")
    Dim mnuToolsCalculator As New _
                    ToolStripMenuItem("&Calculator")
    Dim mnuToolsViewFile As New _
                    ToolStripMenuItem("&View File")
    Dim mnuToolsInternet As New ToolStripMenuItem("&Internet")

    'Add menu and items
    MenuStrip1.Items.AddRange(New ToolStripItem() {mnuTools})
    mnuTools.DropDownItems.AddRange(New _
        ToolStripItem() {mnuToolsCalculator, _
        mnuToolsViewFile, mnuToolsInternet})
    'Set menu and item properties
    'Set shortcut for View File to Ctrl-V
    mnuToolsViewFile.ShortcutKeys =_
                    Keys.Control Or Keys.S
    'Disable Internet option
    mnuToolsInternet.Enabled = False
End Sub
```

Tip

Some menu options will duplicate the effect of other events. For instance, selecting the File|Exit option may be the same as clicking on the Exit button. In such cases, the menu option's Click event should call the procedure for the corresponding event (e.g. mnuFileExit_Click should call btnExit_Click).

Context menus

The **context menus** that are displayed when you right-click on the screen can be added to your program in much the same way as the main menu strip:

1   Drag the **ContextMenuStrip** control from the Toolbox onto a blank area of the form or onto a control. The context menu is added to the component tray.

Take note

You can have different context menus for each part of the form. For example, individual controls (such as labels) can have their own context menu. The context menu for the form pops up when the user clicks on any control that does not have its own context menu.

2   Add items to the context menu in the same way as for a main menu, including access keys where required. Items within a context menu can also lead to sub-menus.

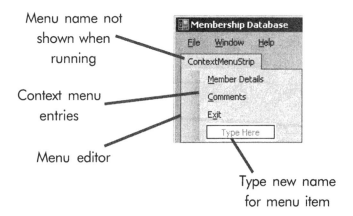

3   In the properties for the form or control to which the context menu is to apply, change the ContextMenuStrip property to the relevant **ContextMenuStrip** control. The available menus are listed in the drop-down box.

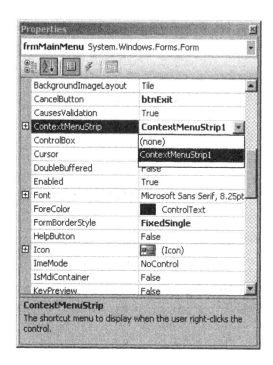

4 Change the properties of the context menu items. The properties are displayed when you click on an item in the menu editor. The same properties are available as for main menu items, including the Name of the individual items.

5 Create Click events for each of the context menu items by double-clicking on the items in the menu editor.

When you run the program, the context menu will be displayed when you right-click on the form or control.

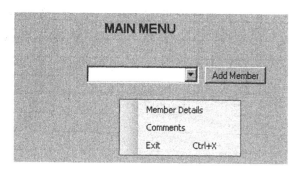

You can also add a context menu while the program is running. The steps required are similar to those for adding the menu at the design stage:

1   Define a ContextMenuStrip object and the required number of ToolStripMenuItem objects.

2   Attach the context menu to the form (or a control) by setting the form or control's ContextMenuStrip property to the name of the ContextMenuStrip object.

3   Add the options to the menu using the context menu object's Items.AddRange method.

4   Specify the text to be displayed in the menu by setting each menu item's Text property. Include an & in front of any access key.

5   Change any other menu item properties (for example, to give the item a shortcut key or to disable it).

6   Create Click procedures for each menu option.

The example procedure below adds a context menu to the Membership Database front-end window, with options to display the other windows or exit the program. This procedure could be called from the form's Load procedure.

The Click events for the three menu items are also given.

Tip

To edit an existing menu, click on its icon in the component tray. The menu temporarily appears below the main menu in the top left-hand corner of the form.

Context menu

```vbnet
Public Sub AddContextMenu()
    'Define context menu and options
    Dim mnuContext As New ContextMenuStrip(Me.components)
    Dim mnuContextMemberDetails As New ToolStripMenuItem
    Dim mnuContextComments As New ToolStripMenuItem
    Dim mnuContextExit As New ToolStripMenuItem
    'Attach context menu to form
    Me.ContextMenuStrip = mnuContext
    'Add the options to the context menu
    mnuContext2.Items.AddRange(New ToolStripItem() _
        {mnuContext2MemberDetails, mnuContext2Comments, _
        mnuContext2Exit})

    'Specify the text to be displayed, including access key
    mnuContextMemberDetails.Text = "&Member Details"
    mnuContextComments.Text = "&Comments"
    mnuContextExit.Text = "E&xit"

    'Change menu item properties as required
    mnuContextExit.ShortcutKeys =_
            Keys.Control Or Keys.X
End Sub

Private Sub mnuContextMemberDetails_Click(...)_
        Handles mnuContextMemberDetails.Click
    btnMemberDetails_Click(sender, e)
End Sub

Private Sub mnuContextComments_Click(...)_
        Handles mnuContextComments.Click
    btnComments_Click(sender, e)
End Sub

Private Sub mnuContextExit_Click(...)_
        Handles mnuContextExit.Click
    Me.Close()
End Sub
```

Exercises

1   Add the following menu options to the Members program's main window:

Menu/option	Access key	Shortcut	Effect when clicked
File	f		(Menu)
Open...	o	Ctrl+O	(Leave empty)
Save...	s	Ctrl+S	(Leave empty)
Exit	x		Ends program
Window	w		(Menu)
Member Details...	m		Displays Details screen
Comments...	c		Displays Comments screen
Help	h		(Menu)
About	a		Displays information box

Change the menu item names and create appropriate Click procedures for these options.

2   Add the following menu options to the Details window:

Menu/Option	Access key	Shortcut	Effect when clicked
File	f		(Menu)
Save...	s	Ctrl+S	(Leave empty)
Abandon	a		Same effect as Cancel
Exit	x		Same effect as OK

Create appropriate Click procedures for these options.

3   Add the following menu options to the Comments window:

Menu/Option	Access key	Shortcut	Effect when clicked
File	f		(Menu)
Save...	s	Ctrl+S	(Leave empty)
Abandon	a		Same effect as Cancel
Exit	x		Same effect as OK
Edit	e		(Menu)
Cut	t	Ctrl+X	Cuts text to clipboard
Copy	c	Ctrl+C	Copies text to clipboard
Paste	p	Ctrl+V	Paste text from clipboard
Clear	l		Deletes highlighted text (asks for confirmation)

Create appropriate Click procedures for these options.

For solutions to these exercises, see page 320.

10 Files

File selection

Visual Basic 2005 provides three standard controls in the Toolbox that give you access to familiar Windows dialog boxes:

- **OpenFileDialog** allows you to access existing files.

- **SaveFileDialog** lets you create new files.

- **FolderBrowserDialog** allows you to select a folder or create a new folder.

There are also controls for other standard dialogs, such as Print, Font and Color. All these dialogs can be found in the Dialogs section of the toolbox.

When you add one of the standard dialogs to a form, the icon appears in the component tray (below the form).

Take note

Earlier versions of Visual Basic had separate controls for selecting a drive, folder and file. These are no longer necessary as all the functionality is included in the standard dialogs.

OpenFileDialog

The OpenFileDialog control has a number of useful properties:

- The **InitialDirectory** property specifies the folder that is displayed when the dialog opens.

- The **Filter** property allows you to restrict the files to those matching a particular file specification. (The filter is shown in the 'Files of type' box.) The value of the filter is in two parts, separated by a vertical bar (|): a description and the file specification.

- The **MultiSelect** property, if True, allows more than one file to be selected from the dialog.

- The **CheckFileExists** property determines whether a warning is displayed if an invalid filename is typed into the 'File name' box.

- The **AddExtension** property, if True, adds an extension to the filename if it does not already have one.

- The **FileName** property contains the name of the selected file; for multiple files, the names are held in **FileNames**. No file is returned if the user clicks on Cancel.

- The **Title** property sets the text for the dialog's title bar. If no value is given, the title defaults to 'Open'.

The **ShowDialog** method displays the dialog box. The procedure containing this statement then waits until the user presses the Open or Cancel buttons. The method returns the value of either DialogResult.OK or DialogResult.Cancel, depending on the button pressed.

For example, the following code sets up a dialog box for selecting a DOC file, starting in the root directory of drive C:

```
OpenFileDialog1.Title = "Select document"
OpenFileDialog1.InitialDirectory = "C:\"
OpenFileDialog1.Filter = "Word files (*.doc)|*.doc"
If OpenFileDialog1.ShowDialog() = _
                        Windows.Forms.DialogResult.OK Then
    strSelectedFile = OpenFileDialog.FileName
Else
    strSelectedFile = ""
End if
```

SaveFileDialog

The SaveFileDialog has similar properties to the OpenFileDialog. There is no MultiSelect property but there is an **OverwritePrompt** property, which determines whether or not a warning is displayed if the filename given already exists.

Tip

You should always turn on the overwrite prompt, so that there is no danger of a file being overwritten accidentally.

FolderBrowserDialog

The FolderBrowserDialog control has the following properties:

- The **Description** property sets the text that is displayed above the folder list in the dialog.

- The **RootFolder** property sets the initial directory from which the search will start. The directory must be one of the standard folder names (such as 'Desktop' and 'My Computers'). These names are held in the Environment. SpecialFolder list.

- The **ShowNewFolderButton** property determines whether the New Folder button is included in the dialog. By default, the property is True, allowing users to create folders from within the dialog.

- The **SelectedPath** property holds the full path of the folder selected by the user. You can also use this property to set the initial directory, if you do not want to use one of the standard folder names.

Note that the SelectedPath value will end with '\' if a root directory is selected but not for any other folder.

The procedure below illustrates the use of the FolderBrowserDialog for retrieving the contents of a folder. When the Select Folder button is clicked, the filenames are added to a list box. This is done using the built-in **Dir** function, which retrieves the first file from the directory specified. Note that you only need to give the file specification once; if no parameter is given, subsequent calls to the function return the next file in the directory.

Tip

The FolderBrowserDialog will appear in most of your programs and when the code has been set up the first time it can be copied easily from one program to another. With these dialogs, you should use the default names rather than make up your own, as this makes the code more transportable.

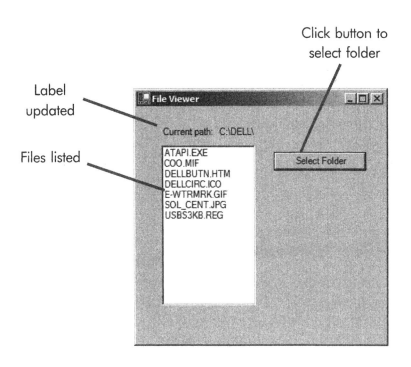

Label updated

Files listed

Click button to select folder

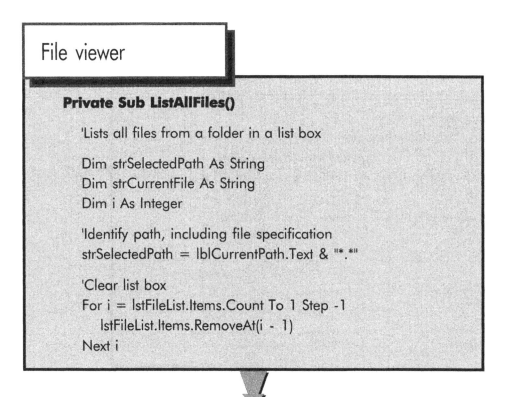

File viewer

Private Sub ListAllFiles()

'Lists all files from a folder in a list box

Dim strSelectedPath As String
Dim strCurrentFile As String
Dim i As Integer

'Identify path, including file specification
strSelectedPath = lblCurrentPath.Text & "*.*"

'Clear list box
For i = lstFileList.Items.Count To 1 Step -1
    lstFileList.Items.RemoveAt(i - 1)
Next i

```
'Get first file from directory
strCurrentFile = Dir(strSelectedPath)
While strCurrentFile <> ""
    'Add file to list and get next file
    lstFileList.Items.Add(strCurrentFile)
    strCurrentFile = Dir()
End While

End Sub

Private Sub btnSelectFolder_Click(...)_
            Handles btnSelectFolder.Click

'Ask for directory, starting in root directory of drive C
FolderBrowserDialog1.Description = "Select folder to view"
FolderBrowserDialog1.ShowNewFolderButton = False
FolderBrowserDialog1.SelectedPath = "C:\"

'Exit procedure if dialog closed or Cancel button pressed
If FolderBrowserDialog1.ShowDialog() =_
            Windows.Forms.DialogResult.Cancel Then
    Exit Sub
End If

'Display path name
If Microsoft.VisualBasic.Right(FolderBrowserDialog1._
            SelectedPath, 1) = "\" Then
    lblCurrentPath.Text = FolderBrowserDialog1.SelectedPath
Else
    lblCurrentPath.Text = FolderBrowserDialog1._
                        SelectedPath & "\"
End If

ListAllFiles()

End Sub
```

248

File operations

Within a program, you may want to delete, rename or copy a file, or carry out directory operations. The file actions can be carried out using methods from the System.IO.File class:

- The **Delete**(*filespec*) method deletes a file.

  The *filespec* is a string containing the name of the file to be deleted. You can use the * and ? wildcards (e.g. *.TMP to delete all TMP files).

- The **Copy**(*source, destination, overwrite*) method copies a file.

  The *source* is a string containing the name of the file to be copied. The *destination* is the name of the new file. Both filenames may include the directory and drive if necessary. Only one file can be copied at a time. If *overwrite* is True the destination file will be overwritten if it already exists.

- The **Move**(*source, destination*) method moves or renames a file. The *source* is the file specification of the file to be moved, the *destination* is its new location and filename. If the *source* and *destination* are in different folders the file will be moved (and its name changed, if a different name is given); if the folders are the same but a different filename is given, the file will be renamed.

- The **Exists**(*filespec*) method returns a value of True if the file exists, otherwise False.

The procedures below demonstrate the use of these methods. The buttons and procedures can be added to the File Viewer program, allowing you to select a folder and then copy, rename or delete any of the files. To be really useful, you should add suitable error-checking code to ensure that new filenames are valid.

File operations

```
Private Sub btnCopy_Click(...)_
         Handles btnCopy.Click

Dim strSelectedFile As String
Dim booCopyFile As Boolean
```

```vbnet
        strSelectedFile = lblCurrentPath.Text &_
                lstFileList.Items.Item(lstFileList.SelectedIndex)
        booCopyFile = False

        If txtCopy.Text <> "" Then
            If System.IO.File.Exists(lblCurrentPath.Text & txtCopy.Text)_
                                            Then
                If MessageBox.Show("Overwrite existing file?",_
                    "Overwrite?", MessageBoxButtons.YesNo,_
                    MessageBoxIcon.Exclamation) = _
                    Windows.Forms.DialogResult.Yes Then
                        booCopyFile = True
                End If
            Else
                booCopyFile = True
            End If
        End If

        If booCopyFile = True Then
            System.IO.File.Copy(strSelectedFile, lblCurrentPath.Text &_
                                txtCopy.Text, True)
        End If

        'Update display
        ListAllFiles()

    End Sub

    Private Sub btnRename_Click(...)_
                Handles btnRename.Click
        Dim strSelectedFile As String

        strSelectedFile = lblCurrentPath.Text &_
                lstFileList.Items.Item(lstFileList.SelectedIndex)

        If txtRename.Text <> "" Then
            If System.IO.File.Exists(lblCurrentPath.Text &_
                                txtRename.Text) Then
```

```
                MessageBox.Show("File already exists - can't rename",_
                                            "Error")
        Else
            System.IO.File.Move(strSelectedFile, lblCurrentPath.Text_
                            & txtRename.Text)
        End If
    End If

    'Update display
    ListAllFiles()

End Sub

Private Sub btnDelete_Click(...) Handles btnDelete.Click
    Dim strSelectedFile As String
    Dim strSelectedName As String

    strSelectedName = lstFileList.Items.Item(lstFileList.SelectedIndex)
    strSelectedFile = lblCurrentPath.Text & strSelectedName

    If MessageBox.Show("Delete " & strSelectedName & " ?",_
        "Delete file?", MessageBoxButtons.YesNo, _
        MessageBoxIcon.Question) =_
        Windows.Forms.DialogResult.Yes Then
            System.IO.File.Delete(strSelectedFile)
            ListAllFiles()
    End If

End Sub
```

Take note

Although these procedures demonstrate the use of the file operations, in any robust application they would also need to include extensive error handling. Dealing with files is always the most unreliable operation.

Folder operations

The System.IO.Directory class has a range of methods for manipulating folders:

- The **Delete** method deletes the specified directory, including any subdirectories and files it contains.

- The **CreateDirectory** method creates the specified directory. If necessary, it will create all the folders specified in the path.

- The **Move** method moves a directory to a new location, renaming the directory if required. You can also use this method to rename a directory without moving it.

- The **Exists** method returns True if a specified directory exists, otherwise False.

File properties

The System.IO.File class has a number of methods that allow you to retrieve a file's attributes and other properties. The attributes (archive, hidden, system etc.) are packed into a long integer as a set of True/False flags. The value contains the following attributes:

Archive	Directory	Hidden	Normal
ReadOnly	System	Temporary	

The attributes are retrieved with the **GetAttributes** method. You can then use the **And** operator to determine whether or not a particular attribute is set. For example:

```
Dim IngFileAtts As Long
Dim booReadOnly As Boolean

IngFileAtts = System.IO.File.GetAttributes(strSelectedFile)
booReadOnly = CBool(IngFileAtts And
System.IO.FileAttributes.ReadOnly)

If booReadOnly = True Then
    MessageBox.Show("Read Only file")
Else
    MessageBox.Show("File is not read only")
End If
```

You can also retrieve dates and times for each file using the following methods from System.IO.File:

- **GetCreationTime**(*filespec*) returns the date and time at which the file was created.

- **GetLastWriteTime**(*filespec*) returns the date and time when the file was last modified.

- **GetLastAccessTime**(*filespec*) returns the date and time when the file was last opened.

The most useful of these is GetLastWriteTime, which tells you when the current version of the file was saved.

The program below uses GetLastWriteTime to compare the contents of two folders and list the files that are different. There are two text boxes, one for each selected folder. Any file that appears in only one of the folders is added to the list for that folder. In addition, for any file that appears in both folders, the modified dates and times are compared; if they are different, the most recent is added to the list.

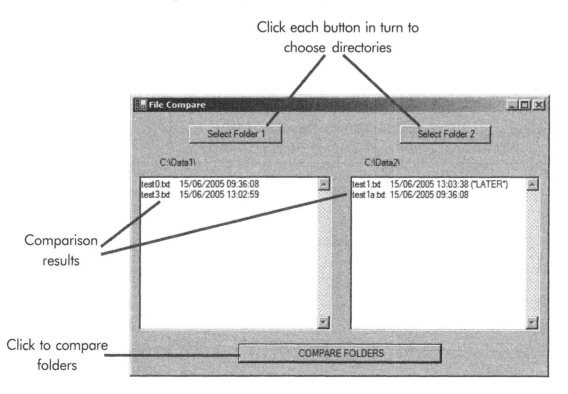

253

```
Private Sub btnSelectFolder_Click(...)_
          Handles btnSelectFolder1.Click
  'Ask for directory, starting in root directory of drive C
  FolderBrowserDialog1.Description = "Select folder to view"
  FolderBrowserDialog1.ShowNewFolderButton = False
  FolderBrowserDialog1.SelectedPath = "C:\"
  'Exit procedure if dialog closed or Cancel button pressed
  If FolderBrowserDialog1.ShowDialog() =_
            Windows.Forms.DialogResult.Cancel Then
    Exit Sub
  End If

  'Display path name
  If Microsoft.VisualBasic.Right(FolderBrowserDialog1._
            SelectedPath, 1) = "\" Then
    lblCurrentPath1.Text = FolderBrowserDialog1.SelectedPath
  Else
    lblCurrentPath1.Text = FolderBrowserDialog1.SelectedPath_
                                        & "\"
  End If

End Sub

Private Sub btnSelectFolder2_Click(...)_
          Handles btnSelectFolder2.Click
  'Ask for directory, starting in root directory of drive C
  FolderBrowserDialog1.Description = "Select folder to view"
  FolderBrowserDialog1.ShowNewFolderButton = False
  FolderBrowserDialog1.SelectedPath = "C:\"

  'Exit procedure if dialog closed or Cancel button pressed
  If FolderBrowserDialog1.ShowDialog() = _
            Windows.Forms.DialogResult.Cancel_Then
    Exit Sub
  End If
```

```vb
        'Display path name
        If Microsoft.VisualBasic.Right(FolderBrowserDialog1._
                            SelectedPath, 1) = "\" Then
            lblCurrentPath2.Text = FolderBrowserDialog1.SelectedPath
        Else
            lblCurrentPath2.Text = FolderBrowserDialog1.SelectedPath_
                                            & "\"

        End If

    End Sub

    Private Sub btnCompareFolders_Click(...)_
                Handles btnCompareFolders.Click
        Dim strSelectedPath As String
        Dim strCurrentFile As String
        Dim strFile1(500) As String
        Dim dteFolder1(500) As DateTime
        Dim dblTimeVal1(500) As Double
        Dim intNumFiles1 As Integer
        Dim intPointer1 As Integer
        Dim strFile2(500) As String
        Dim dteFolder2(500) As DateTime
        Dim dblTimeVal2(500) As Double
        Dim intNumFiles2 As Integer
        Dim intPointer2 As Integer
        Dim booEndOfList As Boolean
        Dim i As Integer

        Const CRLF As String = Chr(13) & Chr(10)
        Const TAB As String = Chr(9)

        'Identify first path, including file specification
        strSelectedPath = lblCurrentPath1.Text & "*.*"
        intNumFiles1 = 0

        'Get first file from first folder
        strCurrentFile = Dir(strSelectedPath)
```

```
While strCurrentFile <> ""
   'Add file and date/time to array and get next file
   'txtFileList1.Text = txtFileList1.Text & strCurrentFile & CRLF
   strFile1(intNumFiles1) = strCurrentFile
   dteFolder1(intNumFiles1) = System.IO.File._
      GetLastWriteTime(lblCurrentPath1.Text & strCurrentFile)
   dblTimeVal1(intNumFiles1) = dteFolder1(intNumFiles1)._
                                 ToOADate

   intNumFiles1 += 1
   strCurrentFile = Dir()
End While

'Identify second path, including file specification
strSelectedPath = lblCurrentPath2.Text & "*.*"
intNumFiles2 = 0

'Get first file from second folder
strCurrentFile = Dir(strSelectedPath)
While strCurrentFile <> ""
   'Add file and date/time to second array and get next file
   strFile2(intNumFiles2) = strCurrentFile
   dteFolder2(intNumFiles2) = System.IO.File._
      GetLastWriteTime(lblCurrentPath2.Text & strCurrentFile)
   dblTimeVal2(intNumFiles2) = dteFolder2(intNumFiles2)._
                                 ToOADate

   intNumFiles2 += 1
   strCurrentFile = Dir()
End While

'Clear text boxes and reset pointers
txtFileList1.Text = ""
txtFileList2.Text = ""
intPointer1 = 0
intPointer2 = 0

booEndOfList = False
```

```
While booEndOfList = False
    'Check current file in first list against next file in second list
    If UCase(strFile1(intPointer1)) <_
                    UCase(strFile2(intPointer2)) Then
        'File in list 1 not in list 2
        txtFileList1.Text = txtFileList1.Text & strFile1(intPointer1)_
            & TAB & dteFolder1(intPointer1) & CRLF
        intPointer1 += 1
    Else
        If UCase(strFile1(intPointer1)) >_
                        UCase(strFile2(intPointer2)) Then
            'File in list 2 not in list 1
            txtFileList2.Text = txtFileList2.Text &_
                strFile2(intPointer2) & TAB &_
                dteFolder2(intPointer2) & CRLF
            intPointer2 += 1
        Else
            'Filenames the same
            If dblTimeVal1(intPointer1) >_
                            dblTimeVal2(intPointer2) Then
                'File in list 1 is later
                txtFileList1.Text = txtFileList1.Text &_
                    strFile1(intPointer1) & TAB &_
                    dteFolder1(intPointer1) & " (*LATER*)"_
                    & CRLF
            Else
                If dblTimeVal1(intPointer1)_
                        < dblTimeVal2(intPointer2) Then
                    'File in list 2 is later (else both the same)
                    txtFileList2.Text = txtFileList2.Text &_
                        strFile2(intPointer2) & TAB &_
                        dteFolder2(intPointer2) & " (*LATER*)"_
                        & CRLF
                End If
            End If
```

```
                intPointer1 += 1
                intPointer2 += 1
            End If
        End If

        'If at end of either folder, add remainder of other
        'folder to list
        If intPointer1 = intNumFiles1 Then
            For i = intPointer2 To intNumFiles2 - 1
                txtFileList2.Text = txtFileList2.Text & strFile2(i)_
                        & TAB & dteFolder2(i) & CRLF
            Next
            intPointer2 = intNumFiles2
        End If

        If intPointer2 = intNumFiles2 Then

            For i = intPointer1 To intNumFiles1 - 1
                txtFileList1.Text = txtFileList1.Text & strFile1(i)_
                        & TAB & dteFolder1(i) & CRLF
            Next
            intPointer1 = intNumFiles1

        End If

        If intPointer1 = intNumFiles1 And intPointer2 =_
                        intNumFiles2 Then

            booEndOfList = True

        End If

    End While

End Sub
```

Sequential files

Sequential files consist of a series of lines of text, and are often referred to as **ASCII files**. Each line of text is terminated by a carriage-return character (ASCII 13) and the file ends with Ctrl-Z (ASCII 26). Although ASCII files can include extended ASCII characters, they are usually restricted to the standard characters, in the range 32 to 126. Sequential files are stored with one byte for each character and can be viewed, edited or created by Notepad or other text editors.

Visual Basic provides a group of instructions for handling sequential files. At their simplest, sequential files are written or read one complete line at a time (a line consisting of everything up to the next carriage-return character). Therefore, they are suitable for storing text: for example, the output from a multi-line text box.

Sequential files can also be saved in **comma-delimited** format. In these files, each line consists of one or more data values, separated by commas. Text items should be enclosed in double quotes. When a line of data is read from a sequential file, each value is assigned to a variable.

Text file (ASCII file)

```
First joined December, 1997
Originally Associate
Became Full member January, 1999
```

Comma-delimited file

```
"Jim Smith", 1023, "Full", 20, "South"
"Jo Edwards", 1036, "Full", 20, "East"
"Ellen Howe", 1045, "Associate", 12, "South"
```

Take note

You cannot both read and write to a sequential file at the same time. Each time you open a file it is for either reading or writing.

Take note

Text in comma-delimited files does not have to be enclosed in quotes but it is less confusing if it is. If the text contains a comma, double quotes must be used around the item containing the comma, otherwise it will be treated as two separate items.

Creating sequential files

There are three stages in creating a sequential file: opening the file, writing the data and closing the file.

The file is **opened** with a statement in the form:

FileOpen(*number, filename,* OpenMode.*mode*)

If the *mode* is 'Output', a new file is created and any existing file with the same name is deleted. If the *mode* is 'Append', the new data is added to the end of the existing file (or a new file is created, if one does not yet exist).

The *number* identifies the file in the rest of the program and must be in the range 1 to 255. The number is linked to the file only as long as the file is open. When the file is closed, the number can be re-used for another file; if a file is re-opened it does not have to be assigned the same number as before.

Data is written to a sequential file with the **Print, PrintLine, Write** or **WriteLine** statements. Each statement writes one line of data to the file. The format of these statements is as follows:

Print(*number, value1, value2, ...*)

PrintLine(*number, value1, value2, ...*)

Write(*number, value1, value2, ...*)

WriteLine(*number, value1, value2, ...*)

The Print statement writes data with tabs between separate items; this statement is suitable for writing text files (with just one item per line). The Write statement stores data in comma-delimited format.

By default, the Print and PrintLine functions write data with a tab between the separate items. The only difference between them is that PrintLine also writes a carriage return sequence to the file; therefore PrintLine is suitable for writing a single line of text to an ASCII file.

You can also include Tab() and Spc() functions in the list of items to output. Tab() prints the next item at the specified column number, while Spc() prints the given number of spaces.

The Write and WriteLine functions store data in comma-delimited format, the only difference being that WriteLine adds a carriage return.

Comma-delimited
file

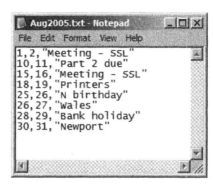

The file is **closed** with a statement in the form:

> FileClose(*number*)

The FileClose statement is essential, as it stores away any unwritten data held in memory.

Reading sequential files

Corresponding to the creation of a sequential file, there are three stages for reading such a file: opening the file, reading the data and closing the file.

The file is **opened** with the following statement:

> FileOpen(*number*, *filename*, OpenMode.Input)

Data is read from the file with one of these statements:

> *variable* = LineInput (*number*)
>
> Input(*number*, *variable1*)

The **LineInput** statement reads an entire line into a *string variable* and is suitable for text files. Each call to the LineInput function reads the next complete line from the file.

The **Input** function should be used where files have been written with the Write or WriteLine functions. Each call to the Input function reads the next item from the file. The function can only read one item at a time, so a series of calls are needed for each line in a comma-delimited file.

The **FileClose** statement is the same as before.

Sequential files are always read from the beginning of the file. You can use the **EOF** function to detect the end of the file. (The function returns a True value when the end-of-file marker has been reached.) The **LOF** function gives you the length of the file (in bytes) and **LOC** returns the current location (in terms of the number of characters read so far). All three functions take the file number as their argument.

The **FileLen** function gives you the length of any file. The function takes the filename as its argument. If the file is open, the function returns the length of the file when it was opened.

The following procedures demonstrate how File|Open and File|Save commands can be used to read and write data entered in the Calendar program from the Chapter 8 Exercises. The File|Save procedure stores the contents of the calendar boxes in a sequential file, with one line for each box. The filename is based on the year and month of the calendar. The File|Open procedure reads the text back into the boxes.

Take note

You can also create binary files, where data is written and read a character at a time. This gives you complete control over the file, without having to worry about the structure imposed by comma-delimited files or record-based files. However, your program must keep precise track of the position and size of data in the file.

Calendar files (1)

```
Private Sub mnuFileSave_Click(...)_
          Handles mnuFileSave.Click
    'Saves when user presses Ctrl-S
    'Should also be called when the month or year
    'is changed or the program is closed

    Dim strCalFile As String
    Dim strCalSpec As String
    Dim i As Integer
    Dim intDayNo As Integer

    'Assume directory already exists for storing files
    Const strCalDir As String = "c:\calendar\"

    'Construct filename for storing calendar contents
    strCalFile = Microsoft.VisualBasic.Left(cboMonth.Text, 3) &_
                                        txtYear.Text
    strCalSpec = strCalDir & strCalFile & ".txt"

    Try
        FileOpen(2, strCalSpec, OpenMode.Output)

        'Write away entries if not blank
        For i = 0 To 36     'Max number of boxes that can be used
            If arrBoxes(i).Text > "" Then      'An entry has been made
                intDayNo = Val(arrLabels(i).Text)    'Get date
                'Write text box number, day number and text
                WriteLine(2, i, intDayNo, arrBoxes(i).Text)
            End If
        Next i

        FileClose(2)
    Catch
        'Cannot save (probably because no directory)
        If Err.Number = 76 Then
            MessageBox.Show("Calendar folder does not exist",_
                    "Save Error", MessageBoxButtons.OK)
        Else
```

```
                'Some other error
                MessageBox.Show("Cannot save file " & strCalSpec,_
                        "Save Error", MessageBoxButtons.OK)
        End If
    End Try
End Sub

Private Sub mnuFileOpen_Click(...)_
            Handles mnuFileOpen.Click
    'Loads calendar data when user presses Ctrl-O
    'Should also be called at end of ViewCalendar procedure so
    'that data automatically loaded when user chooses new month

    Dim strCalFile As String
    Dim strCalSpec As String
    Dim i As Integer
    Dim intDayNo As Integer
    Dim strDiaryEntry As String

    'Assume directory already exists
    Const strCalDir As String = "c:\calendar\"

    'Construct filename for calendar contents
    strCalFile = Microsoft.VisualBasic.Left(cboMonth.Text, 3) &_
                                txtYear.Text
    strCalSpec = strCalDir & strCalFile & ".txt"

    Try
        FileOpen(1, strCalSpec, OpenMode.Input)

        'Read entries until end-of-file reached
        Do While Not EOF(1)
            Input(1, i)
            Input(1, intDayNo)
            Input(1, strDiaryEntry)
            arrBoxes(i).Text = strDiaryEntry
        Loop
```

```
        FileClose(1)
    Catch
        'Cannot open (probably because no file or no directory)
        If Err.Number = 53 Then
            'File does not yet exist so ignore
        Else
            If Err.Number = 76 Then
                MessageBox.Show("Calendar folder does not exist",_
                    "Open Error", MessageBoxButtons.OK)
            Else
                'Some other error
                MessageBox.Show("Cannot open file " & strCalSpec,_
                    "Open Error", MessageBoxButtons.OK)
            End If
        End If
    End Try

End Sub
```

Tip

Sequential files take a little more disk space than random access files but they are much easier to handle and they have the advantage that you can easily check or edit the contents of a file using a program such as Notepad.

Random access files

Random access files store data in a record-based format. The file consists of a number of records, each of which has the same size and layout. The advantage over sequential files is that you can read and write records in any order; records are accessed by specifying a record number. However, random access files are not suitable for variable-length data.

Record structure

You must define the structure of the records before attempting to read or write them. This is done with a **Structure** declaration, which has the following form:

```
Structure recordtype
    Public variable1 As type1
    Public variable2 As type2
    ...
End Structure
```

Any string variables must be given an explicit length by declaring them as follows:

```
<VBFixedString(length)> Public variable As String
```

For example:

```
< VBFixedString(40)> Public CompanyName As String
```

This allows you to store a company name of up to 40 characters. If the string is shorter than the specified length, it is padded with spaces; if it is longer, the string is truncated.

The Structure statement is usually included in the Declarations section of the form or module.

Accessing records

Records are read or written in three stages: opening the file; reading or writing the data; and closing the file.

The **FileOpen** statement has the following format:

```
FileOpen(number, filename, OpenMode.Random, , , recordlength)
```

The easiest way to calculate the *recordlength* is using the **Len** function, whose argument is a record variable of the record type defined in the Structure statement.

Once opened, you can both write to and read from the file; you do not need to close the file in between the writing and reading operations.

To write records, you must first declare a variable of the record type previously defined. This will be in the format:

> Dim *recordvariable* As *recordtype*

You must then fill the record by assigning values to the individual variables, using statements in the format:

> *recordvariable.variable* = *expression*

A completed record is written with a **FilePut** statement, as follows:

> FilePut(*number, recordvariable, recordnumber*)

The *recordnumber* starts at 1 for the first record. If the number is beyond the current end-of-file, the file is extended. (Unused records will contain rubbish unless specifically cleared.)

Data is read from the file using a **FileGet** statement, as follows:

> FileGet(*number, recordvariable, recordnumber*)

The individual variables in the *recordvariable* are filled with the corresponding data from the record. Close the file with FileClose, as before.

The procedures below provide alternative File operations for the Calendar program, this time storing the data in a random access file.

Take note

The EOF, LOC and LOF functions can be used with random access files. EOF is of little use, since you are not usually reading a file from beginning to end. LOF gives the length of the file in bytes. LOC returns the number of the last record read or written.

Tip

You can calculate the number of records in a random access file by dividing LOF by the record length. To get the record length, use LEN with the record variable as its argument.

Calendar files (2)

```
'Insert in Declarations section
Structure CalendarData
    Public shoDayNumber As Short
    <VBFixedString(30)> Public strTextEntry As String
End Structure

Private Sub mnuFileSave_Click(...)_
            Handles mnuFileSave.Click
    'Saves when user presses Ctrl-S
    Dim strCalFile As String
    Dim strCalSpec As String
    Dim i As Short
    Dim shoDayNo As Short
    Dim MonthData As CalendarData

    'Assume directory already exists for storing files
    Const strCalDir As String = "c:\calendar\"

    'Construct filename for storing calendar contents
    strCalFile = Microsoft.VisualBasic.Left(cboMonth.Text, 3) &_
                                    txtYear.Text
    strCalSpec = strCalDir & strCalFile & ".dat"

    Try
        FileOpen(2, strCalSpec, OpenMode.Random, , ,_
                                Len(MonthData))

        'Write away all entries
        For i = 0 To 36
            shoDayNo = Val(arrLabels(i).Text)     'Get date
            'Set up record
            MonthData.shoDayNumber = shoDayNo
            MonthData.strTextEntry = arrBoxes(i).Text
            'Write record to file
            FilePut(2, MonthData, i + 1)
        Next i
```

```vb
    Catch
        'Cannot save (probably because no directory)
        If Err.Number = 76 Then
            MessageBox.Show("Calendar folder does not exist",_
                    "Save Error", MessageBoxButtons.OK)
        Else
            'Some other error
            MessageBox.Show("Cannot save file " & strCalSpec,_
                    "Save Error", MessageBoxButtons.OK)
        End If

    Finally
        'Close file even if an error occurred
        FileClose(2)
    End Try

End Sub
Private Sub mnuFileOpen_Click(...)_
            Handles mnuFileOpen.Click
    'Loads calendar data when user presses Ctrl-O
    'Should also be called at end of ViewCalendar procedure so
    'that data automatically loaded when user chooses new month

    Dim strCalFile As String
    Dim strCalSpec As String
    Dim i As Integer
    Dim MonthData As CalendarData

    'Assume directory already exists
    Const strCalDir As String = "c:\calendar\"

    'Construct filename for calendar contents
    strCalFile = Microsoft.VisualBasic.Left(cboMonth.Text, 3) &_
                                    txtYear.Text
    strCalSpec = strCalDir & strCalFile & ".dat"
```

```
        Try
            FileOpen(1, strCalSpec, OpenMode.Random, , ,_
                            Len(MonthData))

            'Read entries for each possible day
            For i = 0 To 36
                FileGet(1, MonthData, i + 1)
                'Get text entry from record
                arrBoxes(i).Text = MonthData.strTextEntry
            Next i

        Catch
            'Cannot open (probably because no file or no directory)
            If Err.Number = 5 Then
                'File does not yet exist so ignore
            Else
                If Err.Number = 76 Then
                    MessageBox.Show("Calendar folder does not exist",_
                            "Open Error", MessageBoxButtons.OK)
                Else
                    'Some other error
                    MessageBox.Show("Cannot open file " & strCalSpec,_
                            "Open Error", MessageBoxButtons.OK)
                End If
            End If

        Finally
            FileClose(1)
        End Try

    End Sub
```

Simple error handling; the complete appli-
cation should include error handling for
every possible type of error that may occur

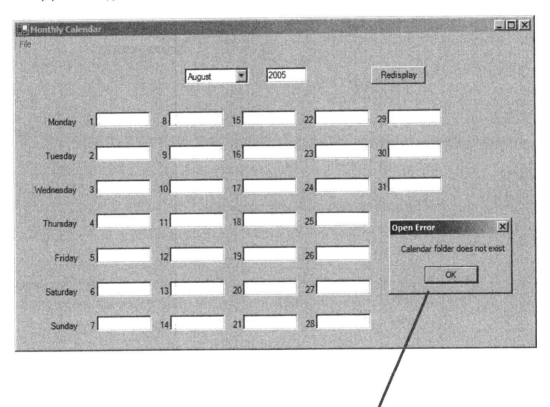

Attempt to open the file for a
particular month fails when the
Calendar folder does not exist in
the root directory of drive C

Exercises

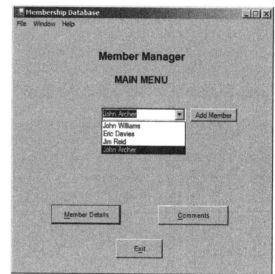

1   In the Membership program, add a combo box to the Main Menu to hold a list of members. Allow new names to be typed at the top of the Combo box. Add a command button which, when clicked, will add any new name to the list in the combo box.

2   Add code to the File|Save As option to create a file with a MEM extension (using a standard dialog box to enter the name). The file should contain the list of members.

3   Add code for File|Save to update the membership file and for File|Open to fill the combo box from the list in the file.

4   Add code for the File|Save option on the Comments screen. The current comments should be added to a text file with a filename based on the member's name. The OK button should also save the comments.

5   Add code so that the current member's comments (if any) are displayed when the Comments screen is loaded.

   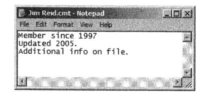

6   Add code for the File|Save option on the Details screen. The member's details should be stored as a single record in a file with the same name as the membership list file but an extension of DTL. The OK button should also save the data.

7   Add code so that the current member's details (if any) are displayed when the Details screen is loaded.

For solutions to these exercises, see page 323.

11 Graphics

Pictures

The **picture box** control displays any type of image file, icon file or metafile.

The **Image** property can be set at design time and specifies the picture to be displayed. In that case, the picture file is incorporated into the form file (and hence in the executable file, making it considerably larger). Alternatively, you can specify the picture at run-time; the picture file is then held separately from the executable file (but must be supplied with the application). The value of the Image property must be specified as a **Bitmap** object.

The **Height** and **Width** properties set the size of the picture box; the **Left** and **Top** properties determine the position of the picture on the form. The **Move** method moves the picture to a new position.

The **SizeMode** property determines the way in which the picture is displayed, as follows:

- **Normal**: The picture is displayed at its normal size and is positioned in the top left-hand corner of the picture box. If the box is not large enough for the whole picture, only the top left-hand corner is shown.

- **CenterImage**: The picture is displayed at normal size in the centre of the box.

- **StretchImage**: The image is stretched horizontally and vertically so that it fills the box.

- **AutoSize**: The picture box is resized to fit the image. The top left-hand corner stays in the same position.

If you need a border around the edge of the picture box, this is applied with the **BorderStyle** property.

The **Visible** property can be set to False to hide the picture.

The procedure below extends the File Viewer program from Chapter 10 to display the contents of an image file. The name of the file is stored in a label above the picture box. The full specification of the filename (including the path) is stored in a string. This string is then used to define a new **Bitmap** object, which in turn is used as the new value for the Image property.

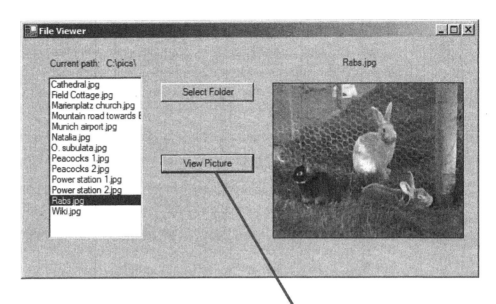

Click button to display picture
of file currently selected

File viewer 2

```
Private Sub btnViewPicture_Click(...)_
        Handles btnViewPicture.Click

    Dim bmpSelectedImage As Bitmap
    Dim strSelectedPic As String

    lblCurrentPic.Text = lstFileList.Items.Item(lstFileList._
                                    SelectedIndex)

    strSelectedPic = lblCurrentPath.Text &_
            lstFileList.Items.Item(lstFileList.SelectedIndex)
    bmpSelectedImage = New Bitmap(strSelectedPic)
    picFileView.Image = bmpSelectedImage

End Sub
```

Lines and shapes

Lines and shapes are drawn on a form or the surface of a control using the **Graphics** object. Drawing is usually done inside an object's Paint event procedure. The first task is to declare a Graphics variable with a Dim statement, following which the object is given a value that is a reference to the form or control's Graphics object; for example:

```
Dim objG As System.Drawing.Graphics
objG = e.Graphics
```

The 'e' parameter supplied with the Paint event has a Graphics property that points to the form or control's Graphics object. The Paint event is called whenever the contents of the object need to be redrawn: for example, when the form is loaded or moved or when the window is brought to the top of the display. You can also force an object to be redrawn by calling its **Invalidate** method.

To draw a line or shape, you can also need to specify the colour, width and other parameters of the drawing. This is done with two further objects:

● The **Pen** object defines the colour, width and style (e.g. unbroken or dotted) of lines.

● The **Brush** object defines the colour and style (solid, hatched etc.) of filled objects. You use a different object for solid filling (**SolidBrush**) and hatched filling (**HatchBrush**).

The pen and brush are created with statements as follows:

```
Dim objPen As New Pen(Color.colour, width)
```

```
Dim objBrush As New SolidBrush(Color.colour)
```

The *colour* value is a standard Windows colour; *width* is a single value representing line width.

When the pen and brush have been created, their properties can be changed. For example:

```
ObjPen.Width = 2.5
ObjPen.Color = Color.Blue
ObjPen.DashStyle = Drawing2D.DashStyle.DashDot
```

The lines and shapes are drawn with the various Graphics methods:

● The **DrawLine** method draws a straight line with a specified pen between two pairs of co-ordinates.

● The **DrawRectangle** method draws a rectangle with a specified pen; the rectangle is defined by the co-ordinates of the top left-hand corner, the width and height.

● The **DrawEllipse** method draws an ellipse with a specified pen; the height and width of the ellipse are determined by a bounding rectangle, defined as above. If the height and width are the same, the result is a circle.

● The **FillEllipse** method draws a filled ellipse with the fill colour defined by a brush.

These are several variations of these methods, depending on what parameters you want to use. There are also a number of other drawing tools.

The program below demonstrates the use of these graphical features. The program also makes use of a timer to generate changes to the display; timers are described in the next section.

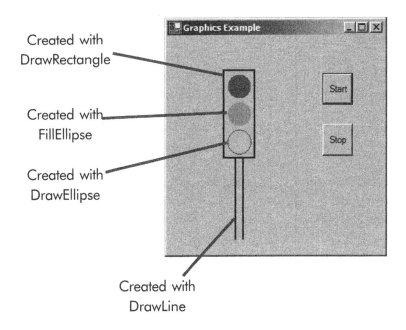

Created with
DrawRectangle

Created with
FillEllipse

Created with
DrawEllipse

Created with
DrawLine

```vb
Public Class frmGraphicsExample
    Inherits System.Windows.Forms.Form

    Dim shoStage As Short

#Region " Windows Form Designer generated code "
#End Region

    Private Sub PictureBox1_Paint(...)_
                Handles PictureBox1.Paint
        Dim objPicture As System.Drawing.Graphics

        'Set up pen, brush and graphics objects
        Dim objPen As New Pen(System.Drawing.Color.Black, 2)
        Dim objBrush As New SolidBrush(Color.Red)
        objPicture = e.Graphics

        'Draw rectangle and vertical lines
        objPicture.DrawRectangle(objPen, 40, 20, 40, 110)
        objPicture.DrawLine(objPen, 55, 130, 55, 350)
        objPicture.DrawLine(objPen, 65, 130, 65, 350)

        objPen.Width = 1
        Select Case shoStage
            Case 0 To 1
                'Draw filled red circle
                objPicture.FillEllipse(objBrush, 45, 25, 30, 30)
                'Draw amber and green circles
                objPen.Color = System.Drawing.Color.Goldenrod
                objPicture.DrawEllipse(objPen, 45, 60, 30, 30)
                objPen.Color = System.Drawing.Color.Green
                objPicture.DrawEllipse(objPen, 45, 95, 30, 30)
            Case 2
                'Red and amber
                objBrush.Color = System.Drawing.Color.Red
                objPicture.FillEllipse(objBrush, 45, 25, 30, 30)
                objBrush.Color = System.Drawing.Color.Goldenrod
```

```
            objPicture.FillEllipse(objBrush, 45, 60, 30, 30)
            objPen.Color = System.Drawing.Color.Green
            objPicture.DrawEllipse(objPen, 45, 95, 30, 30)
        Case 3 To 4
            'Green
            objPen.Color = System.Drawing.Color.Red
            objPicture.DrawEllipse(objPen, 45, 25, 30, 30)
            objPen.Color = System.Drawing.Color.Goldenrod
            objPicture.DrawEllipse(objPen, 45, 60, 30, 30)
            objBrush.Color = System.Drawing.Color.Green
            objPicture.FillEllipse(objBrush, 45, 95, 30, 30)
        Case 5
            'Amber
            objPen.Color = System.Drawing.Color.Red
            objPicture.DrawEllipse(objPen, 45, 25, 30, 30)
            objBrush.Color = System.Drawing.Color.Goldenrod
            objPicture.FillEllipse(objBrush, 45, 60, 30, 30)
            objPen.Color = System.Drawing.Color.Green
            objPicture.DrawEllipse(objPen, 45, 95, 30, 30)
    End Select
End Sub

Private Sub btnStart_Click(...) Handles btnStart.Click
    PictureBox1.Invalidate()
    Timer1.Enabled() = True
End Sub

Private Sub btnStop_Click(...) Handles btnStop.Click
    Timer1.Enabled = False
End Sub

Private Sub Timer1_Tick(...) Handles Timer1.Tick
    shoStage += 1
    shoStage = shoStage Mod 6
    PictureBox1.Invalidate()
End Sub
End Class
```

Using text

You can also draw text on a graphics object. For this you need to define a font using the **Font** object. This object is created in a similar way to the pen and brush:

Dim *fontobject* As New Font(*font*, *size*, *style*)

The style is optional and specifies the use of bold, italic etc. You can combine two or more styles with the **Or** operator (for instance, 'FontStyle.Bold Or FontStyle.Underline'). For example:

Dim objFont As New Font("Arial", 12, FontStyle.Bold)

The text is drawn using the **DrawString** method which has as its parameters the text, font, brush and co-ordinates of the top-hand corner of the text; for example:

objGraphics.DrawString("Lights!", objFont, objBrush, 30, 0)

Note that you can use 'Me.Font' if you want to use the current font from the form or control.

Text added by
DrawString method

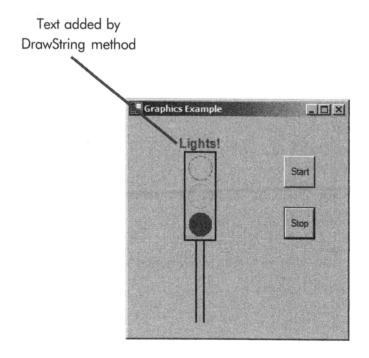

Timers

The **Timer** control allows you to create programs in which events occur at particular times or after specific periods: for instance, clocks, reminder programs and programs that require a sequence of regular events. The previous example used a timer to change the graphics display every two or four seconds.

The Timer control is added to the component tray; it has no visible element. There are two important properties:

● The **Enabled** property is set to True when you want the timer to start running.

● The **Interval** property specifies how frequently you want the timer event to be generated.

The value for the Interval is given in milliseconds (so a value of 5000 would generate an event every 5 seconds). When the specified interval has elapsed the timer's **Tick** event occurs and the timer starts counting again.

The program below demonstrates the use of a timer for generating a reminder at a time entered by the user.

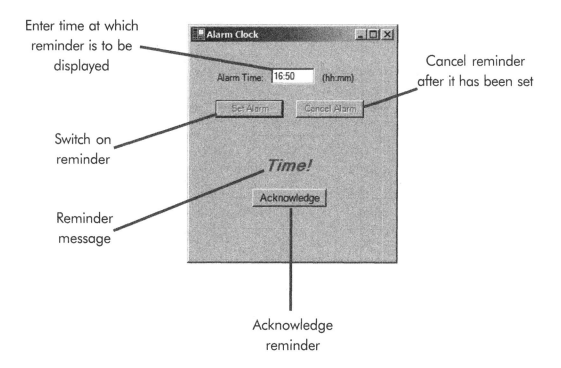

Enter time at which reminder is to be displayed

Cancel reminder after it has been set

Switch on reminder

Reminder message

Acknowledge reminder

Alarm clock

```
Public Class frmAlarm
    Inherits System.Windows.Forms.Form

#Region " Windows Form Designer generated code "
#End Region

    Private Sub btnSetAlarm_Click(...)_
            Handles btnSetAlarm.Click
    Dim objMessageFont As Font

    'Set font for message
    objMessageFont = New Font(lblTimeReached.Font._
                FontFamily, 10, FontStyle.Regular)
    If txtAlarmTime.Text = "" Then
        MessageBox.Show("Must enter a time in the form hh:mm",_
            "Time not set", MessageBoxButtons.OK,_
            MessageBoxIcon.Warning)
    Else
        'Display message when alarm set
        lblTimeReached.Font = objMessageFont
        lblTimeReached.ForeColor = Color.Black
        lblTimeReached.Text = "Alarm is set"

        'Disable Acknowledge button
        btnAcknowledge.Enabled = False

        'Turn on timer
        Timer1.Enabled = True
        'Minimise window
        Me.WindowState = FormWindowState.Minimized
    End If

    End Sub

    Private Sub btnCancelAlarm_Click(...)_
            Handles btnCancelAlarm.Click
    Dim objMessageFont As Font
```

```vbnet
        'Display message when alarm cancelled
        objMessageFont = New Font(lblTimeReached.Font._
                        FontFamily, 10, FontStyle.Regular)
        lblTimeReached.Font = objMessageFont
        lblTimeReached.ForeColor = Color.Black
        lblTimeReached.Text = "No alarm set"

        'Disable Acknowledge button and turn off timer
        btnAcknowledge.Enabled = False
        Timer1.Enabled = False

    End Sub

    Private Sub Timer1_Tick(...) Handles Timer1.Tick
        Dim intCurrentHour As Integer
        Dim intCurrentMinute As Integer
        Dim intAlarmHour As Integer
        Dim intAlarmMinute As Integer
        Dim objMessageFont As Font

        'Get current time
        intCurrentHour = Now.Hour
        intCurrentMinute = Now.Minute
        'Get time entered by user
        intAlarmHour = TimeValue(txtAlarmTime.Text).Hour
        intAlarmMinute = TimeValue(txtAlarmTime.Text).Minute

        If intCurrentHour = intAlarmHour And intCurrentMinute =_
                        intAlarmMinute Then
            'At time specified by user

            'Disable buttons
            btnSetAlarm.Enabled = False
            btnCancelAlarm.Enabled = False

            'Set font and colour of message and display
            objMessageFont = New Font(lblTimeReached.Font._
                FontFamily, 16, FontStyle.Bold Or FontStyle.Italic)
```

```vb
            lblTimeReached.Font = objMessageFont
            lblTimeReached.ForeColor = Color.Red
            lblTimeReached.Text = "Time!"

            'Enable Acknowledge button
            btnAcknowledge.Enabled = True
            'Restore window
            Me.WindowState = FormWindowState.Normal

        End If

    End Sub
    Private Sub btnAcknowledge_Click(...)
            Handles btnAcknowledge.Click
        'Enable Set and Cancel buttons; disable Acknowledge button
        btnSetAlarm.Enabled = True
        btnCancelAlarm.Enabled = True
        btnAcknowledge.Enabled = False

        'Clear text boxes and turn off timer
        lblTimeReached.Text = ""
        txtAlarmTime.Text = ""
        Timer1.Enabled = False

    End Sub

End Class
```

284

Printing

Printing is achieved by creating an instance of the **PrintDocument** class. You can then set the properties of this document and fill it with text, before finally sending it to the printer with the **Print** method.

Text and pictures are added to the document using the methods of the Graphics object, as described earlier. The Graphics object is available as a parameter in the document's **PrintPage** event, which occurs each time the document is required (for example, when previewing or printing the document).

Margins and other document settings are available in the document's **DefaultPageSettings** property.

A number of standard dialog boxes are available as controls to help you set up a document:

- The **PrintDialog** displays a standard Print dialog and can be used to adjust printer settings just before the document is printed.

- The **PageSetupDialog** allows you to change paper size, orientation and margins, as well as giving you access to the printer settings.

- The **PrintPreviewDialog** produces a display of the document as it will appear when printed, with all the standard options available.

- The **PrintPreviewControl** object displays a preview of document in an area on the form, without any of the standard preview options.

In each case, there is a **Document** property, which must be set to the name of your PrintDocument before the dialogs are displayed.

You can also use the FontDialog to change the font for a text selection.

The example below illustrates the use of all these features. Text can be entered in the top left-hand text box to be printed as a title. Below that is a **rich text box**, which allows you to change the font (including typeface, point size and text style) for any part of the text. The following buttons affect the rich text box:

- The Load button calls a standard Open dialog to select an RTF file, which is added to the rich text box.

- The Save button saves the contents of the box in a named file.

- The Font button lets you change the font for the text selected in the box.

On the right of the window is a PrintPreviewControl, which is updated with the current contents by clicking on the Update button. The three buttons below allow you to change the page setup, preview the document in a separate window and print the final document.

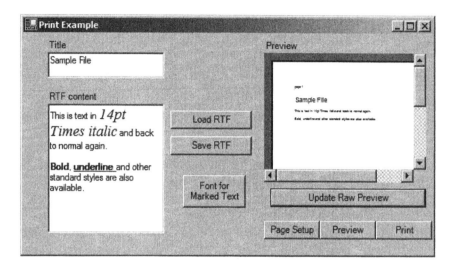

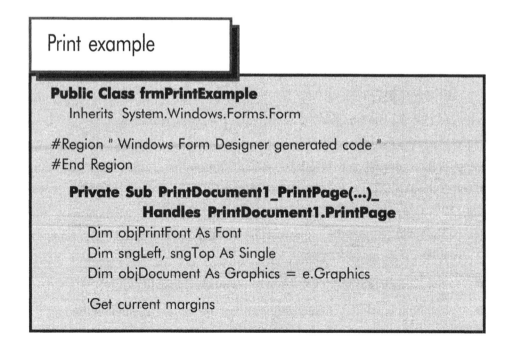

Print example

```
Public Class frmPrintExample
    Inherits System.Windows.Forms.Form

#Region " Windows Form Designer generated code "
#End Region

    Private Sub PrintDocument1_PrintPage(...)_
            Handles PrintDocument1.PrintPage
        Dim objPrintFont As Font
        Dim sngLeft, sngTop As Single
        Dim objDocument As Graphics = e.Graphics

        'Get current margins
```

```vb
        sngLeft = PrintDocument1.DefaultPageSettings.Margins.Left
        sngTop = PrintDocument1.DefaultPageSettings.Margins.Top

        'Build up document
        objPrintFont = New Font("Arial", 10)
        objDocument.DrawString("page 1", objPrintFont,_
                    Brushes.Black, sngLeft, sngTop)
        objPrintFont = New Font("Arial", 20)
        objDocument.DrawString(txtTitle.Text, objPrintFont,_
                    Brushes.Black, sngLeft, sngTop + 50)
        objPrintFont = New Font("Arial", 10)
        objDocument.DrawString(rtbImportText.Text, objPrintFont,_
                    Brushes.Black, sngLeft, sngTop + 110)

    End Sub
    Private Sub btnLoad_Click(...) Handles btnLoad.Click

        'Load existing RTF file
        If OpenFileDialog1.ShowDialog() = _
                    Windows.Forms.DialogResult.OK  Then
            rtbImportText.LoadFile(OpenFileDialog1.FileName,_
                    RichTextBoxStreamType.RichText)
        End If

    End Sub
    Private Sub btnSave_Click(...) Handles btnSave.Click

        'Save contents of rich text box to named file
        rtbImportText.SaveFile("c:\temptest.rtf")

    End Sub
    Private Sub btnFont_Click(...) Handles btnFont.Click

        'Change font for text currently selected in rich text box
        FontDialog1.ShowDialog()
        rtbImportText.SelectionFont = FontDialog1.Font

    End Sub
```

```vb
Private Sub btnUpdate_Click(...)_
        Handles btnUpdate.Click
    'Update print preview control display
    PrintPreviewControl1.Document = PrintDocument1

End Sub

Private Sub btnPageSetup_Click(...)_
        Handles btnPageSetup.Click
    'Change page setup
    PageSetupDialog1.Document = PrintDocument1
    PageSetupDialog1.ShowDialog()

End Sub

Private Sub btnPreview_Click(...)_
        Handles btnPreview.Click
    'Preview current document
    PrintPreviewDialog1.Document = PrintDocument1
    PrintPreviewDialog1.ShowDialog()

End Sub

Private Sub btnPrint_Click(...)_
        Handles btnPrint.Click
    'Print final document
    PrintDialog1.Document = PrintDocument1
    PrintDialog1.ShowDialog()
    PrintDocument1.Print()

End Sub
End Class
```

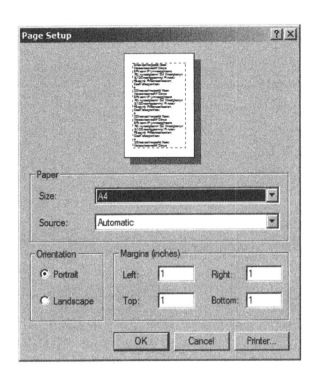

Page Setup dialog,
activated by
PageSetupDialog
control

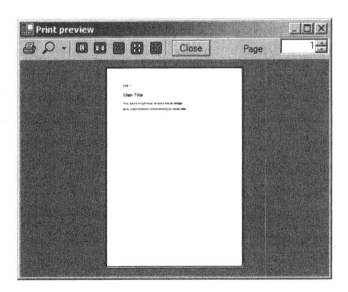

Print Preview dialog,
activated by
PrintPreviewDialog
control

Exercises

1   Add a bitmap to the Members program's main menu.

2   Add a File|Print command to the Members program's Main Menu window, so that the full details, including comments, can be printed.

For solutions to these exercises, see page 332.

12 Solutions to exercises

1 Overview (p24)

1 Click on the Start button and All Programs. Click on the Microsoft Visual Basic 2005 application icon.

Click on the New Project button. In the Name box, replace 'WindowsApplication1' with 'Membership Database' and click on OK.

Select File|Save All. Click on the Browse button, select C:\ as the location and click on Open.

2 Select Window|Reset Window Layout. Click on OK to confirm and then on OK on the Options dialog.

The main window should contain the Form Design tab (containing Form1). The Solution Explorer and Properties windows should be docked and there should be a tab for the Data Sources window. The Toolbox window should be hidden.

3 Click on the Toolbox button to show the window, then click on ▣.

Drag the Data Sources tab into the main window, then click on its Close button.

Click on the 🔲 button to show the properties in alphabetical order.

Move windows by dragging the title bar; resize by dragging the edges or corners. Maximise by clicking on the Maximise button.

4 Click on the Help menu, then on Index. In the 'filtered by' box, select 'Visual Basic'; in the 'Look for' box, type 'properties w'; click on 'Properties Window' at the top of the list of topics. After using the help, click on the Close button on the help page.

5 Click on the Minimise button in the main window. Then click on the Membership Database button in the taskbar.

6 Click on File in the main window menu bar and then on Exit. If you are asked to save the changes, click on Yes.

2   Forms (p46)

(Note that the dimensions of these forms do not have to be exactly as given below.)

1   Click on the Start button and then on the Microsoft Visual Basic option. On the Start Page, double-click on Membership Database.

2   Change the properties for Form1 as follows:

Name:	frmMainMenu
Text:	Membership Database
FormBorderStyle:	FixedSingle
MinimizeBox:	True (default)
MaximizeBox:	False
Location	0, 0 (default)
Size:	450, 425
ShowInTaskbar:	True

Save using File|Save Form1.vb As in the Membership Database directory, giving it the name 'frmMainMenu'. In Windows Explorer, delete the two Form1 files.

3   Use Project|Add Windows Form to add a form. In the Add New Item dialog, enter a name of 'frmDetails'. Change the properties as follows:

Name:	frmDetails
Text:	Member Details
FormBorderStyle:	FixedSingle
MinimizeBox:	True (default)
MaximizeBox:	False
Location:	100, 100
Size:	500, 350
ShowInTaskbar:	False
StartPosition:	Manual

Save the form in the Membership Database directory with the name 'frmDetails'.

4   Use Project|Add Windows Form to add a form. Change the properties as follows:

Name:	frmComments
Text:	Comments

FormBorderStyle:	Sizable (default)
MinimizeBox:	True (default)
MaximizeBox:	True (default)
Location:	200, 200
Size:	500, 250
ShowInTaskbar:	False
StartPosition:	Manual

Save the form in the Membership Database directory with the name 'frmComments'.

5 Click on Membership Database in the Solution Explorer window, then change the Project File in the Properties window to 'Members.vbproj'.

6 Use File|Save All.

7 Right-click on the Membership Database entry in the Solution Explorer window and select Properties. List the forms in the Startup Object box and select frmMainMenu. Click on OK.

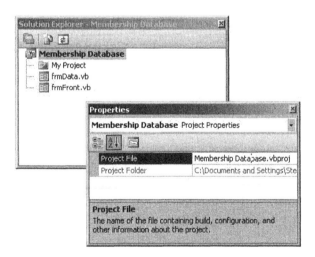

8 Press [F5] to run the application. The first window should be displayed. Click on the Close box to close it down. Click on the Close box on the Output window.

3 Controls (p78)

1   Control properties are as follows:

Labels

Name:	lblTitle	lblMainMenu
Text:	Member Manager	MAIN MENU
TextAlign:	TopCenter	TopCenter
Font:	14 point, bold	12 point, bold
Location:	50, 24	48, 64
Size:	345, 25	345, 25

Buttons

Name:	btnMemberDetails	btnComments
Text:	&MemberDetails	&Comments
Location:	66, 288	250, 288
Size:	120, 32	120, 32

Name:	btnExit
Text:	E&xit
Location:	176, 344
Size:	80, 32

Form

Name:	frmMainMenu
AcceptButton:	btnMemberDetails
CancelButton:	btnExit

2   Use Project|Add New Item to add a new Windows Form. Change the properties as follows:

Name:	frmPassword
Text:	Password
FormBorderStyle:	FixedDialog
ControlBox:	False
Location:	180, 180
Size:	280, 190
ShowInTaskbar:	False

Add the following controls:

Label

Name:	lblEnter
Text:	Enter your &password:
Font:	Arial, 10pt
Location:	64, 24
Size:	140, 20

Text box

Name:	txtPassword
Text:	(blank)
Font:	Arial, 10pt
PasswordChar:	*
Location:	64, 24
Size:	140, 25

Buttons

Name:	btnOK	btnCancel
Text:	&OK	&Cancel
Location:	32, 104	152, 104
Size:	80, 32	80, 32

Save the form as frmPassword.vb in the Membership Database directory. Amend the form properties as follows:

AcceptButton:	btnOK
CancelButton:	btnCancel

3   Control properties are as follows:

Group boxes

Name:	grpPersonal	grpMType
Text:	Personal Details	Membership Type
Location:	32, 72	32, 248
Size:	380, 150	130, 80
Name:	grpSubs	
Text:	Subscription	
Location:	176, 248	
Size:	150, 80	

Label (form)

Name:	lblMemNo
Text:	&Member No:
TextAlign:	TopRight
Location:	32, 20
Size:	64, 18

Text box (form)

Name:	txtMemNo
Text:	(blank)
Location:	104, 16
Size:	105, 25

Labels (Personal Details)

Name:	lblName	lblAddress
Text:	&Name:	&Address:
TextAlign:	TopRight	TopRight
Location:	16, 28	16, 68
Size:	80, 18	80, 18

Text boxes (Personal Details)

Name:	txtName	txtAddress
Text:	(blank)	(blank)
Multiline:	False	True
Location:	136, 96	136, 136
Size:	218, 25	218, 75

Radio buttons (Membership Type)

Name:	radFull	radAssociate
Text:	&Full	A&ssociate
Checked:	True	False
Location:	32, 24	32, 48
Size:	80, 18	80, 18

Labels (Membership Type)

Name:	lblAmount	lblPaidOn
Text:	Amoun&t	&Paid on:
TextAlign:	TopRight	TopRight
Location	16, 20	16, 52

Size:	50, 18	50, 18

Text boxes (Membership Type)

Name:	txtAmount	txtPaidOn
Text:	(blank)	(blank)
Location:	72, 16	72, 48
Size:	65, 25	65, 25

Buttons (form)

Name:	btnOK	btnCancel
Text:	&OK	&Cancel
Location:	344, 256	344, 296
Size:	65, 32	65, 32

Amend the form properties as follows:

AcceptButton:	btnOK
CancelButton:	btnCancel

4   Control properties are as follows:

Text box

Name:	txtComments
Text:	(blank)
Multiline:	True
ScrollBars:	Vertical
Location:	0, 0
Size:	446, 185

Buttons

Name:	btnOK	btnCancel
Text:	&OK	&Cancel
Location:	96, 200	269, 200
Size:	80, 32	80, 32

5   Save using File|Save All. Run the program by pressing **[F5]**. You can click on any of the three Main Menu buttons but they will have no effect as yet.

Close the program with Debug|Stop Debugging or by clicking on the Close button. Close the Output window.

4 Coding events (p114)

(Note that, to save space, most blank lines have been removed from program listings.)

1 Display the frmMainMenu form, double-click on the Member Details button and enter the following procedure in the Code window:

```
Private Sub btnMemberDetails_Click(...) Handles
btnMemberDetails.Click
    Dim frmvDetails As New frmDetails
    frmvDetails.Show()
End Sub
```

2 Double-click on the Comments button and enter the following procedure:

```
Private Sub btnComments_Click(...) Handles btnComments.Click
    Dim frmvComments As New frmComments
    frmvComments.Show()
End Sub
```

3 Double-click on the Exit button and enter the following procedure:

```
Private Sub btnExit_Click(...) Handles btnExit.Click
    Me.Close()
End Sub
```

4 At the design stage, change the StartPosition property to CenterScreen

5 Display the frmDetails form and add a combo box control with the following properties:

Label	
Name:	lblRegion
Text:	Region:
TextAlign:	TopRight
Location:	264, 20
Size:	40, 17

Combo box	
Name:	cboRegion
Text:	(blank)
DropDownStyle:	DropDownList

Sorted:	True
Location:	312, 16
Size:	100, 22

Double-click on a blank part of the form and add the following procedure:

```
Private Sub frmDetails_Load(...) Handles MyBase.Load
    cboRegion.Items.Add("North")
    cboRegion.Items.Add("South")
    cboRegion.Items.Add("East")
    cboRegion.Items.Add("West")
End Sub
```

6   Double-click on the OK button and enter the following procedure:

```
Private Sub btnOK_Click(...) Handles btnOK.Click
    Me.Close()
End Sub
```

Double-click on the Cancel button and enter the following procedure:

```
Private Sub btnCancel_Click(...) Handles btnCancel.Click
    Me.Close()
End Sub
```

7   Display the Comments form and double-click on it. In the Procedure box in the top right of the window, select Resize and enter the following procedure:

```
Private Sub frmComments_Resize(...) Handles MyBase.Resize
    txtComments.Top = 0
    txtComments.Left = 0
    txtComments.Height = Me.Height - 72
    txtComments.Width = Me.Width - 8
    btnOK.Top = Me.Height - 64
    btnCancel.Top = btnOK.Top
    btnOK.Left = Me.Width / 2 - 55 - btnOK.Width
    btnCancel.Left = Me.Width / 2 + 55
End Sub
```

(Later, you will need to add instructions to cope with the window being minimised or made too small to display the text box.)

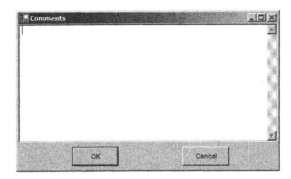

8   Double-click on the OK button and enter the following procedure:

```
Private Sub btnOK_Click(...) Handles btnOK.Click
   Me.Close()
End Sub
```

Double-click on the Cancel button and enter the following procedure:

```
Private Sub btnCancel_Click(...) Handles btnCancel.Click
   Me.Close()
End Sub
```

5 Variables (p144)

1 Set up the form and add the following procedures:

```
Option Strict Off
Option Explicit On
Friend Class frmUnits
    Inherits System.Windows.Forms.Form
#Region "Windows Form Designer generated code "
#End Region

    Private Sub btnCmInch_Click(...) Handles btnCmInch.Click
        Dim decInches As Single
        Dim decCm As Single
        Const decCmPerInch As Single = 2.54
        decCm = Val(txtEntry.Text)
        decInches = (Int((decCm / decCmPerInch * 100) +_
                                            0.5)) / 100

        txtResult.Text = Str(decInches)
        lblEntry.Text = "cm"
        lblResult.Text = "Inches"
    End Sub

    Private Sub btnExit_Click(...) Handles btnExit.Click
        Me.Close()
    End Sub

    Private Sub btnInchCm_Click(...) Handles btnInchCm.Click
        Dim decInches As Single
        Dim decCm As Single
        Const decCmPerInch As Single = 2.54
        decInches = Val(txtEntry.Text)
        decCm = (Int((decInches * decCmPerInch * 100) +_
                                            0.5)) / 100

        txtResult.Text = Str(decCm)
        lblEntry.Text = "Inches"
        lblResult.Text = "cm"
    End Sub

    Private Sub btnKgLb_Click(...) Handles btnKgLb.Click
        Dim decPounds As Single
```

```
        Dim decKg As Single
        Const decKgPerPound As Single = 0.453
        decKg = Val(txtEntry.Text)
        decPounds = (Int((decKg / decKgPerPound * 100) +_
                                          0.5)) / 100

        txtResult.Text = Str(decPounds)
        lblEntry.Text = "Kg"
        lblResult.Text = "Pounds"
End Sub

 Private Sub btnLbKg_Click(...) Handles btnLbKg.Click
        Dim decPounds As Single
        Dim decKg As Single
        Const decKgPerLb As Single = 0.453
        decPounds = Val(txtEntry.Text)
        decKg = (Int((decPounds * decKgPerLb * 100) + 0.5)) / 100
        txtResult.Text = Str(decKg)
        lblEntry.Text = "Pounds"
        lblResult.Text = "Kg"
End Sub

Private Sub btnLitrePint_Click(...) Handles btnLitrePint.Click
        Dim decPints As Single
        Dim decLitres As Single
        Const decLitresPerPint As Single = 0.568
        decLitres = Val(txtEntry.Text)
        decPints = (Int((decLitres / decLitresPerPint * 100) +_
                                             0.5)) / 100

        txtResult.Text = Str(decPints)
        lblEntry.Text = "Litres"
        lblResult.Text = "Pints"
End Sub

Private Sub btnPintLitre_Click(...) Handles btnPintLitre.Click
        Dim decPints As Single
        Dim decLitres As Single
        Const decLitresPerPint As Single = 0.568
```

```
        decPints = Val(txtEntry.Text)
        decLitres = (Int((decPints * decLitresPerPint * 100) +_
                                        0.5)) / 100

        txtResult.Text = Str(decLitres)
        lblEntry.Text = "Pints"
        lblResult.Text = "Litres"
    End Sub

    Private Sub txtEntry_TextChanged(...) Handles_
                                        txtEntry.TextChanged

        lblEntry.Text = "(Entry)"
        lblResult.Text = "(Result)"
        txtResult.Text = ""
    End Sub
End Class
```

The result box's Enabled property should be False. The form's AcceptButton property is '(none)'.

2   Add a text box called lblRep and then insert the following procedure:

```
Private Sub cboRegion_SelectedValueChanged(...)_
    Handles cboRegion.SelectedValueChanged
    Dim strReps(3) As String
    Dim intSelectedRegion As Integer
    Dim strRep As String
    'Fill array (assume list box is sorted)
    strReps(0) = "M. Williams" 'East
    strReps(1) = "R. Walker" 'North
    strReps(2) = "J. Evans"    'South
    strReps(3) = "D. Clarke" 'West

    'Get selection number and display
    'corresponding rep
    intSelectedRegion = cboRegion.SelectedIndex
    strRep = strReps(intSelectedRegion)
    lblRep.Text = "Rep: " & strRep
End Sub
```

3 The following program uses two text boxes for entering the dates (txtDate1 and txtDate2) and two for showing the results (txtDays and txtWeeks). The calculation is initiated by clicking on a button (btnCalculate).

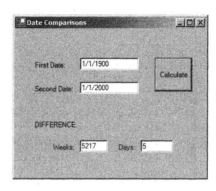

```
Public Class frmDateComparisons
    Inherits System.Windows.Forms.Form

#Region " Windows Form Designer generated code "
#End Region

    Private Sub btnCalculate_Click(...) Handles btnCalculate.Click
        Dim dteDate1, dteDate2 As DateTime
        Dim intTotalDays As Integer
        Dim shoNumWeeks, shoNumDays As Short
        'Get dates into date/time variables
        dteDate1 = DateValue(txtDate1.Text)
        dteDate2 = DateValue(txtDate2.Text)
        'Get difference in number of days
        intTotalDays = dteDate2.ToOADate - dteDate1.ToOADate
        'Convert to weeks and days
        shoNumWeeks = Int(intTotalDays / 7)
        shoNumDays = intTotalDays Mod 7
        'Put answers back in text box
        txtWeeks.Text = shoNumWeeks
        txtDays.Text = shoNumDays
    End Sub
End Class
```

6 Basic instructions (p178)

1   The function is as follows:

```
Public Function PasswordValid(strPassword As String) As Boolean
    'Add code here to read password from file (Assume "pass")
    If strPassword = "pass" Then
        PasswordValid = True
    Else
        PasswordValid = False
    End If
End Function
```

2   The procedure is as follows:

```
Public Sub AddDate(ByRef dteDateIn As DateTime,_
        ByRef strPeriod As String, ByRef shoExtra As Short,_
        ByRef dteDateOut As DateTime, ByRef shoWDay As Short)
    Dim strUnits As String
    Dim shoMonthIn, shoDayIn, shoYearIn As Short
    Dim shoMonthOut, shoYearOut As Short
    strUnits = UCase(VB.Left(LTrim(strPeriod), 1))
    shoDayIn = dteDateIn.Day  'Extract date components
    shoMonthIn = dteDateIn.Month
    shoYearIn = dteDateIn.Year
    Select Case strUnits 'Calculate new date
        Case "D"
            dteDateOut = System.DateTime._
                    FromOADate(dteDateIn.ToOADate + shoExtra)
        Case "W"
            dteDateOut = System.DateTime._
                FromOADate(dteDateIn.ToOADate + shoExtra * 7)
        Case "M"
            shoMonthOut = shoMonthIn + shoExtra
            dteDateOut = DateSerial(shoYearIn, shoMonthOut,_
                                            shoDayIn)
        Case "Y"
            shoYearOut = shoYearIn + shoExtra
            dteDateOut = DateSerial(shoYearOut, shoMonthIn,_
                                            shoDayIn)
```

```
    End Select
    shoWDay = Weekday(dteDateOut) 'Calculate weekday
End Sub
```

The following event procedure calls the calculation procedure:

```
Private Sub btnCalculate_Click(...) Handles btnCalculate.Click
    Dim dteDateOut, dteDateIn As Date, shoWeekOut As Short
    dteDateIn = DateValue(txtDateIn.Text)
    AddDate(dteDateIn, (txtType.Text), Val(txtAdd.Text),_
                                    dteDateOut, shoWeekOut)
    txtResult.Text = CStr(dteDateOut)
    txtDayNumber.Text = CStr(shoWeekOut)
End Sub
```

3   The function is as follows:

```
Function SimplifyText(ByVal strTextIn As String) As String
    Dim strTextOut As String, chr1 As Char
    Dim booWordStart As Boolean, i As Integer
    booWordStart = True
    i = 1
    strTextOut = ""
    Do While i <= Len(strTextIn)
        chr1 = Mid(strTextIn, i, 1)
        If UCase(chr1) >= "A" And UCase(chr1) <= "Z" Then
            If booWordStart Then  'Character is a letter
                chr1 = UCase(chr1)
                booWordStart = False
            End If
            strTextOut = strTextOut & chr1  'Add to output string
        Else
            'Character not letter - therefore next is start of new word
            booWordStart = True
        End If
        i += 1
    Loop
    Return strTextOut
End Function
```

7 Classes (p204)

1   The new class is as follows:

```
Public Class clsNumericLabel
    'Derived class of label that displays numeric values on right of
    'label in black or red and text on left in blue
    'Base class on existing label class
    Inherits System.Windows.Forms.Label
    'Use private variables to store property value
    Private dblLabelValue As Double  'Numeric value of text
    Private strLabelValue As String  'Actual text

    Public Sub New()
        'Procedure called when label object is created
        'Change default colour to blue and alignment to Left
        Me.ForeColor = System.Drawing.Color.Blue
        Me.TextAlign = ContentAlignment.MiddleLeft
        'Change background colour to white
        Me.BackColor = System.Drawing.Color.PowderBlue
        'Set default label text
        Me.Text = "blank"
    End Sub

    Public Property LabelValue() As String
        'Create property to hold label value
        Get
            'Return stored value of property
            Return strLabelValue
        End Get
        Set(ByVal strValue As String)
            'Store new value of label's property
            dblLabelValue = Val(strValue)
            strLabelValue = strValue
            'Set text colour to black for positive number or zero,
            'red for negative number or blue for non-numeric
            Select Case dblLabelValue
                Case Is > 0
                    Me.ForeColor() = System.Drawing.Color.Black
```

```
                Me.TextAlign = ContentAlignment.MiddleRight
                Me.Text = dblLabelValue
            Case Is < 0
                Me.ForeColor() = System.Drawing.Color.Red
                Me.TextAlign = ContentAlignment.MiddleRight
                Me.Text = dblLabelValue
            Case Else
                If strLabelValue = "0" Then
                    Me.ForeColor() = System.Drawing.Color.Black
                    Me.TextAlign = ContentAlignment.MiddleRight
                    Me.Text = dblLabelValue
                Else
                    Me.ForeColor() = System.Drawing.Color.Blue
                    Me.TextAlign = ContentAlignment.MiddleLeft
                    Me.Text = strLabelValue
                End If
            End Select
        End Set
    End Property

    Public Sub ClearBox()
        'Clear current value
        'Change in value results in call to Property procedure
        Me.LabelValue = ""
    End Sub
End Class
```

2   The three controls at the top of the window have the following properties:

Combo box
Name: cboMonth
Sorted: False
DropDownStyle: DropDownList

Text box
Name: txtYear
Text: (blank)

Button
Name: btnRedisplay
Caption: Redisplay

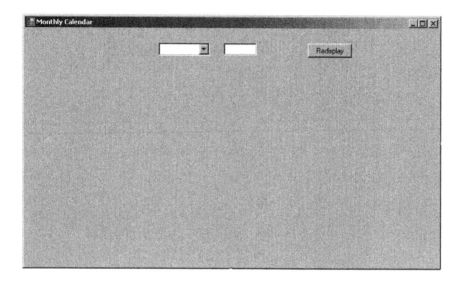

Add the following code module:

```
Module modCalendar
    'Use code module to store values that are needed by both
    'the form and the class
    'Latest box and label to be clicked or created
    Public intCurrentBox As Integer
    Public intCurrentLabel As Integer
    'Latest day label to be created
    Public intCurrentDayLabel As Integer
End Module
```

Add a class to handle the array of text boxes:

```
Public Class clsBoxArray
    'Handles creation and use of arrays of boxes
    'Box array is held as a collection
    Inherits System.Collections.CollectionBase
    'Variable to identify form containing boxes
```

```
Private ReadOnly ThisForm As System.Windows.Forms.Form
'Box width and height, horizontal and vertical gaps,
'offset of first box
Const intBoxWidth As Integer = 75
Const intBoxHeight As Integer = 25
Const intBoxHGap As Integer = 25
Const intBoxVGap As Integer = 20
Const intHOffset As Integer = 110
Const intVOffset As Integer = 80

Public Function AddBox() As System.Windows.Forms.TextBox
    'Function to add a box to the form
    'Create new instance of Text Box class
    Dim itxtNew As New System.Windows.Forms.TextBox
    'Define box co-ordinates, box space requirement
    Dim intX, intY As Integer
    Dim intHSpace, intVSpace As Integer
    'Add box to collection list
    Me.List.Add(itxtNew)
    'Add box to the form's controls collection
    ThisForm.Controls.Add(itxtNew)
    'Calculate space used by each box
    intHSpace = intBoxWidth + intBoxHGap
    intVSpace = intBoxHeight + intBoxVGap
    'Calculate box co-ordinates for 5 x 7 grid
    intX = Int(intCurrentBox / 7)
    intY = intCurrentBox Mod 7
    'Set properties for the new button
    itxtNew.Left = intHOffset + intX * intHSpace
    itxtNew.Top = intVOffset + intY * intVSpace
    itxtNew.Width = intBoxWidth
    itxtNew.Height = intBoxHeight
    'Store index number in Tag
    itxtNew.Tag = Me.Count - 1
    'Display button number in button caption
```

```
                intCurrentBox += 1
                Return itxtNew
        End Function

        Public Sub New(ByVal AForm As System.Windows.Forms.Form)
            'When array is created, generate 42 boxes
            'Define count variable
            Dim i As Integer
            'Identify current form
            ThisForm = AForm
            'Add 42 boxes
            For i = 1 To 42
                Me.AddBox()
            Next i
        End Sub

        Default Public ReadOnly Property Item(ByVal Index As Integer)_
                As System.Windows.Forms.TextBox
            'Programmer can get value of Item property but not change it
            'Set available properties for list items to standard
            'button properties
            Get
                Return CType(Me.List.Item(Index),_
                                    System.Windows.Forms.TextBox)
            End Get
        End Property
    End Class
```

Add a class to handle the array of labels:

```
Public Class clsLabelArray
    'Handles creation and use of arrays of labels
    'Label array is held as a collection
    Inherits System.Collections.CollectionBase
    'Variable to identify form containing labels

    Private ReadOnly ThisForm As System.Windows.Forms.Form
    'Box width and height, horizontal and vertical gaps,
```

312

```
'offset of first box - same as box class
Const intBoxWidth As Integer = 75
Const intBoxHeight As Integer = 25
Const intBoxHGap As Integer = 25
Const intBoxVGap As Integer = 20
Const intHOffset As Integer = 110
Const intVOffset As Integer = 80
'Label width and height
Const intLabelWidth As Integer = 20
Const intLabelHeight As Integer = intBoxHeight
'Day label width and offset
Const intDayLabelWidth As Integer = 80
Const intHDayOffset As Integer = 5


Public Function AddLabel() As System.Windows.Forms.Label
    'Function to add a label to the form
    'Create new instance of Label class
    Dim ilblNew As New System.Windows.Forms.Label
    'Define label co-ordinates, label space requirement
    Dim intX, intY As Integer
    Dim intHSpace, intVSpace As Integer
    'Add label to collection list
    Me.List.Add(ilblNew)
    'Add label to the form's controls collection
    ThisForm.Controls.Add(ilblNew)
    'Calculate space used by each label
    intHSpace = intBoxWidth + intBoxHGap
    intVSpace = intBoxHeight + intBoxVGap
    'Calculate label co-ordinates for 5 x 7 grid
    intX = Int(intCurrentLabel / 7)
    intY = intCurrentLabel Mod 7
    ilblNew.Text = intCurrentLabel
    'Set properties for the new button
    'Shift label to left of box
    '(leaving 1 pixel between label and box)
```

```
        ilblNew.Left = intHOffset + intX * intHSpace_
                                  - intLabelWidth - 1
        ilblNew.Top = intVOffset + intY * intVSpace
        ilblNew.Width = intLabelWidth
        ilblNew.Height = intLabelHeight
        ilblNew.TextAlign = ContentAlignment.MiddleRight
        'Store index number in Tag
        ilblNew.Tag = Me.Count - 1
        'Display button number in button caption
        intCurrentLabel += 1
        Return ilblNew
    End Function

    Public Function AddDayLabel() As_
                System.Windows.Forms.Label
        'Function to add a day label to the left of the form
        'Create new instance of Label class
        Dim ilblNew As New System.Windows.Forms.Label
        'Define label space requirement
        Dim intHSpace, intVSpace As Integer
        'Add label to collection list
        Me.List.Add(ilblNew)
        'Add label to the form's controls collection
        ThisForm.Controls.Add(ilblNew)
        'Calculate space used by each label
        intHSpace = intBoxWidth + intBoxHGap
        intVSpace = intBoxHeight + intBoxVGap
        'Set properties for the new label
        'Display label on left
        ilblNew.Left = intHDayOffset
        ilblNew.Top = intVOffset + intCurrentDayLabel * intVSpace
        ilblNew.Width = intDayLabelWidth
        ilblNew.Height = intLabelHeight
        ilblNew.Text = WeekdayName(intCurrentDayLabel + 1)
        ilblNew.TextAlign = ContentAlignment.MiddleRight
```

```
                    'Store index number in Tag
                    ilblNew.Tag = Me.Count - 1
                    'Display button number in button caption
                    intCurrentDayLabel += 1
                    Return ilblNew
                End Function

                Public Sub New(ByVal AForm As System.Windows.Forms.Form)
                    'When array is created, generate 49 labels
                    'Define count variable
                    Dim i As Integer
                    'Identify current form
                    ThisForm = AForm
                    'Add 42 labels for boxes
                    For i = 1 To 42
                        Me.AddLabel()
                    Next i
                    'Add day labels
                    For i = 1 To 7
                        Me.AddDayLabel()
                    Next i
                End Sub
                Default Public ReadOnly Property Item(ByVal Index As Integer)_
                                    As System.Windows.Forms.Label
                    'Programmer can get value of Item property but not change it
                    'Set available properties for list items to
                    'standard button properties
                    Get
                        Return CType(Me.List.Item(Index), _
                                            System.Windows.Forms.Label)
                    End Get
                End Property
            End Class
```

Add procedures to the form code so that it reads as follows:

```
Public Class frmMonthlyCalendar
    Inherits System.Windows.Forms.Form
    'Declare arrays of boxes and labels based on
    'clsBoxArray and clsLabelArray classes
    Dim arrBoxes As clsBoxArray
    Dim arrLabels As clsLabelArray

#Region " Windows Form Designer generated code "
#End Region

    Private Sub frmMonthlyCalendar_Load(...) Handles_
                                    MyBase.Load
        'When form is loaded, create box array object
        Dim i As Integer
        'Create box array - results in class's New procedure being
        'called and array filled with boxes
        arrBoxes = New clsBoxArray(Me)
        'Similarly, create labels array
        arrLabels = New clsLabelArray(Me)
        'Fill Month combo box with months
        For i = 1 To 12
            cboMonth.Items.Add(MonthName(i))
        Next i
        txtYear.Text = Now.Year
        cboMonth.SelectedIndex = Now.Month -1
        ViewCalendar(Now.Month, Now.Year)
    End Sub

    Public Sub ViewCalendar(ByRef shoCalMonth As Short,_
            ByRef shoCalYear As Short)
        'Redisplay calendar for given month (1 to 12) and year
        Dim shoDayNo As Short
        Dim shoRow, shoCol, i As Short
        Dim booStarted, booFinished As Boolean
        Dim dteFirstDay, dteLastDay As DateTime
```

```vbnet
Dim shoNumDays As Short
'Get first day of month
dteFirstDay = DateSerial(shoCalYear, shoCalMonth, 1)
'Calculate last day of month
dteLastDay = dteFirstDay.AddMonths(1)
dteLastDay = dteLastDay.AddDays(-1)
'Calculate number of days in month
shoNumDays = DateTime.DaysInMonth(shoCalYear,_

'Set initial values
booStarted = False
booFinished = False
shoDayNo = 1
For shoCol = 0 To 5
   'One col for each week
   For shoRow = 0 To 6
      'One row for each day of the week
      'For first column, check to see if is first day of month
      If shoCol = 0 Then
         If shoRow + 1 = Weekday(dteFirstDay,_
               FirstDayOfWeek.Monday) Then
            booStarted = True
         End If
      End If
      'Calculate day number
      i = (shoCol * 7) + shoRow
      'Display text box and label; increment day number
      If booStarted And Not booFinished Then
         arrBoxes(i).Visible = True
         arrBoxes(i).Text = ""
         arrLabels(i).Text = shoDayNo
         arrLabels(i).Visible = True
         shoDayNo = shoDayNo + 1
      Else
         arrBoxes(i).Visible = False
```

```
                    arrLabels(i).Visible = False
                End If
                'Stop when last day has been displayed
                If shoDayNo > shoNumDays Then
                    booFinished = True
                End If
            Next shoRow
        Next shoCol
    End Sub

    Private Sub txtRedisplay_Click(...) Handles txtRedisplay.Click
        Dim shoCalendarYear, shoCalendarMonth As Short
        'Get year and month
        'NB SelectedIndex = 0 for January
        shoCalendarYear = Val(txtYear.Text)
        shoCalendarMonth = cboMonth.SelectedIndex + 1
        ViewCalendar(shoCalendarMonth, shoCalendarYear)
    End Sub

    Private Sub cboMonth_SelectedIndexChanged(...)_
                    Handles cboMonth.SelectedIndexChanged
        txtRedisplay_Click(sender, e)
    End Sub

    Private Sub txtYear_Leave(...) Handles txtYear.Leave
        txtRedisplay_Click(sender, e)
    End Sub
End Class
```

8 Error handling (p222)

1. Display the Code window for the Member Details form. In the cboRegion_SelectedValueChanged procedure, click on the first line of executable code below the Dim statements and comment and press **[F9]**.

Press **[F5]** to run the program, click on the Member Details button and on the Region drop-down arrow. Click on any entry in the list to break into the program.

Highlight lblRep.Text on the last line of the procedure, right-click and select Add Watch. Right-click on cboRegion in the code and select Add Watch; click on cboRegion in the Watch window and edit it to become cboRegion.Text.

Press **[F8]** to single-step through the program and note the values as they change in the Watch window.

2. Amend the ViewCalendar procedure as follows:

```
Public Sub ViewCalendar(ByRef shoCalMonth As Short,_
        ByRef shoCalYear As Short)
    'Redisplay calendar for given month (1 to 12) and year
    Dim shoDayNo As Short
    Dim shoRow, shoCol, i As Short
    Dim booStarted, booFinished As Boolean
    Dim dteFirstDay, dteLastDay As DateTime
    Dim shoNumDays As Short
    'Get first day of month
    Try
        dteFirstDay = DateSerial(shoCalYear, shoCalMonth, 1)
    Catch When Err.Number = 5
        MsgBox("Invalid year - assuming this year")
        shoCalYear = Now.Year
        dteFirstDay = DateSerial(shoCalYear, shoCalMonth, 1)
        txtYear.Text = Now.Year
    End Try
    'Calculate last day of month
    dteLastDay = dteFirstDay.AddMonths(1)
    dteLastDay = dteLastDay.AddDays(-1)
    ' /// Rest of procedure unchanged ///
End Sub
```

9 Menus (p242)

1 The menus and procedures are as follows:

```
Private Sub mnuFileExit_Click(...) Handles mnuFileExit.Click
    btnExit_Click(sender, e)
End Sub

Private Sub mnuWindowMemberDetails_Click(....)_
        Handles mnuWindowMemberDetails.Click
    btnMemberDetails_Click(sender, e)
End Sub

Private Sub mnuWindowComments_Click(....)_
        Handles mnuWindowComments.Click
    btnComments_Click(sender, e)
End Sub

Private Sub mnuHelpAbout_Click(....)_
        Handles mnuHelpAbout.Click
    MsgBox("Membership Database v1.0",_
        MsgBoxStyle.Information, "About Membership Database")
End Sub
```

 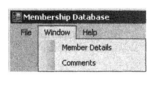 

2 The menus and procedures are as follows:

```
Private Sub mnuFileAbandon_Click(...)_
        Handles mnuFileAbandon.Click
    btnCancel_Click(sender, e)
End Sub
```

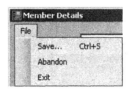

```
Private Sub mnuFileExit_Click(...) Handles mnuFileExit.Click
    btnOK_Click(sender, e)
End Sub
```

3 You may need to adjust the sizes of the window and text box:

```
Private Sub frmComments_Resize(....) Handles MyBase.Resize
    txtComments.Top = 24
    txtComments.Left = 0
    'Revised to allow for menu
    txtComments.Height = Me.Height - 92
    txtComments.Width = Me.Width - 8
    'Revised to allow for menu
    btnOK.Top = Me.Height - 62
    btnCancel.Top = btnOK.Top
    btnOK.Left = Me.Width / 2 - 55 - btnOK.Width
    btnCancel.Left = Me.Width / 2 + 55
End Sub
```

The menus and procedures are as follows:

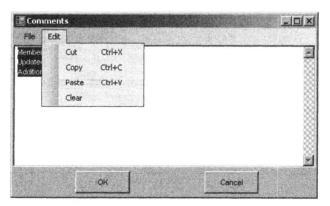

```
Private Sub mnuEditCut_Click(...) Handles mnuEditCut.Click
    Clipboard.SetDataObject(txtComments.SelectedText)
    txtComments.SelectedText = ""
End Sub
```

```
Private Sub mnuEditCopy_Click(...) Handles mnuEditCopy.Click
    Clipboard.SetDataObject(txtComments.SelectedText)
End Sub

Private Sub mnuEditPaste_Click(...) Handles mnuEditPaste.Click
    Dim iData As IDataObject = Clipboard.GetDataObject()
    txtComments.SelectedText = CType(iData._
                        GetData(DataFormats.Text), String)
End Sub

Private Sub mnuEditClear_Click(...) Handles mnuEditClear.Click
    Dim bytButtonVal As Byte
    bytButtonVal = MessageBox.Show("All text in Comments box _
        will be deleted!", "Delete all text",_
        MessageBoxButtons.OKCancel)
    If bytButtonVal = Windows.Forms.DialogResult.OK Then
        txtComments.Text = ""
    End If
End Sub
```

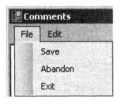
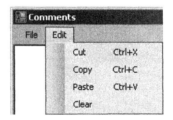

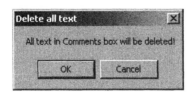

10 Files (p272)

1   Add the following controls:

Combo box

Name:	cboMemList
Style:	DropDown
Text:	(blank)
Location:	152, 128
Size:	144, 21

Button

Name:	btnAddMember
Text:	Add Member
Location:	304, 128
Size:	80, 21

You will also need to move the labels for the titles.

Add the following procedure:

```
Private Sub btnAddMember_Click(...)_
                Handles btnAddMember.Click
    cboMemList.Items.Add(cboMemList.Text)
End Sub
```

2.   Add a SaveFileDialog control to the front-end form:

Name:	SaveFileDialog1
Filter:	Membership files (*.mem)|*.mem

Add the following line to modMainCode:

```
Public Const strSaveDir As String = "C:\Members"
```

Add the following procedures to frmMainMenu:

```
'At top of code
Dim strFilename As String

Private Sub SaveMemberList()
    'Save contents of list box to sequential file
    Dim i As Integer
    Dim strMember As String
    Dim strError As String
```

```
'Create new file or replace existing file
Try
    FileOpen(2, strFilename, OpenMode.Output)
    'Repeat for each item in list
    For i = 0 To cboMemList.Items.Count - 1
       'Get item and write to file
       strMember = cboMemList.Items.Item(i)
       WriteLine(2, strMember)
    Next
Catch ex As Exception    'A file error has occurred
    strError = "Error " & Str(Err.Number) & ": " &_
                            ErrorToString(Err.Number)
    MsgBox(strError)
Finally
    FileClose(2)
End Try
End Sub

Private Sub mnuFileSaveAs_Click(...)_
            Handles mnuFileSaveAs.Click
    'Set up dialog
    SaveFileDialog1.Title = "Save membership details"
    SaveFileDialog1.InitialDirectory = strSaveDir
    If SaveFileDialog1.ShowDialog = _
                Windows.Forms.DialogResult.OK Then
       'Filename selected
       strFilename = SaveFileDialog1.FileName
       'Check that extension has not been changed
       If Microsoft.VisualBasic.Right(strFilename, 4) <> ".mem"_
                                        Then
          strFilename = strFilename & ".mem"
       End If
       'Call procedure to save list
       SaveMemberList()
    End If
End Sub
```

3 Add an OpenFileDialog control to the front-end form:

Name: OpenFileDialog1

Filter: Membership files (*.mem)|*.mem

Add the following procedures to frmMainMenu:

```
Private Sub mnuFileSave_Click(...) Handles mnuFileSave.Click
    'Call procedure to save list
    SaveMemberList()
End Sub

Private Sub GetMemberList()
    'Retrieve contents of list box from sequential file
    Dim strMember As String
    Dim strError As String
    'Open file and read contents
    strMember = " "
Try
        FileOpen(1, strFilename, OpenMode.Input)
        'Repeat until end of file
        Do Until EOF(1)
            'Get item from file and add to list
            Input(1, strMember)
            cboMemList.Items.Add(strMember)
        Loop
    Catch ex As Exception
        'A file error has occurred
        strError = "Error " & Str(Err.Number) & ": " &_
                                    ErrorToString(Err.Number)
        MsgBox(strError)
    Finally
        FileClose(1)
    End Try
End Sub

Private Sub mnuFileOpen_Click(...) Handles mnuFileOpen.Click
    'Set up dialog
    OpenFileDialog1.Title = "Get membership details"
```

```
        OpenFileDialog1.InitialDirectory = strSaveDir
        If OpenFileDialog1.ShowDialog = _
                        Windows.Forms.DialogResult.OK Then
            'Filename selected
            strFilename = OpenFileDialog1.FileName
            'Call procedure to retrieve list
            GetMemberList()
        End If
    End Sub
```

4   Add the following labels:

Name:	lblCurrentMem1	lblCurrentMem2
Text:	Current member:	(blank)
Location:	72,248	168,248
Size:	96,23	160,23

Add the following code to modMainCode:

```
Public strCurrentMem As String
Public intMemberNum As Integer
```

Change btnComments_Click in frmMainMenu:

```
Private Sub btnComments_Click(...) Handles btnComments.Click
    Dim frmvComments As New frmComments
    If lblCurrentMem2.Text <> "" Then
        frmvComments.Show()
    Else
        MsgBox("Select member first")
    End If
End Sub
```

Add the following code to frmMainMenu:

```
Private Sub cboMemList_SelectedIndexChanged(...)_
            Handles cboMemList.SelectedIndexChanged
    'Display name of selected member
    'Get index number and corresponding member name
    'Store in global variables
    intMemberNum = cboMemList.SelectedIndex
```

```
        strCurrentMem = cboMemList.Items.Item(intMemberNum)
        'Update label
        lblCurrentMem2.Text = strCurrentMem
    End Sub
```

Add the following code to frmComments:

```
Private Sub mnuFileSave_Click(...) Handles mnuFileSave.Click
    Dim strCommentsFile As String
    Dim strError As String
    'Create filename from current member name
    strCommentsFile = strSaveDir & "\" & strCurrentMem & ".cmt"
    Try
        'Write current comments to file
        FileOpen(3, strCommentsFile, OpenMode.Output)
        PrintLine(3, txtComments.Text)
        MsgBox("Comments saved for " & strCurrentMem)
    Catch ex As Exception
        'A file error has occurred
        strError = "Error " & Str(Err.Number) & ": " &
ErrorToString(Err.Number)
        MsgBox(strError)
    Finally
        FileClose(3)
    End Try
End Sub
```

Change btnOK_Click:

```
Private Sub btnOK_Click(...) Handles btnOK.Click
    mnuFileSave_Click(eventSender, eventArgs)
    Me.Close()
End Sub
```

5   Add the following procedures to frmComments:

```
Private Sub frmComments_Load(...) Handles MyBase.Load
    Dim strCommentsFile As String
    Dim strError As String
    Dim booFirstLine As Boolean
```

```
        Dim strTextIn As String
        Const CR As String = Chr(13) & Chr(10)
        'Create filename from current member name
        strCommentsFile = strSaveDir & "\" & strCurrentMem & ".cmt"
        booFirstLine = True
        Try
            FileOpen(4, strCommentsFile, OpenMode.Input)
            Do While Not EOF(4)
                strTextIn = LineInput(4)
                If booFirstLine Then
                    txtComments.Text = strTextIn
                    booFirstLine = False
                Else
                    txtComments.Text = txtComments.Text & CR &_
                                              strTextIn

                End If
            Loop
        Catch ex As Exception
            'A file error has occurred
            If Err.Number <> 53 Then
                'Error other than file not found
                strError = "Error " & Str(Err.Number) & ": " &_
                                      ErrorToString(Err.Number)
                MsgBox(strError)
            End If
        Finally
            FileClose(4)
        End Try
    End Sub
```

6   Change the following procedure in frmMainMenu:

```
    Private Sub btnMemberDetails_Click(...) Handles
    btnMemberDetails.Click
        Dim frmvDetails As New frmDetails
        If lblCurrentMem2.Text <> "" Then
            frmvDetails.Show()
```

```
        Else
            MsgBox("Select member first")
        End If
    End Sub
```

Add the following code at the top of frmDetails :

```
    Structure DetailsRecord
        Public intRecordNo As Integer
        <VBFixedString(8)> Public strMemberNo As String
        Public shoRegion As Short
        <VBFixedString(40)> Public strName As String
        <VBFixedString(200)> Public strAddress As String
        Public bytMemType As Byte
        Public sngAmount As Single
        Public dtePaidOn As DateTime
    End Structure
```

Add the following procedure to frmDetails :

```
    Private Sub mnuFileSave_Click(...) Handles mnuFileSave.Click
        Dim intRecNo As Integer
        Dim strDetailsFile As String
        Dim intRecLen As Integer
        Dim DetailsRec As DetailsRecord
        Dim strError As String
        'Construct filename
        strDetailsFile = strSaveDir & "\" & strCurrentMem & ".dtl"
        'Record number = combo box index + 1
        intRecNo = intMemberNum + 1
        'Build record
        DetailsRec.intRecordNo = intRecNo
        DetailsRec.strMemberNo = txtMemNo.Text
        DetailsRec.shoRegion = cboRegion.SelectedIndex
        DetailsRec.strName = txtName.Text
        DetailsRec.strAddress = txtAddress.Text
        DetailsRec.bytMemType = radFull.Checked
        DetailsRec.sngAmount = Val(txtAmount.Text)
```

```
            DetailsRec.dtePaidOn = txtPaidOn.Text
            intRecLen = Len(DetailsRec)   'Write record
            Try
                FileOpen(3, strDetailsFile, OpenMode.Random, , ,_
                                                    intRecLen)

                FilePut(3, DetailsRec, intRecNo)
            Catch ex As Exception
                strError = "Error " & Str(Err.Number) & ": " &_
                                        ErrorToString(Err.Number)

                MsgBox(strError)
            Finally
                FileClose(3)
            End Try
        End Sub
    Change btnOK_Click::

        Private Sub btnOK_Click(...) Handles btnOK.Click
            mnuFileSave_Click(eventSender, eventArgs)
            Me.Close()
        End Sub
```

7. Add the following procedures to frmDetails:

```
    Private Sub frmDetails_Load(...) Handles MyBase.Load
        Dim intRecNo As Integer
        Dim intRecNoFromFile As Integer
        Dim strDetailsFile As String
        Dim intRecLen As Integer
        Dim DetailsRec As DetailsRecord
        Dim strError As String
        cboRegion.Items.Add("North")
        cboRegion.Items.Add("South")
        cboRegion.Items.Add("East")
        cboRegion.Items.Add("West")
        strDetailsFile = strSaveDir & "\" & strCurrentMem & ".dtl"
        'Record number = combo box index + 1
        intRecNo = intMemberNum + 1
        intRecLen = Len(DetailsRec)   'Read record
```

```
Try
    FileOpen(3, strDetailsFile, OpenMode.Random, , ,_
                                        intRecLen)
    FileGet(3, DetailsRec, intRecNo)
Catch ex As Exception
    If Err.Number <> 5 Then
        'File other than record not existing
        strError = "Error " & Str(Err.Number) & ": " &_
                                ErrorToString(Err.Number)
        MsgBox(strError)
    End If
Finally
    FileClose(3)
End Try
'Unpack record
intRecNoFromFile = DetailsRec.intRecordNo
If intRecNo = intRecNoFromFile Then
    'Record exists so can unpack other fields
    txtMemNo.Text = Trim(DetailsRec.strMemberNo)
    cboRegion.SelectedIndex = DetailsRec.shoRegion
    txtName.Text = Trim(DetailsRec.strName)
    txtAddress.Text = Trim(DetailsRec.strAddress)
    radFull.Checked = DetailsRec.bytMemType
    radAssociate.Checked = Not radFull.Checked
    txtAmount.Text = DetailsRec.sngAmount
    txtPaidOn.Text = DetailsRec.dtePaidOn
Else
    'Record number wrong, so record contains rubbish; clear it
    txtMemNo.Text = ""
    cboRegion.SelectedIndex = -1
    txtName.Text = strCurrentMem
    txtAddress.Text = ""
    radFull.Checked = True
    DefaultSubscription()
End If
End Sub
```

11 Graphics (p290)

1 Add a picture box control to frmMainMenu. Use its Image property to select a bitmap. Set SizeMode to StretchImage to make the bitmap fit the image area.

2 Add a Print option to the File menu. Add a PrintDialog control and PrintDocument control. Enter the following procedures:

```
Private Sub mnuFilePrint_Click(...) Handles mnuFilePrint.Click
    PrintDialog1.Document = PrintDocument1
    PrintDialog1.ShowDialog()
    PrintDocument1.Print()
End Sub

Private Sub PrintDocument1_PrintPage(...)_
            Handles PrintDocument1.PrintPage
    Dim objDoc As Graphics = e.Graphics
    objDoc.DrawString("Membership Details", Me.Font, _
                Brushes.Black, 100, 200)
    'Add other instructions to place individual records on the page
End Sub
```

Index

Trapping errors, 216
Try statement, 220
Type (variables), 118

U

Unload event, 97
Unloading forms, 97
Until statement, 171
Upgrade Wizard, 23
Upgrading projects, 23
User-defined functions, 158
Using properties, 89

V

Val function, 132
Value property
    progress bars, 75
    progress bars, 76
    scroll bars, 74
Value variable, 185
Variables, 116
    declaring, 116
    form-level, 117
    forms, 88
    local, 117
    module, 154
    names, 116
    non-numeric, 124
    object, 125
    order of precedence, 121
    passing to procedures, 155
    private, 154
    public, 154
    scope, 117
    string, 124
    type, 118
    watching, 215
VB files, 26
VBPROJ files, 22, 40
Version numbers, 112

Vertical property, 75
View options, 11
Visible property
    forms, 33
    controls, 64
    menus, 231
    pictures, 274
Visual Basic functions, 129
Visual Basic installation, 2
Visual Basic versions, 2
Visual Studio, 3
    display, 7
    exiting, 21
    leaving, 21
    main window, 8
    restarting, 22
    running, 3
    suspending, 21

W

Watch window, 215
Watching variables, 215
WeekdayName property, 134
While statement, 171
Width property
    controls, 58
    forms, 31
    pictures, 274
Window tabs, 11
Windows, 26
    floating, 10
    focus, 63
    hidden, 10
    initial position, 93
    open, 9
    tabs, 11
Write statement, 260
WriteLine statement, 260
Writing random access files, 267
Writing sequential files, 260

X

Y

Printed and bound by CPI Group (UK) Ltd, Croydon, CR0 4YY

17/10/2024

01775677-0004